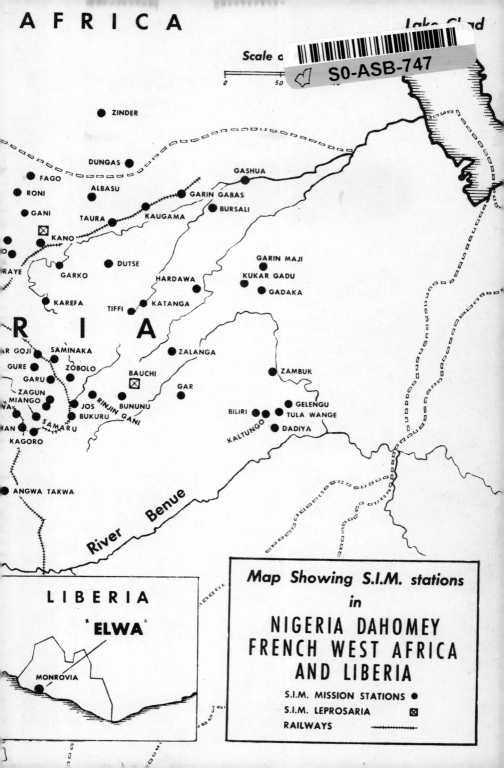

AFRICA

Lake Chad

Scale

SO-ASB-747

0   50

ZINDER

DUNGAS

GASHUA

FAGO

ALBASU

GARIN GABAS

RONI

BURSALI

GANI

TAURA   KAUGAMA

KANO

GARIN MAJI

RAYE

GARKO   DUTSE

KUKAR GADU

HARDAWA

GADAKA

KAREFA

TIFFI   KATANGA

R I A

SAMINAKA   ZALANGA

AR GOJI

GURE   ZOBOLO

ZAMBUK

GARU

BAUCHI

ZAGUN   GAR   GELENGU

MIANGO   BILIRI   TULA WANGE

JOS   RINJIN GANI   KALTUNGO   DADIYA

BUKURU   BUNUNU

SAMARU

KAGORO

ANGWA TAKWA

River Benue

LIBERIA

'ELWA'

MONROVIA

Map Showing S.I.M. stations

in

NIGERIA DAHOMEY
FRENCH WEST AFRICA
AND LIBERIA

S.I.M. MISSION STATIONS   ●

S.I.M. LEPROSARIA   ⊠

RAILWAYS   ┼┼┼┼┼

SPLINTERS

from an

AFRICAN LOG

Gertrude
Frink
Reed

1960

SPLINTERS
from an
AFRICAN LOG

By

MARTHA WALL

MOODY PRESS • *Chicago*

Printed in the United States of America

CONTENTS

DIAGRAM SHOWING COMPOUND ARRANGEMENTS

  Trees.

Thatched roofs. Large ones represent houses, small ones are over granaries. Medium-sized roofs may be open shelters for animals, or small dwellings for aged or infirm dependents.

S The *shigifa* or mud-roofed type of dwellings, one for each wife on the compound, have but one room. Note that the women in compound D are denied even the light from their single doorways. There are no windows.

Z Entrance *zaures*. Men outside the family circle do not trespass beyond the *zaure,* the doors of which are so situated that no man can see beyond the wall that separates the outer court from women's quarters.

Note that if I have a service in compound A, women from compound B and D could look over the wall to see us, but I would have no way of knowing which *zaure* would lead me to those women. Compound walls are 7 to 10 ft. high.

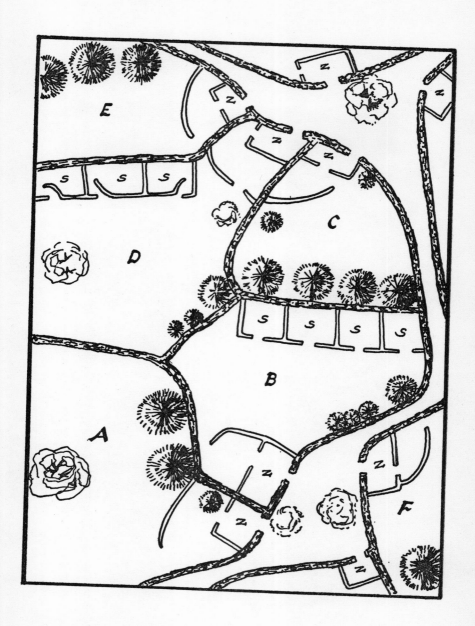

INTRODUCTION

FOR AN AUTHOR TO SUCCEED with the African and with the English reading public in mid-twentieth century she must possess several unique qualities.

Deep spiritual experience without taking life and self too seriously is indispensable. Thorough professional training along the line of interest and dedication is also important. Miss Martha Wall is a deep Christian and a fully recognized registered nurse. Her Christian experience and her professional experience fit her in a special way to write this thrilling story.

Deep love for Africa and for every African, whatever his stage of development, bubbles over from the author's radiant personality all along the way. A gift to see and to help the reader see Africa in stimulating word pictures makes enjoyable and profitable reading for people of varied backgrounds.

Deep appreciation of the New Africa (and it is New, how new it is I ought to know since I have lived there since 1922), an Africa that is vibrant and going places, lives before you as you take the trail with this gifted woman who knows and cares. Never once will you find her sparing herself—always pressing on, always looking for the best and finding it. The very fact that Martha Wall is so loved by Africans in all walks of life is the best commentary about how well she has succeeded in entering into the deeper hopes and prayers of those who are now coming into power.

I attempt in a humble way to say a word in introducing this thrilling book, *Splinters from an African Log,* because I believe that it is a true picture by a dedicated life, the like of which Africa stands in great need. It is a chance to take a look through vivid eyes and a mind that can smile and cry as together we back off a little and look at Africa, my beloved Africa.

It is my hope and prayer that many young people, seeking for reality and for something big to which they can give their all, will find their place with Miss Wall seeking to train the thousands in Africa who seek training to do what only those thousands can do.

ALBERT D. HELSER, PH.D.
General Director
Sudan Interior Mission

PREFACE

L ET ME LEAD YOU through a land that lies just under the lower fringes of the Sahara Desert. I promise you high adventure on uncharted bush trails—trails worn smooth by bare feet of people who will spring out to meet you, as if by magic, from apparently unpeopled wilderness. Africa throbs with life—and emotion. You will become conscious at once of the intricate and varied rhythm of drums whose cadence forms a background for all that transpires, for it is the heartbeat of Africa. You will need someone to interpret the throb of joy and that of tears, of barbarous dancing and of communal labor. You will be intrigued by the efficiency of tom-toms as a syndicated news agency.

I invite you to stand with me, at nightfall, on the brow of a hill overlooking a Moslem village, to watch the flickering glow of many great campfires, reflected ruddily from trees and thatch, casting a radiant web of enchantment over a scene picturesque and wild. I would draw you even nearer—so that you may see what is going on under those trees.

As we approach the village, you will want me to explain the grave significance of the fires, and of the distant hum of voices chanting in unison. Your eyes may grow dim, with pain or tears, as the flames' romantic glory fades to an ominous crimson haze of stark realism. I would linger there, with you, until God uses a coal from those fires to sear into your heart a realization of Africa's great need—and the urgency of it.

11

I would take you farther. Though others labor long for proficiency, I would not grudge you a miraculous gift of tongues. As I draw closer to the people, you will need to understand their languages, and the motives and the customs behind their words. I should like to take you so near that you will feel the grimy softness of tiny brown hands clinging confidingly to yours, and feel, too, the tug of responsibility for lives that will go on for all eternity.

In one book, I cannot show you all of Africa, nor even of the small area in which I worked for twelve years. But, by throwing a short, sharp flash of light on various scenes here and there, perhaps I can give a fairly clear idea of what is going on in the stretches of darkness that we must pass by because there is still so much of darkness.

That is why I am writing down this log—a somewhat chronological record of what I saw while I worked in the West African interior during three terms as a medical missionary. It is also the record of the grace of God in the life of one who had much to learn, and who was slow in learning it—a "saint" on whom a helmet fitted far better than a halo.

This record is no autobiography. It is not really even a log. Just splinters.

ONE

SO FALLS THE PROUD TREE

> I will bring the blind by a way that they knew not;
> I will lead them in paths that they have not known;
> I will make darkness light before them, and crooked
> things straight. These things will I do . . . *and not*
> *forsake them.*—Isaiah 42:16

THE LETTER I TORE OPEN so excitedly was the very first one
I had ever received from home. But that was natural—
I had never been away from home before. The missive was
brief. It shook in my hand, as I read it over the second time.

"If you join that church," my father had written, "I shall
disown you!"

My father's angry ultimatum reached me at a nurses' training school halfway across the state from my home. My reaction
to his unexpected threat was not so much grief as defiance.
My decision had been formed. It was right. I would allow
nothing or no one to deter me from my course!

Well! I can take care of myself!

I was eighteen. And I was proud. How sure I was of myself! How completely oblivious of any way to the right goal
than the one that meant slashing cruelly across old scars, and
piling one more barrier of antagonism between my father and
his acceptance of my Saviour.

Fortunately, the pastor of the church I proposed to join
saw the letter I had written my father in answer to his curt
warning. He persuaded me to change a few phrases, and to
add a postscript.

If there is ever anything I can do, please let me know.
I will be only too glad to be of help.

In God's wonderful providence, my father did need the care I could give him not too long after Pastor Nikkel dictated those lines.

During those last months of his life, he accepted the Lord against whom unworthy believers had embittered him.

Actually, my ignorance of true Christianity was, and remained for some time, as gross as my lack of Christian tact. I remained in such ignorance, perhaps because the church of which I had become a member was in a German Mennonite community, and all of the services were still carried out in that language of which I understood pathetically little!

Nor had I had anyone to counsel me at the time I had taken Christ as my Saviour. I had been at home—quite alone—four years previously, when I accepted the challenge of Sheldon's book, *In His Steps,* to begin to do everything "as Jesus would do." I knew just enough of the Gospel to understand that Jesus alone can save. I had come, by faith, to the cross for forgiveness, but, alas, I thought that from the cross to Heaven depended on *me!*

Later, when I actually doubted whether I really had been a Christian at all during this time, I was led to check through an old diary. I was surprised to see, on almost every one of its pages, a record of unfeigned love of Christ, and earnest, sincere effort to live the austere life I thought was required of a Christian. My father's disinheritance seemed to me but a test of my sincerity. I was willing to give up all pleasures, my home—or anything—to please God.

That diary also carried the record of my baptism and of my ludicrous efforts to give my testimony beforehand, first in German—which *nobody* could understand—then in the Dutch dialect that had been my mother-tongue, which was not much better. Finally, the Mennonite elders, though convinced of their duty to uphold the language of the fathers, decided that if they were going to have any kind of testimony out of me, it had better be in English!

Since I lacked a clear understanding of my spiritual resources, my failures soon became a great millstone of discouragement. I had tried to live as Jesus would. I couldn't. I did not make a good hypocrite. I would not pretend a piety I did not know. And so I gave up.

My next diary, a blue one with a little golden key, was the diary of a person who was no longer very seriously "trying to follow Jesus' steps." I still indifferently went through the motions of being a respectable church member, but my interests were with the world.

I had failed to attain the ideals of Christianity I had set for myself. I slipped easily from a rigidly circumscribed path of narrow legalism into a broader road, one shared by many professing Christians. I thought, "If they can get by, maybe— maybe—I can, too." I tasted warily of the leeks and garlic of Egypt, saying I just wanted to put flavor—spice—into life. But the aftertaste was always bitter, for it brought regret, uncertainty and fear.

I was living the days of that last diary when, several years later, I went back to school. I had entered a Christian school only because it was in my home town, so expenses would be far less than elsewhere. Tabor College was just a stepping stone. I planned to get my degree, with its greater prestige, from California University.

In Tabor, I took Bible courses because they were obligatory. I signed the required statement promising to refrain from worldly diversions such as smoking, drinking, dancing, and attending theaters, with the honest intention of keeping my word—for I was very honorable! But I maintained my own "superior and broadminded" mental reservations. During the school year I would comply with these rigid and narrow rules, then . . .

Perhaps it salved my conscience, perhaps it gave me a faint hope that my virtues would outweigh my weaknesses—whatever the reason—I was glad to be assigned as Sunday school teacher to a class of high school girls. That I can have been the source of any spiritual refreshing to those girls seems doubtful, for who can draw water from a dry well? But no one can delve deeply into the Word of God without receiving rich and unexpected blessings from Him.

I recall clearly, as though it were but a few days ago, a truth that God brought to my heart, not while I was studying the lesson—that had probably been done with far too much haste—but while I was standing before the girls.

My purpose was to keep the girls' interest by dramatizing

the account of Israel breaking up camp, on the desert side of Jordan, to cross over to Canaan. I skillfully evaded the question about why, after forty years in the desert—forty years during which there had not failed to be a season when the bed of Jordan becomes a sluggish and shallow stream bed —now God's people were required to walk right into the Jordan in high flood! I little dreamed that I should learn, from experience, that it is often during high flood that God gives His marching orders to move forward into greater blessing.

Moses, I reminded the girls, was not there to raise his rod, nor was Elijah there to strike the waters with his mantle. The waters did not divide to make a path for the priests bearing the ark into the raging, flooded Jordan. Yet God had said, "This is the day!"

We tried to imagine the commotion that must have prevailed on the east bank of the river that day.

> And it came to pass, when . . . the feet of the priests that bore the ark were dipped in the brim of the water (for Jordan overfloweth all his banks all the time of harvest), that the waters . . . were cut off . . . until all the people were passed clean over Jordan.—Joshua 3:14-17

God did not make their obedience easy for them. The Jordan writhed there before them, treacherous and threatening. God did not sweep it aside *until the soles of their feet touched the water!*

"This is *faith!*" I exclaimed, almost breathlessly. "Faith isn't something we say we believe, but don't really. These people risked life itself on the faithfulness of their God!"

Did I make them see it—those girls? I don't know. Perhaps only the Sunday school teacher went away bearing a new realization of what practical faith may involve. How little did she dream, that day, that she was nearing the same type of "Jordan" test!

Such blind faith was contrary to the carefully planned structure of my life. I had never stepped forward at God's leading. I had always walked only where I could see my own way ahead. I had planned. I had set the goals. Because those goals were high, I had not been ashamed to ask God to bless my ideals and help *me* attain them. Not that I had much assurance that God would actually intervene with anything fate might bring into my way. But then, I had never come to a place where I felt I really needed God. I was doing pretty well. *I could take care of myself!*

Even at the time, I was enrolled in Tabor to get the degree I thought would smooth my path to future security and—I hoped—even make me a bit prominent in the nursing profession.

That winter I attended the school's Bible conference services, which were evangelistic in nature. One evening, during those services, I felt impelled to speak to one of the fellows with whom I worked on the diminutive *Tabor Spectator's* editorial staff. Victor was clearly not a Christian. I urged him to give his life to Christ.

I was glad when several young men from the school's Mission Band took Vic in tow, leading him to their room in an earnest determination to win him for Christ. I told Vic I was going home to pray for him.

But I could not pray. My worldly reservations, especially about the theater, stood between me and God like a heavy barrier.

"Behold, the Lord's hand is not shortened, that it cannot save; neither His ear heavy, that it cannot hear: but your iniquities have separated between you and your God, and your sins have hid His face from you, that He will not hear." Thus spoke the Spirit.

And I argued, "But I don't even go to shows now. I am keeping my promise to the school."

But the barrier was still there, for my reservations were

unmoved. I had always chosen my shows carefully. I felt that I was strong enough to close my mind to suggestiveness or immoral trends of thought that, I admitted, often crept into even the "best."

For an hour and a half I battled with the Holy Spirit, stubborn, self-righteous—and miserable. At last the Spirit showed me my great responsibility to others. I knew at least one person, my Little Sis, who felt that what I did could not be wrong. The Lord urged, Perhaps *I* was strong and wise—would she always be? If my stubbornness would mean the straying of just one other soul, though I myself were saved, would I persist in my own way?

At last, twelve minutes before midnight, I yielded, in unconditional surrender, to the Spirit's voice. And then I was able to pray for Vic.

Next day, Vic hailed me and told me that my prayers were heard. "But," he said, "it was twelve minutes to twelve before I gave in to Christ."

In my paltry, wilderness experience as a child of God, this evidence of God's having heard my prayer was so glorious that I sat down to write a letter to my Little Sis, who lived with her husband in California. I told her of the happiness and peace that had come when I had yielded my will and my reservations to God, and the tangible proof that God had put His blessing on my new relationship with Him.

Some weeks passed. Then I received a cold, curt note from my sister telling me that married women have to think also of their husbands' pleasure and diversion during the few hours they are free from work. Such narrowness as mine might lead to separation, and surely that wasn't Christian, was it?

The letter dropped from my hand as I finished reading it. I stared at it in dismay. I was very fond of Little Sis. I had had no intentions of preaching to her when I had written my letter! I had just been sharing a very precious experience.

I could see that her letter was a revolt against her hitherto
devoted acceptance of my leadership. She had taken my
letter as my signal for her own compliance, as my actions had
so often before inspired imitation.

I was sad that, as months went by, Little Sis did not write
again. I knew—because she had always followed me so closely
—that I was the one who had led her to her present attitude!

Meanwhile, school routine took up my time and interest.
I took a more active part in Christian school activities, though
I still did not visit Mission Band meetings, most of which
were open for members only. The organization accepted as
members only missionary candidates or students who were
willing to serve as missionaries if the Lord should so lead. I
belonged to neither category.

I had grown up in a rural area where we rarely saw a missionary, and those few who came, bored us with statistical
"reports"—as a hireling reporting to his masters. The attitude, toward these missionaries, of church members who had
occasionally given a dime or a quarter to the general missionary treasury was one of proprietorship. A holier-than-thou
attitude on the part of one or two members of the Mission
Band at Tabor did nothing to alleviate my prejudice.

I held the idea that missionaries are voluntary applicants
for public charity, misfits of society who seek service in a
foreign land because they are afraid to face life's realities, or
because dealing with ignorant heathen is the only thing such
maladjusted persons are capable of doing.

I tithed my earnings, and a good share of this money went
to foreign missions, but I suppose I should have given less if
I had analyzed my opinion of missionaries. Since I considered
myself well able to make my own way in the world, the idea
of *my* becoming a missionary was not only odious—it just did
not enter my mind.

Then, one day, Jake Eitzen, a former Tabor student, came

to speak in chapel. He was a two-fisted, vigorous, intelligent man.

Jake Eitzen told of a *man's* work in a frontier missionary field that no misfit could ever handle! In fact, he presented an objective great and rewarding, and challenged others to join the fray. He described treks over rugged trails through bush country. He spoke of opposition and danger. He talked of lepers, and their pitiful physical needs.

I felt as though a hand had been laid on my shoulder to arrest my attention; I saw another hand, a nail-scarred hand, point toward Africa.

"All these years you have been praying every day, 'Lord, make me the kind of nurse that You want me to be.' Well, I am showing you now. *This* is the kind of nurse I want you to be."

"But," I protested, "the missionary said that no medical work is permitted in French West Africa!"

My argument was true—*then*. But God, you see, is omniscient. He knew how He would arrange events of many years to fall into that pattern some people might dare to call "coincidence." And so, though medical service in French West Africa was *impossible,* God kept saying, "This is the place. You have asked. I have answered. All that has gone before was only preparation. You will serve me here."

I could not know, at the time, that my greatest service—a magnificent career far beyond my highest dreams—waited for me in that forbidden land, French West Africa.

A group of students had gathered about the missionary as soon as the chapel hour had closed. I edged toward them, tempted to miss my next class. I could have done so without losing credit, since a few unexcused absences were permitted each semester. I longed intensely to ask questions, as these other students were doing. I picked up a few tracts from the missionary's literature display, and tore myself away.

For all the attention I gave Professor Weimer's science

class, I might as well have missed it! I looked at one of the tracts I still held in my hand. It was titled, "The Cry of the Leper." From this leaflet I gained the information that though medical work was not permitted in French West Africa, the Sudan Interior Mission did have several leper colonies in Nigeria. The tract was an urgent plea for nurses to help in this work.

So that is why, my heart told me, though the speaker's message had led me to think there was no opening for my specialized training, I had still felt the Lord's hand on my life. It wasn't a missionary's message I was fighting, and I knew it. The Lord had revealed a need to my heart before factual evidence had confirmed the need! But now I knew.

"A missionary is going to show pictures in church tonight," my mother said that evening. "I think he's from Africa. Don't you want to go?"

I would not go. I pleaded a school assignment. I did not want to be reminded of the needs of Africa. My life was all planned. Those plans did not include missionary service.

Did I think that I could so easily evade the One who sought my love? I am reminded of Thompson's magnificent allegory *The Hound of Heaven*. The following Sunday I heard Mother mutter, as she fiddled with the radio, "Well, it's the wrong program, but it doesn't sound so bad. Leave it." And she left it on, loud enough for me to hear it in another room.

That "wrong" program was a voice telling of the need for nurses in Africa. The voice told of lepers waiting, barred from leper settlements that remained small because they were understaffed. Lepers waiting, Carl J. Tanis said, while the disease consumed their bodies for lack of care.

"Put yourself in my place," Mr. Tanis challenged, quoting an African idiom, as spoken by one of those lepers. I did. And I knew what I had to do.

The wrong program? A mistake? I knew differently. God had caused my mother to tune in on this program.

So the Hound of Heaven pursued. And I fled before Him.

I'm not the kind of person God wants on the mission field. I don't even belong to Mission Band. Scores of far better Christians think it's wonderful to go to a foreign field as a missionary. Why doesn't God call one of them?

To get an endorsement of my views, or to gain encouragement for a final commitment, I posed a question, casually tossed into a group of students during a laboratory period in which we were free to talk.

"You go out as a missionary?" one of the boys jeered.

"I hope you enjoy the trip," said another, laughing.

I muttered something, self-consciously, about the need for nurses, but no one took me seriously. I was definitely not the type. I knew it. Everybody knew it. So I tried to dismiss the entire subject from my mind.

But the Hound of Heaven still pursued. I grew thin as the chase lengthened. I was like Jonah fleeing from his responsibility to Nineveh—*anything,* Lord, but that!

People began asking what was the matter with me. Wasn't I well? I looked somehow as though I'd lost interest in everything. I knew I had lost interest in food. For the first time in my life I was not able to sleep well. I plunged with feverish energy and frivolity into extra-curricular activities. But it was all just a race to keep myself from facing the issue.

Yet it was ridiculous—this obsession that I must go to Africa! I was not good enough to be a missionary. Surely God knew that.

To get my degree from California University, I must transfer to that school the following year. I had worked in a California hospital. It paid better wages than did the local hospital, and I needed money. I knew that I was well liked, and would be almost sure to get a job if I wrote soon enough, so I wrote to that hospital.

The California hospital did not answer my letter. Weeks went by. Two months. I was becoming very uneasy, for I had to have work as soon as school closed. It was March.

The nail-scarred hand was on my shoulder again. I had never quite succeeded in shrugging that hand from my consciousness.

"You've written to the hospital for work. What about the lepers in Africa? You have the address of Sudan Interior Mission. Why not write the mission, too? Do you love your own plans more than you love Me?"

That was the only argument I could not resist. I owed the Lord my faithful services, even if I could not give them eagerly, or even very willingly. If God really wanted me in Africa, then that is where I must go.

The next day I wrote a letter to the board of the Sudan Interior Mission. It was as businesslike as the one I had written to California. I understood, I wrote, that they needed nurses in their leper work. If there was still an opening, I would be willing to serve under their supervision for a term. I understood the term is four years . . .

I wrote that letter under duress, because I had no peace otherwise. Then I prayed, "Now, Lord, please make me willing *to be made willing.*" I was still far from being a missionary at heart.

I waited anxiously, dreading the word that would say that nurses were still in demand—that I must go out to Africa. Days wore away into weeks. I began to feel easier. If they did not need nurses enough to acknowledge a letter offering my services, then they did not need nurses very badly!

Time was slipping by. Now that I had eased my conscience by writing the mission, I decided that I would drop my California hospital another note reminding them that I had applied for a position. I could not believe that they would not give me work.

The scarred hand was back on my soul. "You've sent a

second letter to the hospital in California. Do you love Me enough to send a second letter?"

Yes, I loved Him. But I was proud. My greatest deterrent was still my prejudiced idea that missionary service entailed my becoming a subject of charity—a beggar!

I feared neither heat, nor head-hunters, nor the danger of contracting leprosy, but I cringed from the ignominious calling of the missionary. Did I love God enough for *that?* I, who need not beg—I, who was on the way to a successful career—would I become a pauper for Him?

I shall never be able to forget that evening in the hospital lounge (I often worked on week ends) when I faced the issue squarely at last. I knelt at a window to watch the glow of a setting sun fade in the western sky. That sun set forever on my proud independence. I yielded my destiny, definitely, into God's hands.

God waited for me to be willing to take the life of a beggar —for His sake. Then, as the shadows lengthened, He blessed the offering I had placed on the altar by giving joy. And He gave peace, too, by taking away also a small, nagging fear of insecurity in an unknown future. He urged me to trust Him, to depend on His faithfulness. His children never beg or suffer want, He assured me (Ps. 37:25). How gracious He was, knowing how little I had ever tested His faithfulness, to give me this assurance!

And so next day I wrote another letter. This time I wrote out the whole sorry story. I withheld nothing. I ended, "I don't know much about missionary calls, but if you think that is what this is, I am willing to go to Africa."

Since I had not had a reply to my previous letter, I registered this one and sent it special delivery. My time was growing very short.

A few days later I had an answer from Sudan Interior Mission headquarters. *They knew nothing about that first letter,* though I had used a correct address. Someday I shall ask the Lord what happened to that unworthy offer of service.

On June 6, I made out the forms of application. The letter from the office informed me that if the committee approved my application, I would be asked to go east in August for a period of probation.

TWO

"AS A GRAIN OF MUSTARD . . ."

Lord, I believe; help thou mine unbelief.—Mark 9:24

A WEEK PASSED. Two weeks! Three! Four!
The tempter whispered, "It's taking that committee an interminable time to decide they need you, isn't it? If they could use a person like you, it would not take them all this time to make up their minds. Did you ever really think they would accept you as a missionary—*you?* This is a vacation during which you should be working in California, getting funds for school. You are wasting time, delaying all the plans you have made for a wonderful career."

Or was it the tempter? Wasn't it just plain common sense that told me that the council had not been impressed with my application? It was probably pigeon-holed, or perhaps it had been filed in the mission office waste basket by this time. I told the bare truth about my ignorance of even what missionary call is. I wasn't the type.

I waited out the tense, silent weeks entirely alone, confiding in no one, not even my mother. I did not want the disgrace of anyone knowing that I had applied to serve as a missionary, and had been rejected.

I began to remember instances which illustrated that when man relinquishes some treasure to God, He gives it back, with interest. Had God just wanted to test my love? How glad I should be, indeed, if God did not really want me in Africa,

27

and I could go on with my own plans. The more I thought
of it, the more convinced I became that this was the case. I
began to chafe at the passing of the time that I should be
using to earn money for the expenses of the coming school
year. I needed that money.

I counted the days left in this vacation. I also counted the
days left in July, for with the passing of July, I should be freed
from responsibility regarding the mission, as they would meet
candidates during August. On July 18, I made this entry in
my diary:

> Counting days, and waiting for a letter. $31 - 18 = 13$.
> It will take four days to travel. $13 - 4 = 9$. Nine days
> before I should start for New York—if I am accepted! Is
> this what James meant when he said that the "trying of
> faith worketh patience"?

July 22 brought a wire—*from California*. Little Sis was ill.
She did not ask for me to come, but she knew I had been
planning to go west. She had seldom written since that short,
resentful letter written during the winter. Now she needed
me. By loving service, I might show her the reality of my new
relationship with God.

On that same afternoon, someone offered me a ride to
California on July 27. This was the exact date I had calculated as the deadline of my going to New York. I had five
days left to pack. I packed for a school term in California.

God had indicated, I was thoroughly convinced, through
the Mission Board's silence, and through this provision coming at the very end of my waiting on His will, that He had
finished His test and was going to let me have my own way
—to follow my own precious plans—after all!

When Abraham offered up Isaac, I reminded myself, God
had supplied a substitute lamb at the very last minute, when
all had seemed lost. *Just like that wonderful career I had
thought I would have to give up!* Now He had shown me

Little Sis' need, and had even provided a free way to reach her. How good of God! I did love Him more for this test, and thanked Him for it.

With such short notice before my trip west, I was occupied with packing, visiting, and general merrymaking. Mother was planning to follow me later for a visit, so she was content with my plans, and rather proud of my ambition.

I packed, all the while scheming how I should manage to make up for the weeks that had passed. I had lost so much time, just waiting. Still, the loss of a summer was nothing. What if God had really held me to my offer of serving Him in Africa? Now I was free!

Since I knew so little of mission matters, I had not the slightest idea that a mission council is a group of men from various addresses who meet just once to consider all applications at one time, preferably just before a candidating period, so that all candidates can be considered. I visualized them as a black-clothed group of gaunt and sternly solemn men deliberating over the affairs of the mission and the missionaries. The decreasing count of days made brighter my increasing hope that I should never have to meet this bunch of somber individuals.

A messenger brought the bomb, well timed to blow up in the midst of last-minute merriment and leave-taking. The wire from New York arrived just a matter of hours before that double deadline, July 27.

APPLICATION FAVORABLY CONSIDERED. PROCEED TO
NEW YORK WITHOUT DELAY. NOTIFY TIME AND PLACE
OF ARRIVAL. WILL MEET YOU.

Application favorably considered. What a disquieting note of reservation hanging over the final decision that would come only after I had been subjected to a month's probation! I could never pass that test! Could I act—*even for a month*—like a missionary?

Like a wet blanket flung onto a timid flame, the telegram smothered the newly restored ardor of my burning ambition. I had the whole battle to fight all over again, and now I must decide without delay. I must make a choice between a free trip westward to my fondest dreams, or a train journey east that would take most of my summer's meager savings and another month of my time that would end, at best, in the postponement of plans I might as well take up now.

I had promised God that if the mission wanted my services, I would be willing to go. But I had spent most of the summer in uncertainty. Was there any good reason for plunging back into that agony, now adding also the greater embarrassment of openly going east as a missionary candidate, only to be rejected? I could not slip away quietly, as I had once planned, for my friends and neighbors all knew of my proposed trip west. And what mission board would accept me? I must only come back, now openly disgraced.

My inclinations and desires—even my better judgment—pointed west. Only one still small voice held me to the promise I had made my Lord. Now it seemed a foolish vow, a false gesture of religious emotionalism that could only end in public humiliation. I grew cold at the very thought of facing either the ironic amusement of the straight-laced church crowd, or my own mocking friends, when I returned from New York.

Had not God Himself opened the way west by showing me a more immediate family need, opening a way both toward this duty and a fulfillment of my heart's desire? Or was it possible that God had permitted all these circumstances to come as a test of my sincerity? Or had Satan ingeniously contrived this tempting "but" for me?

If I made a weak decision now, I faced more months of unrest, a loss of the inner peace I had had ever since I had asked God to make me willing to go to Africa. I could sooner face the scorn and ridicule of my neighbors than the proddings of a conscience that warned me that I was out of touch with God's will. Yet if I went to Africa, what lay ahead? After a term, I would be almost too old to go back to school. That term would change the entire shape of my future. I would work in a leprosarium. *What if I should contract leprosy?*

God had never been able to trust me with testings or difficulty, for my faith had not been great enough to bear them. So I knew little, from experience, of His faithfulness. My decision was hard, for I must choose between my own way—a way clear and pleasant to my vision—and God's way, a path obscure and frightening except as faith could draw my look upward.

So far, my gaze was on the ruggedness of the unknown, uncharted trail. I feared hidden pitfalls; I feared the steepness of the climb. Most of all, I feared myself, for I knew much of my weakness and little of the strength and comfort of taking the hand of the One who has never asked more than that we follow as He goes before.

The choice was difficult, but I shall never cease to praise God for drawing me to make the right decision. The more I look back at my own feeble floundering along the path God challenged me to take, the greater grows my wonder that God—though foreseeing all my stumbling and my slowness of heart—should have deigned to invite me to walk this glorious road with Him. Great beyond expression is His longsuffering and patience!

With my decision made, and a suitcase packed to go west, I had still to tell my mother about my letter to the Sudan Interior Mission, and the invitation to spend a month at the Monterey Bible Conference on a probationary basis. It is not surprising that she was shocked by the suddeness of my revelation just a day or two before I must leave her, grieved at the possibility of prolonged separation.

"I hope they don't accept you," she said.

I had little expectation that they would. I pledged her to secrecy. I doubted more and more, now that I was about to face these members of a mission council, that I should be accepted as a foreign missionary. I did not want to have people know that I had even considered such an illogical possibility.

So I went east on what must inevitably be an ill-fated errand to appease a tender conscience. Once in Monterey, though, I discovered that the other missionary candidates— there were ten or twelve others—were not long-faced, sancti-monious ascetics who walked about mumbling prayers. They swung brooms and tea towels, at floors and dishes respectively, and sometimes at each other. Such levity, to my preconceived notions of missionaries, seemed somehow shockingly improp-er. Was it possible that missionaries would be permitted a sense of humor? I was amazed, incredulous, *and delighted* when I saw Mrs. Trout, our mission-mother, look on serene-ly with a smile when she surprised a couple of the boys in the midst of some horseplay. Could it be possible that even she did not disapprove?

Gradually the truth penetrated into my mind that these missionaries were just plain human beings who loved the Lord enough to serve Him where they were most needed. *And I fitted into that category!* Being a missionary began to appear far less distasteful. I began to ask eager questions about the country of Nigeria, of the history of the work, of the opportunities for service. In a few days, all my reluctance had melted away, and I was eager to be accepted as a mis-sionary.

I learned many other things during those days. I was be-ginning to see that these young Christians, as well as the older ones, were *living* the life of faith that I had glimpsed, theoretically, in Israel's Jordan crossing. The speakers at Berkshire Bible Fellowship were some of God's choice saints: Dr. J. Sidlow Baxter, Rowan Pearce, Dr. Thomas Lambie, a medical missionary from Ethiopia, and a man whom I remember only as Dr. Palmer, who radiated God's very presence wherever he moved, and who brought Him very near to us as he spoke to us of Him. I heard of others struggling against God's voice; I began to learn of His faithfulness to those who do yield to Him!

Then I met our own Dr. Rowland Bingham, founder of the Sudan Interior Mission. I had thrilled to the amazing story of the faith of this man who had gone to the African continent, with two others who shared his burden for unreached souls inland. Though his two companions died during the first year, and he was invalided home, Rowland Bingham's vision burned ever more brightly, because he himself had seen the great need. Another attempt failed, but Rowland Bingham's faith never failed. I quote from my diary: "Now, 45 years later, the S.I.M. has 321 missionaries—not counting us!"[1]

To my utter amazement, I heard of God's provision of financial needs in a practical way that I had never dreamed of. Not one of these people acted like paupers talking about reluctant handouts from *people*, but they spoke as the King's favored children, praising Him for His foreknowledge, for His provision—and for His testings. At last I was given a glimpse into the spiritual Canaan—the promised land of every consecrated believer. *And I gloried in it!*

Ah, yes! By this time I wanted nothing more than to be a missionary. Now the paltry idea of my once-precious career paled in contrast to the glow of the adventure of serving in utter reliance on God's grace and goodness. I had been warned about the precarious financial policies of *faith missions* which had no guaranteed salary—a "hand-to-mouth" existence. At this Bible conference, I learned that it always would be *God's hand—my mouth*.

But Mrs. Nanna Trout was a very discerning woman. One

[1]The present count is 1294.

day she took me aside and asked me gently if I felt that I knew enough about the Word to be a missionary. The perception that I was unworthy—the rejection that I had once hoped for —had it come? Now I did not want it to happen. I wanted to be a missionary.

"I know a good school," said Mrs. Trout, "where . . ."

I was relieved. I had sensed a difference in the conversation and outlook of these other missionary candidates who had had training in Bible schools, but I was so ignorant of the vital issues of practical Christianity, and the way these truths are taught in a Bible school, that I did not even know how ignorant I was! I told Mrs. Trout that I had taken Bible courses. I said I would be willing to take an examination.

Mrs. Trout said no more, but I could see that she was not satisfied. Had I already been weighed in the balances and found wanting? Had Mrs. Trout seen that a faith mission's practical application of Biblical doctrines was an idea as utterly strange to me as it was thrilling? Yes. She could have seen. She could not know that in my heart I had determined to pursue this marvelous and blessed path of faith until I knew it well, yes, even to the end of my days. Would my present ignorance exclude me from this now-coveted experience of pursuing it in Africa?

My diary of those days reveals how eagerly I was drinking in the riches revealed by the testimonies and by the type of preaching at the Berkshire fellowship that was so new to me.

"Oh, if I could only keep fresh in my soul the blessed knowledge that God can do mighty things through me if I but cease trying to do them in my own way," I wrote. "I shall never forget the challenge Dr. Bingham gave us candidates. To do great things? No. But to yield ourselves fully to God, so that *He* can work miracles of power through us. . . . If only I knew how to step aside to let God work."

As missionary candidates, we were to meet members of the council near the end of our probationary period. Dr.

Bingham talked to me quietly about my spiritual experiences and of my call.

"The need for nurses is urgent," he said, "but do you think you are really ready to go to Africa?"

My heart stood still. Again that question. Had Mrs. Trout spoken to him? I knew that, because of Mrs. Trout's close daily contact with all the candidates, one word from her regarding the personality or spirituality of any of us would bear great weight with the council.

Because I had hoped to hide the spiritual deficiencies of which I myself had become painfully conscious, I had actually restrained my urge to ask questions about this way of life that appealed to me so much. I could not know that my spiritual immaturity was obvious to these discerning people who spoke to me.

Dr. Bingham's eyes were kind, but they were also searching. He thought I was not "ready" to be a missionary. He had uncovered my secret and knew that I lacked experience in the practical Christianity of which I had just begun to learn. Was he telling me tactfully that I should never see Africa?

"I am eager to go to Africa," I said, dodging his question.

Later in the conversation, I further exposed my ignorance of a faith mission's policies by bringing up the subject of finances. Dr. Bingham had made the statement that God endorses the council's official acceptance of a candidate by providing outfit and passage funds. "These are not supplied from the general funds of the mission."

"I belong to a denomination that has its own missionary program," I said. "I am sure that its regulations will not allow it to take on my support. I am known only in my own community. Will it be all right if I earn the money I need for passage?"

"That will take a good bit of time, won't it?"

"Well, yes," I said, trying to do a bit of rapid calculation. I can save money better than some if I set my heart to it.

Before I had my estimate of the time I might need to earn and save that much money, Dr. Bingham spoke again.

"Have you ever tried faith?" His tone was gentle.

I looked up at this great giant of faith, startled and speechless. All these days I had been learning about faith, yet I had not really learned. Dr. Bingham could not know, I thought. My case was one of impossibility. Even God could not supply when nobody would know of my needs. Money, after all, has to come from *people!*

I must have stammered out some of these thoughts, for Dr. Bingham left me with the understanding that he would not mind if I worked to pay my way. He had also extracted from me the promise to place my needs before God, asking Him to provide for these needs.

Looking back, seeing my immaturity as Dr. Bingham saw it, the great miracle seems that there was ever any need for my obtaining either outfit or passage funds! It is only by God's grace that I ever learned—from my own missionary experience—that the God who made the universe out of *nothing* does not need a tangible, earthly *something* to provide our needs. I was inexperienced enough to think that God could answer my prayer only when there was some faint human possibility for Him to start on.

At the end of the conference in Monterey, the missionary candidates were taken to the Brooklyn headquarters of Sudan Interior Mission. All of us would be required to pass a physical examination given by the mission doctor. I drew hope that I was still being considered as a possible missionary from the fact that I was on the list for examinations. But then, the final verdict would be passed by the council after they had the doctor's report.

Emma Snyder who had been converted far later than I, but whose radiant testimony had been an inspiration to all of us, held up one of the forms that we were to fill in while we waited our turn in the doctor's office.

"The doctor's questionnaire requires a statement of the probable date we'll be leaving this country," she said. "I've heard that they intend to send out a group in December. Let's put down that date."

Was Emma being rash? After all, she had not been officially accepted any more than I, though none of us doubted that she would be. But Emma did not have her support, either. She looked confident—almost sure—that December was the right date.

What date could I put down, knowing my circumstances? Since I had no definite possibilities in sight, would it be presumptuous to put down a date as she had said she was doing "in pure faith"? With some qualms of conscience about prevarication on an official form, I also wrote down December.

All too soon we scattered to return to our homes to prepare for the field or to await God's further guidance, for official word of our acceptance would probably not reach us for some days. Never before had I known this kind of Christian fellowship, and I hated to leave the stimulus of my new friends' faith. I had been reveling in a mountaintop experience that seemed too wonderful to be true. Now I must go home to face "reality." Would I forget, there in the valley, what I had learned of God's faithfulness?

I had told no one that, after my train ticket had been paid, I had only enough money for very frugal lunches on my way back. I believe I had not even mentioned it to God, for I had counted carefully, and felt I could manage on what I had. To my surprise, Mrs. Trout drew me aside, a few minutes before I left, and slipped a bill into my hand.

"Just in case you have a need on the way," she said.

I thanked her, though I planned to be no less careful of my funds on my trip. This money would be applied on further travels than those to Kansas, I determined. When I arrived in Kansas City, however, I learned that the passenger train for which my ticket had been purchased had been discontinued.

"You'll have to go by bus," said the ticket agent. "Your refund for your ticket cannot be made here, either," he continued. "You have to write to the central office."

Without Mrs. Trout's bill I should have been stranded, for I would not have had money for a bus ticket. So the Lord demonstrated His foreknowledge and His provision before a need was known to me. A warm sense of His loving presence flooded my heart and I praised God silently as I paid my bus fare.

When I got back to my home town, I was on my own, as far as encouragement in my faith was concerned. My sailing at all began to seem somewhat unlikely. Mother met me at the station with the information that she had already approached our pastor about my support.

"It is entirely impossible," she said.

I spoke to her then as though I were Emma Snyder, but in my heart, alas, I was still Martha Wall! How would I ever reach Africa, when the only people who knew me were not interested in getting me to the field? It would take an enormous sum to provide passage and an outfit. I would have to work harder and save more carefully than I ever had. What could Dr. Bingham mean—in a case like mine—by "trying faith"?

Mother's house was just across the street from Tabor College campus. I wandered into the familiar halls a day or so after I returned home, at the time of the daily chapel period. Before I left the building, I was offered my old position as school nurse.

I agreed to work, with the understanding that if I were accepted by the Sudan Interior Mission, and were asked to leave town for some reason, that I should not be bound by my responsibilities in the school. The president of the school arranged for me to be given an assistant, whom I was to train to help the school doctor with physical examinations if I were to leave. The school's president clearly did not fear an interruption to my duties, and I—I am sorry to admit—shared his opinion!

On Friday of that week, I set up my equipment for examinations. On Saturday I assisted our doctor alone. On Monday my student assistant came to help with the examinations.

That noon when I went home, Mother rushed across the lawn to meet me. She was filled with excitement. "They've taken you on as their missionary! You're accepted!"

But who? Where? How?

She did not know. She had been too excited even to check the radio station over which my name had been mentioned. She had not noticed the name of the church that would take on my support. We were both in a dither of happiness and relief. Mother had had time to pray about my being a missionary by then, and was no longer averse to my going to Africa, though she dreaded the lonely years ahead for her.

A wire ended the agony of our suspense. By Tuesday afternoon, I was on my way to Salina to meet a wonderful group of people who not only promised to meet my needs of outfit and passage, but to support me while I served in Africa.[2] I also met Carl J. Tanis, deputation secretary for Sudan Interior Mission, whose radio message about Africa's need Mother had inadvertently found that Sunday so many weeks before. With him was Dr. Thomas Moody, veteran missionary from the Congo, who influenced me more than I understood during those days.

As a rebuke to my unbelief—or more probably, because our Lord is very gracious and, knowing the smallness of my faith, wanted to encourage me—God had sent my support only a few days after my return to Kansas, even before my official acceptance notification from the mission had arrived. While

---

[2]The group, now known as Salina Bible Church, has faithfully supported me financially and by prayer throughout all my years in Africa. At the time, they were just a small handful of Christians meeting in a rented hall.

I was in Salina, most of my outfit was supplied, much of it lovingly stitched by the women of the church.

This log must travel quickly past many stirring shadows and shining memories to settle in the heart of Africa. The deepest shadow of those days lay in the heart of my mother. I had kissed her good-by lovingly, but I had been impatient to be off to the adventure of faith that lay before me. Much later, I understood the price of stark loneliness Mother paid for my years in Africa. She paid them bravely. I saw only her smile. She kept her tears to shed where no one saw, as she took up the unsung labor of intercession.

Late in November, I returned to the Brooklyn Home to join Emma Snyder, the girl who had had the audacious faith to believe for both of us that we would sail with the December group. We were the largest single group of new missionaries the Sudan Interior Mission had ever sent to Africa up to that time. During that one year, 1938, 50 recruits had joined the ranks of a work that, in 45 years, had drawn some 300 missionaries to Africa. About a score of us spent a delightfully hectic week getting our immunizations, packing last-minute purchases, and meeting people who would share in our work by "holding the ropes" at this end.

I received a great stack of mail to be reserved for the boat, but I tore open eagerly one letter that came to New York. Little Sis had written me!

"Do you think," she wrote—a question tucked casually between trivial notes of personal affairs and best wishes for a good trip—"that what you wrote me about had anything to do with your going out now as a missionary?"

She did not need to be explicit. I knew she referred to the letter about my first surrender and the ensuing happiness of which I had witnessed to her. I answered her letter before I left New York, not knowing that my answer would change the course of her whole life.

"Dear Sis," I wrote, "I think my surrender to Christ in

Tabor of a very small thing still had *everything* to do with my becoming a missionary. That was just one step, a small one. But I believe that if I had not taken the first step when God showed it to me, He might never have shown me the second. And the going is good, Mabel! This step is much nearer Heaven than that first one was!"

THREE

LEOPARDS, LANGUAGE—AND A CHUNK OF ICE

> Behold, the Lord's hand is not shortened, that it cannot save; neither his ear heavy, that it cannot hear. . . . Thus saith the Lord, . . . Call unto me, and I will answer thee, and show thee great and mighty things, which thou knowest not.—Isaiah 59:1; Jeremiah 33:2, 3

WHAT! NO SCORPIONS?"

Wilma Robison shook her mosquito boots again. Still no scorpions.

Actually her gesture, as well as her exclamation, was a facetious comment on one of Wushishi's precautionary rules: *Never put on your shoes before you shake out the scorpions!*

We had been sternly warned about scorpions more than once. Until we met someone who had discovered through painful experience how long it seems to take to pull off a tight boot with an angry and active scorpion inside it, we strongly suspected the older missionaries of being fussy and overcautious.

That illusion faded when we had seen a strong man writhe in an agony that the Bible uses as a criterion for pain. Even morphine, or a locally injected anaesthetic agent such as novocaine, gives only short periods of incomplete relief.

Another of the rules of the station was that we must be particularly careful to tuck our mosquito nets well in around

our mattresses, and learn to slip into bed without allowing any
opening for these silent killers; for the tiny African anophe-
line mosquito means business, and does not sing about her
deadly work.

The almost imperceptible sting that may have alerted a
person of her presence was no warning, but a signal that *Annie*
had already made her contribution toward adding another
victim to the high mortality record in Africa. Death by
malaria was the foremost reason that Africa had gained its
title of *white man's grave*. Those were the days before quinine was put to prophylactic use.

A mosquito is small, though, and can be crushed with a
finger. We were far more afraid of the hyenas that seemed to
lurk all about us in the bush, and who were not unwilling to
advertise their presence nightly by their ghoulish, blood-chill-
ing serenade. Wilma and I were happy to spend our nights
inside our room. Others of our group of neophytes were

initiated to sleeping outdoors immediately, for they shared quarters with older missionaries, all of whom insisted that it was more wholesome to sleep in the open. Wilma and I agreed to choose the less healthful manner of living. And we locked our door!

Even the doubtful security of a hooked screen door had to be relinquished. The room we had been given in the school was a temporary accommodation. We were to have a house.

We watched with great interest as our dumbbell house went up. Sun-baked balls of clay were lined up in a double row and plastered over with more mud to form the walls. Two round huts, probably nine feet across, were built with a nine- or ten-foot gap between them. A thatched roof was built over the whole, giving us a fine airy porch under which to study—and under which to sleep!

We slept there, too, though the bush was separated from our dumbbell house the mere width of a narrow driveway. We had to, for there was not enough room in our houses for a cot and table. We must have the table, for our purpose in Wushishi was to study Hausa. And then, of course, we were cowed to conformity of accepted custom by a general contempt of our timidity.

Miss Clark, who had survived nearly twenty-five years of outdoor sleeping, laughed at our unadmitted fears.

"All wild animals are afraid of the white mosquito nets, and will never bother you," she said. "Hyenas are cowardly creatures. It is only an exceptional one that will take a baby or a very old person in their sleep."

I still felt uneasy. I did not feel old, but I was not certain whether some indiscreet hyena might not misjudge my age.

Both Wilma and I were careful to bring our flashlights to bed with us (ostensibly to look for scorpions and snakes if we had to get up during the night) and kept them under our pillows. I often fell asleep with my hand clutching the torch that might just possibly intimidate an attacking lion or leopard, since hyenas, I was then partially convinced, would hesitate to disturb us. Lions, we knew, sometimes wandered into houses. Leopards are more daring and more vicious than lions.

One night a frightful, agonized cry rang out sharply across Wushishi compound. For several seconds—and it seemed much longer—I thought it was the shrieking of a child in an extremity of terror or pain. My first thought was that a wild animal had gotten into the orphanage, for the cries came from that direction. The dreadful sound ended with wild yelping that quickly died to whimpers—then silence.

Wilma and I flung our mosquito nets off simultaneously, and dashed for the safety of our house. My heart had constricted with a fear I should have hated to admit, and I wondered if Wilma could hear its telltale pounding. Excited voices, here and there, gave evidence that others were also up, and, reassured by the cluster of flashlights near Miss Clark's house, we joined the group there.

Miss Clark, we learned, had been up with one of the tiny orphans. She had just gotten back into her bed—was still sitting up in it—when a leopard snatched a dog from under her bed. Miss Clark was quite upset. She had been keeping this dog for a missionary who was home on furlough.

I was upset, too. But not because of the dog. Miss Clark's house is in the very *center* of Wushishi compound. The leopard not only left tracks near some of the mosquito nets that held nice, young, juicy missionaries, but he walked right up to one where the occupant was still moving about.

Shattered was the delusion that the mosquito net is a fortress of safety. And shattering was the knowledge that the bush reached to within six yards of our beds. More shattering—the compound was now fresh out of dogs. The leopard, once having found an appetizing tidbit, might return for whatever else was obtainable.

Nights were just short periods of comparative oblivion

between days, each of which was packed with the romance and novelty of living in Africa. I pinched myself often to prove that it was actually I who was having the unbelievable privilege of being a missionary in this wild, primitive land. I prayed that I might be made worthy of the high honor I so little deserved.

We roamed the dusty paths of the nearby village and practiced our greetings of *sanu, ina kwana,* or *ina yini,* remembering—most of the time—to use each one at the time of day for which it applies.[1] Our vanity was inflated by the respectful way most of the villagers courtsied, by dropping down on one knee.

We took scores of pictures during those first days, and we did well. All new missionaries should make a special attempt to capture the wonder and romance of their first days in a strange land. All too soon the picturesque attire ceases to impress, the queer customs cease to amaze, the novelty of the entire scene becomes commonplace. We become blind to local color that must still be a background for our letters home if our friends are going to get any sort of an idea of our surroundings or our experiences.

We loved the orphans, especially the toddlers. Children are sweet in any language, and these were no exception. Their dark eyes, flashing friendliness, entwined them to our hearts as much as did the chubby softness of their clinging hands.

At first glance, people of another race look very much alike. Our first impression was that we would never learn to tell people apart. The children began to show us that Negroes are by no means alike.

Little Dido flirted his way into our hearts, his huge eyes reflecting personality plus. Benjamin was deaf, a result of a high fever that had nearly taken his life. He would have been

---

[1]*Ina kwana?* How did you sleep? *Ina yini?* How did you spend the day? *Sanu* is a general greeting that may mean "Hello!" or "So sorry!"

buried had not a local Christian noticed a sign of life and rescued him from his parents' intentions. He won his way into our affections by his quiet devotion.

Comfort, the problem child whose actions often belied her name, was into so much mischief because she had an imaginative mind. But she was no more resourceful than Biya Muradi, the housemother for the girls! One day, when Comfort howled incessantly, listening to neither comfort nor persuasion, Biya Muradi settled the trying situation by hanging a bucket under Comfort's chin.

"All those tears are being wasted. We can water flowers with them."

Comfort stubbornly refused to weep another tear.

We watched Biya Muradi serve the children their huge helpings of *tuwo*. She scooped the heavy mush from a great, blackened earthen *tukunya* into the children's little enamel bowls. Then she dipped a dark, stringy, and odoriferous gravy over the *tuwo*, from a smaller earthen pot that still steamed over the fire.

Tuwo da miya is the staple food of a large portion of Africa, though it may be called by many names, and may be composed of a variety of grains or gravies. It is delicious, but in those days we used to hold our noses and say, "I dodt see how they cad eat it!"

Daudawa, the seasoning responsible for the high aroma of the *miya,* is made from the seed pod of a tree, and aged, with the pungent result cheese manufacturers obtain with Limburger. The *miya* used at Wushishi was of crude palm oil, an egg-yolk colored product, for which a taste and smell approval must also be acquired with patient determination. Onions, okra, tomatoes, baobab leaves or other vegetation, were added to the *miya,* with local seasonings selected with the care of a connoisseur, always including a liberal amount of the small, fiery, red peppers. The okra gave it that revolting slimy quality—revolting, that is, until one has acquired a taste, as I did, for just that special kind of *miya*. After that, one shops carefully for just the right tender pods that will melt into delightful, savory mucilage.

The girls of the school pounded the guinea corn or millet that was used in their *tuwo*, as well as some that was used for our breakfast cereal. Hours of strenuous work handling the heavy pestles provided the girls with all the exercise they needed, and may have had a great deal to do with their lithe, well-developed figures.

This guinea corn cereal was the source of one of my first missionary hardships. To make this grain more easily crushable, the girls soaked it in water. The resulting flour was brought into the hot kitchen in a covered container. By morning it was sour. It was served to us as a thin, unappetizing paste.

I had never cared much for cooked cereal. I found this *kunnu* nauseating, almost impossible to swallow. At our first breakfast, I looked surreptitiously at the other girls. Everyone was calmly eating her helping of *kunnu*. It had been served in wide soup plates that expedited the cooling and congealing of the awful porridge into a heavy, gelatinous cake.

Ah, now would come the test of a true missionary! Would I flunk it? Would I gag and say I couldn't eat this food that all *missionaries* ate without quibbling? I could not expect to fill up on something else. Bread in those days was definitely a luxury. It was *kunnu* or nothing.

The first morning I was slow finishing my breakfast. Gradually, however, I learned to take large spoonfuls and eat quickly. And later, because some of the others did the same, I dared to ask for a small helping. So modest, in fact, was my demand for *kunnu*, that my helping was termed a "dirty dish." In the five months or more that I remained in Wushishi, I never lost my distaste for this breakfast staple.

Miss Emily Clark was a frail, blue-eyed woman who looked

The author

Moving a "bed-patient" to hospital unit
Haruna (left), Arzika (right)

The encircling bush hovers watchfully as the head builder thatches the roof of our dumbbell house.

Madugu, the patient who took the gospel to Gidan Magaji

Woman at well. The baby is uncomfortable, but secure.

Meat market

Granaries and a *Rumfa*

Jadi, a star pupil

Dan Naito, the cook, and my kitchen stove

far older than her years because she was so tired. Head of the station, superintendent and teacher in her girls' school—for which she had entire responsibility for financial and general maintenance, mother to a score or more of orphans, many of whom were brought to her in a sad state of disease or under-nourishment, she had been asked to teach six or more of us the Hausa language. She took on this added burden cheerfully and did her job well.

Our first class in Hausa grammar started the morning after we arrived. We had no unpacking to do, as our luggage had been delayed, so we were free to concentrate on making sense out of what seemed an unintelligible garble, but which we must conquer if our time in Africa would be of any value to our Lord, or to the people whom we had come to serve.

On our first day, we were just beginning to have an inkling of the task that lay ahead. The size of Bargery's Hausa-English dictionary was awesome. Completely new sounds and intonation would complicate a quick accumulation of vocabulary. A new order of sentences must be acquired, and rules, and exceptions to rules, and most challenging—idiom.

We had an hour with Miss Clark, who gave us assignments to work on for the rest of the day, except for two one-hour periods with our tutors who were for the most part illiterate natives of Wushishi whom we paid a penny an hour. The pennies, we discovered, were larger coins than an American half-dollar and had a hole through the center for convenience, so that a man could carry his wealth on a string.

Miss Clark suggested that we confine our periods with our *malams*, that day, to acquiring the names of common objects about us. For this she gave us the simple question, *"Minene wannan?"* (What is this?) Unfortunately, I was impatient to get at the language. I would get a few simple verbs, too, I thought. So I asked Miss Clark to give me the sentence for "What am I doing now?" She did, with a hesitation that I began to understand as the morning progressed.

Audu, the *malam* who would help me each morning, was a pert, intelligent young man from the chief's household. I recall a sense of complete helplessness when he appeared, for all I could say to him was a limited variety of greetings. In my notes from Miss Clark's class, I had my two questions, so I began pointing at things, listening to his pronunciation, and writing down the result. Some of those results, when later checked, were not in the dictionary at all because I had not heard correctly, and others were entirely wrong, since it is easy to get the word for *wood* when one points to a table, or *shoe* when one points to a foot, or vice versa.

I had repeated, *"Minene wannan?"* so monotonously, that I was sure Audu must be bored. In fact, he had yawned openly. So, carefully, syllable by syllable, I read my second question from my notes. *"Mi ni ke yi yan-zu?"* I asked, throwing a stone.

"Kina jefa dutse."

"Kina jefa dutse," I echoed, as well as I could, and began to write.

A series of staccato ejaculations showed me I was definitely off somewhere. I threw the stone again and read my question even more carefully from my notes.

"Mi ni ke yi yanzu?"

"Kina jefa dutse."

Again I repeated, and again Audu was emphatic in his disapproval, shaking his head and rolling his eyes while he explained something eagerly and at length. I was nonplused. I could not understand what was the matter with my verbs. I tried other actions with the same discouraging result. I had had no such trouble getting my nouns, for when I had made a mistake in pronounciation, Audu had corrected it, and we had proceeded to the next one.

Audu was no longer sleepy, but I seemed to be getting nowhere with Hausa verbs. Thwarted in my ambition to learn the whole language at once, I concentrated the rest of the period in learning nouns.

Had I stumbled onto the challenge of plurals, I might have found my nouns more interesting. For instance, the word for woman, *mace,* is *mata* in the plural; *miji* (husband) becomes *maza* in the plural; *kaza* (hen) becomes *kaje*; *itace* (tree), *itatuwa*; *rago* (goat), *raguna*; *maciji* (snake), *macizai.* This list simply suggests irregularities that exist and by no means exhausts the possible variations.

When the British government educational system put the Hausa language into print, it did an excellent job simplifying spelling. All vowels are, phonetically, like those in Latin. *C* is allowed to stand for *ch,* since the hard *c* is always written *k,* while the soft *c* sound is invariably represented by *s.*

Hausas cannot pronounce consonantal diphthongs, so the most fascinating of the nouns, and usually the most difficult to read, are those incorporated into the Hausa language from English. The plural of those words, as well as their spelling, makes an intriguing study. For example, *tica, ticoci; duroba, durobobi; mota, motoci; sitam*—I don't know the plural for *stamp,* because, as far as I know, no African ever asked me for more than one at a time. If the above commonplace English words are not quite clear, they are *teacher, driver,* and *motor,* respectively, with their plurals.

When I asked Miss Clark, on that first day, why Audu had objected so strenuously to my verb forms, though he accepted my nouns quite calmly, she explained that Audu's objection had been because I had repeated the feminine second person pronoun he had naturally given me, and, of course, no Hausa male would ever allow me to address a feminine pronoun to himself!

So, after we had memorized the declensions of pronouns, we were ready to start on the conjugations of verbs, many of which are far more irregular than our own verbs. I have always enjoyed the study of foreign languages, and I particularly liked to study Hausa, perhaps because our study was not limited to textbook exercises.

I was not such a good student, however, that I was not entirely taken aback when, after only three weeks in the country, Miss Clark asked me if I would take a class in simple arithmetic each afternoon.

"But," I cried in consternation, "I don't know how to talk! And I wouldn't understand their questions."

"You'll have to learn your numbers," she said, "and a few words denoting that the work is addition or subtraction. The vocabulary required is not so great."

When I continued to hesitate, she explained that a few men from the town had requested this class and it was a point of contact that she hated to lose. By granting them the help they desired, they might also be drawn to our services. More capable staff members were too busy to take the class.

So, though my eyes longingly followed the other girls when they passed by the school window on their way to visit in the town, where they would absorb the vocabulary of the homes, I was laboriously teaching sums and multiplication tables. One day, Audu, also part of my class, spoke up.

"Teach us money. Our idea is to learn to work with money."

So the tables had to be complicated with inserted pounds, shillings, and pence. By multiplying them, we got a wealth of money—British money. This made even the arithmetic difficult for me, for I had to learn to figure pounds in English before I translated my problems into Hausa.

I got a wealth of good from the class, if no one else did. My students did not want naked figures, they wanted applied problems. I worked hard to put such problems into words. In spite of the fact that I envied the girls who went to the village, I think I made nearly as much progress as most of them.

When we had been in Wushishi three months, Miss Clark gave us a language test to see what progress we had made. I remember little of the test questions now, but I do remember the story of a little boy who pulled his kitten's tail. I had learned two Hausa words for *pull*, but, as is rather common at examination time, one of those words had escaped me. I had an uncomfortable feeling that the elusive word was the right one. It was. I used the word *ciri* instead of the shorter word *ja,* and that left the kitten without any tail at all, for *ciri* means to uproot or pull out.

Miss Clark was suffering under our attempts at language study and her many other duties far more realistically than the imaginary kitten. Frail as she was, she was carrying so heavy a schedule that even a strong person would have broken under it. Four of us in Wushishi were nurses, but that seemed of little consequence the day she showed us an ugly red edematous spot on her leg. It was erysipelas!

In the days before sulfas and antibiotics, erysipelas was a serious matter indeed. The treatment in our hospitals at home was ice packs. But where, in that part of Africa, was there any ice?

Quickly we had cool cloths evaporating over the area, and we had put Miss Clark to bed, where she should have been when her unadmitted fever had begun. In spite of our best efforts, the fever rose and the area of redness spread so alarmingly that each of us knew the almost inevitable prognosis. Without ice, Miss Clark would die. And we could not hope for ice.

Naturally, we had dropped all our other duties and concentrated on our one great anxiety. We nurses organized shifts for Miss Clark's care, for she would need constant attention around the clock—as long as our ministrations would be needed. I had already begun the cool compresses, so I was allowed the first shift.

"How is she?" whispered Nyleta Stilwell, when I came out of Miss Clark's room to get fresh water. All three of the other nurses were there in tense concern.

I shook my head. I had had the disease myself, and had

been very near death with an infection far less virulent, for this was spreading three or four times as fast.

"Only a miracle can save her," I answered sadly. "And what kind of miracle can help? We need ice."

Ice. Kerosene refrigerators, so common on the field today, could not be found even in the homes of highest government officials in 1939. To send for ice was out of the question. We had no car and we had no means of communicating with anyone with a car unless we sent a runner. And no one knew of a refrigerator closer than Lagos, two days down country by train, and trains ran only twice a week.

We looked into each others' faces, appalled at the certainty we read in every one. Then we joined our hands and prayed tearfully and without much hope.

Even another and very unwelcome complication arose that afternoon. Only once before, in all the time we had been there, had we had callers. This would be the day that a government official would drop in to have a cup of tea with Miss Clark, whom he said he knew. As anxious as we all were, someone had to entertain him. I was glad that it was not I, for I was still on duty. The man seemed sorry to hear of Miss Clark's illness, and he did not stay too long. Everyone was relieved when he left.

Word of Miss Clark's illness was spreading rapidly, and quiet groups of Africans gathered here and there on the compound. Though we had not discussed Miss Clark's condition with them, our faces had betrayed the dreadful truth.

Death stalks with fearful reality on a tropical station where there are no men. I glanced at the tall cupboard made out of a large packing box that had been built to conform to certain measurements with deliberate foresight. Miss Clark had shown it to us during our first days in Wushishi.

"We have to be prepared for all emergencies. Nobody here could make a coffin. *This is the one.*"

I was to learn, all too soon, of death in the tropics and of the haste that is necessary where a body is not embalmed.

Not more than an hour after our visitor had left us, a car again entered the long driveway to our compound. It was the same man, and he carried a heavily wrapped parcel. Unknowingly, the girls had entertained the manager of Nigerian Railways, the only man in the country with authority enough to stop a train and demand all the ice it carried. That is exactly what he had done.

That day we began to learn to know our God, His power, and His faithfulness. Neither chance nor coincidence could have brought this one man to visit us on the day of our great need of ice, on the day the train made its trip up country, and just before the hour it would pass Wushishi station, three miles from the village.

Looking back at the experience now, it also becomes obvious that it is as great a miracle that this one supply of ice should have been effective in staying the virulent infection in one who had little physical reserve to fight it. Miss Clark has continued to serve her Lord and her beloved people in Africa until she is nearly an octogenarian. I think that one large cupboard is still there!

Though all else has changed, unalterable is the loving-kindness of the omnipotent God who did not need ice at all, but who saw that *we* needed a reassurance that nothing—not even the impossible—is too hard for our Lord.

Miss Clark wanted each one in the language class to have the experience of a trek into a bush village. Though she was planning to protect us from the shock of raw village life by sending us to a government rest house, the prospect of a trek sounded like a real adventure. We could now speak well enough to get about a little, and she was sending with us her own personal boy, Iliya (Elijah), who was used to interpreting our clumsy attempts at Hausa.

At first glance, it would appear that such a trek offered no greater advantage than a highly coveted escape from school routine. However, we would be visiting a place that had not been contacted for Christ for six or more years, as nobody from Wushishi station could be spared for trekking. Iliya would preach. We could read portions of Scripture we had practiced with our *malams*. And we would take a phonograph. Christian Hausa records, made by Harold Germaine and others by Gospel Recordings, were—and continue to be—an excellent means of evangelization. One side of each record heralded choice selections from God's Word, quoted in a challenging and convincing manner. The other side played well-chosen Gospel music. Everyone knows the power of one phrase of a song running in the mind day after day. We could hope for such results. And we could pray for them.

To many people, a trek suggests a safari or a camel caravan. The term, as it is used in Nigeria, refers to any journey in bush country that entails taking equipment for cooking and sleeping. Our camping outfit was hoisted to an already over-loaded lorry. Then it remained for us to squeeze our way into the mass of baggage and passengers that already threatened the groaning axles. Lydia Jantz, Beth Smith, Wilma Robison, and I were the happy ones whom Miss Clark had chosen for this trip. Miss Clark herself explained to the driver that our destination was the rest house at Babban Zaure.

In most inland towns and villages there are no accommodations suitable for white people. European governments have built rest houses here and there, primarily to provide sleeping quarters for their own officials, though other Europeans are allowed to use them. In those days, most of these rest houses were just large, round, native-style huts with an extension of roof to form an airy veranda. They were cleaner and better ventilated than accommodations one could find among the people. So, though we would be "roughing it," we anticipated no difficulties during the week we were to be away.

We thoroughly enjoyed our trip to Babban Zaure, for even the crush on the lorry offered much of interest. The newness of all that was African had not yet worn off, and even what was later to become commonplace still held a high and exciting luster to our uninitiated eyes. We intercepted the curious stares of our fellow travelers, and gazed with equally open curiosity at them, their attire—or lack of it—and at their baggage, which included some agitated chickens and bright enamel pots of reddish palm-oil *miya*, among which we moved cautiously to avoid too much commotion. We commented on our observations in our tongue; they commented in theirs.

When the truck stopped, opposite a small village, and the driver motioned for us to alight, we looked at each other in mystification. The man must have gotten Miss Clark's directions wrong. She had explicitly told us that the truck would stop right in front of the rest house, which was some distance from the village.

"Babban Zaure?" we asked, pointing.

"Babban Zaure *ne*," said the driver, with some impatience, waving us down. Iliya was down below, with the driver. He nodded.

But he must be wrong!

"Rest house. Rest house." We did not know how to say it in Hausa.

The driver and his assistant paid no attention to us, but kept unloading our baggage, which included an oblong galvanized "bathtub" full of kettles and foodstuffs, our duffel bags, phonograph, and suitcases.

There is something frightening about the inability to communicate your questions to someone who, for the moment, has you in his power. After a hurried consultation, we all refused to get down from the lorry, and kept repeating *rest house, rest house*, knowing that the driver understood a bit of English. Finally he shrugged expressively and, leaving our loads exactly where they were at the side of the road, drove off with us!

Already slightly schooled to the ways of the land, we now realized that someone, at least, should have remained with the loads. Our concern over our belongings soon melted in greater consternation. The rest house where Miss Clark had bargained to send us was there, but in complete ruins. There was no roof of any kind, and the mud walls had melted into mounds of straw-matted clay. The driver motioned us, now with finality, to get off. He had known all the time, of course, that there was no government rest house in Babban Zaure!

There would be no lorry past Babban Zaure, probably, until the return trip of this rascal who had bargained to take us back to Wushishi at the end of a week. What would we do? When things go wrong, the language barrier looms in sinister threat, leaving the most resourceful person helpless and sometimes terrified. We made our way back to our equipment, but though we hurried breathlessly, most of it had vanished from the side of the road. We saw the last things being carried toward the native village, where we lost sight of them. We stood there on the road and looked at each other, not quite ready to share our thoughts.

Iliya strolled back to the roadside, seemingly neither confused by the turn of events nor surprised. He smiled blandly, as though he had been a party to a conspiracy. Of course he had known, as well as the driver, that the rest house had long ago ceased to exist, but for him, as well as for us, this trek had been a keenly anticipated interruption from monotonous routine. Had he explained the situation, he might have missed this holiday. And so would we!

"Come!" he said. He had everything under control.

Babban Zaure means *large entrance hut.* The enclosed compounds of Moslems have but one opening, and that through a large hut with two doors. The *zaure* is the gather-

ing place of men, for adult males are not allowed to enter the
inner section of the compound that is screened from either
door of the *zaure* by another wall.

For the most part, the inhabitants of Babban Zaure were
pagans for whom Hausa was not the mother tongue. The
compounds were open and the huts scattered. Nearly all the
local population had turned out to meet us, or—as our still
uneasy minds suggested—to make a quick estimate of the loot.
We arrived at the nearest cluster of dwellings to find some
goats being evicted from a large, roomy hut where they had
been tethered. Young boys were industriously raising a cloud
of dust as they swept the earth floor with brooms made of
handfuls of coarse grass bound together.

My mind went back nearly two thousand years to a time
when another stable was probably swept out to make room
for human occupants, though I doubted that the hand that
held that broom was as eager or as energetic as were these
black ones!

Iliya explained, and we understood as well as our joint

Kitchen

knowledge of Hausa could piece together, that the chief of the town was making us welcome as his guests. We giggled at what Miss Clark would think, and settled down to enjoy ourselves.

Our quarters were uncommonly spacious, for there was room for all three cots, and floor space to spare. Very few native huts are so large. The span of the roof was so great that a supporting pole had been erected in the center of the hut.

Gifts began to arrive from our eager hosts, the villagers—eggs, milk, chickens—and when the people discovered that we liked mangoes, a great pile began to accumulate around the center pole of our hut. Women brought water and wood, and Iliya began to busy himself with such chores as would produce a meal.

In the meantime we attacked the heap of mangoes. All of us enjoyed them, though they have a flavor for which some people do not readily acquire a taste. Because of limited foot space when our metal bathtub was set inside, one of us occupied the tub, proving once and for all, by experiment, that the best place to eat a mango is in a bathtub.

A mango was never meant for civilized eating, and more than one that has been attacked in a dining hall, properly with a knife, has shot out of control only to strike another diner who was not agile enough for a quick dodge. A good mango is very juicy and as slippery as a fish. It should definitely be eaten in unconventional circles, or in private, with a wash basin handy. We ate mangoes until the juice dripped from our elbows.

While we had our supper outside where there was elbow room, the inhabitants of the entire district for miles around began to appear in a tight circle that held itself at a respectful distance. To these people, who have never seen tableware used, our deft manipulation of knife and fork must have been the source of great wonder—or so it seemed by the inflections of voices raised in comment.

As I recall this first trek, I wonder at our irresponsible attitude. We were bored language students on vacation. Nobody expected much of us, least of all we ourselves. We were still just playing at being missionaries, it seems now, though we were very serious as we opened our Bibles to follow Iliya's reading of a passage we had selected for him. Then we sang choruses in Hausa, and finally played the phonograph records. We had a great crowd of people there for that service, which continued until we had played all our records over again and again and Iliya was quite hoarse.

In the morning we were awakened by a new and eager audience, much of which was composed of children, since adults were working at their various dry-season occupations. By midafternoon the crowd began to form once more, and were demanding *karatu*.

Now *karatu* can mean—and their request for it probably did mean—preaching or reading from the Word such as had been done the previous evening. But God had so managed that the four who came to these needy people would misunderstand their demand to mean *education*, the only meaning of that Hausa word *karatu* with which we were then familiar. How proud we were that these people, mostly young adults, would have a desire to learn to read!

"We can't possibly teach them to read in a few days," someone said. Then someone else had that magnificent idea that we would make them *think* they were learning to read. For everyone who came for *karatu,* we prepared a slip of paper on which we wrote a well-chosen Gospel text. We made no duplicates. Then we sat down with each eager student and reread his verse until he had learned it by heart. That night our students could not be persuaded to leave. Even after we had gone into the hut and had closed the mat door, we heard them reciting their *karatu.*

"Give them the Word of God," Dr. Moody, the old mis-

The reading class

sionary from the Congo, had said. "It is the Word that giveth light."

For the following days we kept busy with our *karatu*. How little did we dream, in our ignorance of the country, that those little strips of paper would be carefully treasured for several years, and their messages repeated over and over again to all who would listen; they were finally brought out again when a native pastor was found to go and shepherd a flock that God had been able to draw to Himself through our untutored, fumbling methods. There are so few messengers of the truth, you see, that God needs often to perform a miracle with the weaknesses that are yielded to His use.

We were entirely unaware of any truly worth-while effects of our contacts with the friendly people of Babban Zaure, except that one man, Malam Shehu, from Laga, accepted a Gospel of John. He brought it to Wushishi not many days later asking for more literature. He had read his book eleven times. He was given a Testament. When Miss St. Germaine contacted him later, he said he had read it through 25 times.

Malam Shehu was probably the only man in that entire district who could read. When one reads, in Africa, it is very often done aloud, with an eager audience hanging on every word. *Karatu* was still a miracle which people longed for but which was out of reach. Time has changed even this.

FOUR

COMMENCEMENT EXERCISES— *A L'AFRIQUE*

> Now unto him that is able to do exceeding abundantly above all that we ask or think, according to the power that worketh in us, unto him be glory in the church by Christ Jesus throughout all ages, world without end.—Ephesians 3:20, 21

KANO. Citadel of Islam, city of 150,000 souls. Fortified with massive walls of mud 30-50 feet high, and barricaded against the Gospel of salvation with walls of hatred and antagonism—insurmountable, invulnerable, as hard as adamant—Kano. Rowland Bingham's first objective—Kano.

"You will never see Kano," a missionary of the coast had bluntly warned Dr. Bingham. "Your children will never see Kano. Your grandchildren may!"

Many centuries before, in blind obedience to a command of God, another young man led a march around fortified walls of another city. His course must have seemed foolish to many. Yet, by the simple "folly" of his obedience, Joshua conquered Jericho and gained a foothold in the land of Canaan.

Rowland Bingham and his friends had pushed inland into the vast Sudan, toward Kano, in obedience to Jesus' marching orders: "Go ye into all the world and preach the gospel to every creature." Their objective, like Joshua's, was to break down walls—walls of prejudice against Christ—and to take the Gospel to those millions of souls in the heart of Africa who had never once heard of the salvation Jesus died to provide for them. Their motto became *To preach the Gospel, not where Christ is already named* (Rom. 15:20).

Kano! And I was going there! I would live there for a few weeks. I would have a small share in Dr. Bingham's dream of witnessing to these people in the north of Nigeria.

Some of those early missionaries died as they pressed into the interior, but other dedicated young men and women courageously stepped into the gaps until great congregations of believers, some of them converted head-hunters, were worshiping the Lord Jesus Christ in many languages.

But the great Moslem area of North Nigeria—where one language, Hausa, could be used to evangelize millions—remained closed against the Gospel of Christ. Repeated petitions to the British and the Moslem government leaders alike were as ineffectual as beating with bare fists against gates of brass. Antagonism to the cause of Christ was unyielding and bitter. But our leader, under the Lord, was appealing at the courts of a higher Magistrate for admittance to this city whose need had caused him once and again to risk his life, and that had taken the lives of his first two companions in the work. While Rowland Bingham strove before God for souls, he remembered that Jesus had also said, "Heal the sick; cleanse the lepers . . ."

After successfully demonstrating heartening results in the care of lepers in southern Nigeria, the Sudan Interior Mission offered—in obedience to Christ's command—to take over a leprosarium in Katsina, near the very northern boundary of Nigeria. With blind and disfigured lepers begging in every market place, lying by nearly every main thoroughfare, hobbling about on unbandaged, ulcerated stumps of feet at the very doors of the emirs' palaces—200,000 of them—the rulers of the North cautiously opened their doors to medical missionaries, with the hope that they would be rid of the stench and the cry of these professional beggars.

Until this time, the total advance in the North was three bush stations—Garko, Malumfashi, and Roni. The leper work in Katsina, followed by the opening of similar settlements near Sokoto and Kano, spearheaded mission activity into three dominant areas of concentrated population. At first, restrictions against the primary objective of evangelical missions were so stringent that it seemed almost foolish to send laborers into an area so fanatically determined to prevent the witness of Christ from being disseminated.

Still, far-sighted leaders were praising God for a wedge into the land. One by one, too, souls were coming to the knowledge of Christ. More help was offered the sick in general dispensaries. Loving care and kindness broke through the ramparts of antagonism and hatred in many areas, and our own large group of recruits had actually ridden in on a great crest of opportunity that swept across the land like a tidal wave. The next decade was to see an approximate tripling of our missionary force on the field. Churches, schools, bookshops, and radio have joined the medical aspect of the work, and thousands have been won to Christ in the "closed" North.

The sudden surge of new recruits put a great strain on all accommodations. Housing became a problem of emergency proportions, business and shopping services at headquarter stations were swamped with the novel task of sending building and living supplies to isolated bush stations. Language schools felt the same pressure. After we had been in Nigeria for five months, both Minna language school and the one in Wushishi gave examinations to eliminate students who might possibly be able to get along by continuing their study on a station without a language teacher.

As we took that examination, we were torn between the desire to make the best grade possible and the knowledge that if we made a good showing we would have to exchange this wonderful fellowship in Wushishi for some unknown, unnamed station, facing, at last, the realities of missionary life. We all had known that Lydia Jantz would come out with the top grade. It came as a shock that I was to be "evicted" at the same time!

Until 1937, one doctor had served the Sudan Interior Mission's medical needs; sick missionaries had to go to government hospitals where bedside care was notoriously poor, or they were sent to Vom, on the southern plateau, where the Sudan United Mission kindly opened its already overtaxed hospital to our people.

When the Sudan Interior Mission had been granted access to North Nigerian territory, through its offer to work among lepers, one requirement had been a resident doctor for the settlement. Dr. Raymond Jotcham had responded to the urgent challenge. On his death, not many months after his arrival on the field, Dr. and Mrs. Charles L. Entner had been rushed right to Katsina, with no chance to study Hausa before they reached the settlement.

Arrangements had now been made for Dr. Entner and his wife to go to Minna language school for six months after he had established his residence in the colony. He would return to Katsina at specified intervals, or in case of emergency, to superintend the work and do any surgery that would be needed. Miss Susan Hooge, an intelligent and level-headed nurse, was left in charge of the patients, then numbering somewhat over 300. I was to help her with the medical work during the doctor's absence from the station. In my spare time—if there would be any—I should continue my language study. So I was being stationed temporarily in Katsina Leper Colony. I was not surprised. Had not the Lord shown me that He had such work for me?

I have already mentioned the housing shortage. Until the Entners left Katsina, I was assigned to remain in Kano, then a small station erected outside the walls of the great city that was, and remains, a stronghold of Mohammedanism.

The chief advantage of building a station in such a difficult and antagonistic area was that Kano was one of the few places in the North where there were either British or Syrian canteens. Kano station was needed to supply the widely scattered new outposts of Christian witness with building and household supplies not available in the bush, and to relay to these stations, by messenger or by lorry delivery, any mail that came, as well as their allowances—in cash; checks or bills were useless in the villages.

Padlocked "chop" boxes went out from Kano containing lemons and screws, flashlight bulbs and shoe polish, a bag of shillings and pennies, a pineapple, a hard, unwrapped cone of sugar that would have to be pounded to powder (for granulated sugar was then almost unobtainable), matches, carrots, a tin of tea—and mail!

Always it was mail for which missionaries reached first, and —because meager allowances were often direly needed long before they arrived (they were rarely the full $35.00 a month in those days), the contents of the little bag were quickly counted and carefully locked away.

Luxuries such as tinned food and ready-to-wear clothing, or knickknacks from the "dime" store, were prohibitively expensive, rare, or entirely absent from Nigerian canteens.

Kano station was an important link between headquarters in Jos and the people in Northern Nigeria, though the station itself, with its five or six buildings—including a combination storehouse and garage—was smaller than Wushishi station.

A small medical work had been begun and was carried on in a storage room off the single garage. The class in religious education met in the building that was then used as chapel, and though it drew only a few adults who came irregularly, it was probably better attended than were the Sunday services. Most evangelical activity had to be done by those who trekked to outlying villages.

I arrived there one afternoon and was taken to the guest house, built especially for transient missionaries such as I, or those who were ill, or who had come to Kano on imperative business. It was a long, tin-roofed building that was divided into four or five separate rooms, all of which opened onto a common front porch facing the "main" house, where meals were served.

After five months in Wushishi, with its thatched roofs and verandas of beaten earth, the strip of concrete porch seemed almost palatial luxury. More, each of those five rooms had a glass window, a luxury that I had not seen for five months; for in Wushishi, tin shutters shielded us from storms, and expanding metal grating protected us from thieves and wild animals while the shutter was opened to let in light. The windows in Kano did have the expanding metal gratings, too, so that the glass windows could be left open.

My room contained a chair or two, a table, and a bed, over which hung the inevitable mosquito net frame. After our crowded dumbbell hut that had no place for a bed, the room seemed spacious and grand. A wardrobe built of roofing "pan" and locally hewn wood, provided space enough to hang my clothes, and became a partition between the bedroom and a niche that was used as a bathroom. Shelves in the wardrobe took the place of a dresser, for drawers were a luxury I did not know throughout the years of that term. I marveled at the space I had to lay out my personal and toilet necessities.

The "bathroom" included the convenience of an indoor toilet. In Wushishi our toilet had been an outhouse, described, quite appropriately by someone, as a "telephone booth." Like those in Wushishi, the *bucket* was a five-gallon kerosene tin that had to be *flushed* with enough sand to keep the top always dry. Kano had the added magnificence of a handle attached to the tin can that was used to scoop sand, and the bucket was serviced from outside, through a small aperture that could be fastened, I noticed, by a sliding bolt on the inside. The bathtub, in Kano as in the bush, was a portable galvanized laundry tub, oblong in shape, and large

enough for an adult with an average build and limber joints.
Water for washing was in another of the square kerosene tins,
with a coffee tin *dipper* floating in it. I hung my clothes on
the hangers that had been cleverly made of stiff rolls of news-
paper bent slightly where a string was tied about the center.

A shadow passed my glass window facing the veranda.

"Malama!"

The magic of a compliment—in this case it may have been
deliberate flattery—brought my drooping spirits to attention.
The eager, male voice outside carried a sense of urgency. But
then, of course, the man, whose billowing robes I now
glimpsed through the window, was asking for someone else
in one of the other rooms, for I could certainly not qualify
for the title of respect that is due only a woman who has become known as a religious teacher. But the title was repeated.

"Malama!"

Since I still made no answer, the trader outside probably
decided that I knew no Hausa at all, so he tried his best English on me.

"Come. See. Good sings. Nice! Lookut here!"

Relieved at the diversion a trader would offer and genuine-
ly curious to know what he had to sell, I was easily drawn to
the door. The trader, seeing me appear, threw the cumber-
some loose sleeves of his gown back onto his shoulders, and
took the lid from a great, colorful, hand-woven basket. Quickly he spread out a colorful Indian print *zane,* and scooped
his wares from the basket for better display.

In Wushishi, I had seen the little compacts made of goat-
skin, with the bristly hair to the outside, in which the women
keep black antimony crystals that are applied directly to the
unpigmented edge of the eyelids to enhance the size and
brightness of their eyes. I had seen beaded bracelets there,
too. But the Kano trader had many articles I had never seen.
Most beautiful—and most expensive—was a string of ivory

elephants that had been ingeniously and masterfully carved from a single giant tusk.

"What's that?" I wondered, audibly, pointing to a bone elephant that looked somewhat like a porcupine.

"Toos picks," said the trader, picking up the queer figure and pulling one of its quills. "Ibory toos picks." And he demonstrated the efficacy of the dental requisite by picking at his *kola*-reddened teeth. Ebony plaques also featured elephants or well-carved Negro faces. What interested me far more was a set of bookends, each side a highly polished ebony elephant, one with trunk upraised, the other with his trunk below his feet. Ivory tusks glowed whitely against the smoothly carved ebony. Another set of bookends were in the form of a Hausa man and woman, realistically performed, even to the typical headdress of the best set of Hausa society.

As my eyes wandered over his display, the trader lifted up for me to handle the beautiful cushions and hassocks made of kid with a symbolic design, typically Hausa, repeated on most of them. The finest kid in the world comes from North Nigeria, near Sokoto. However impractical a creamy white hassock might be, the most beatiful were white with appliqués of lizard skin.

Beverly Pegg,[1] the girl who was doing the medical work in Kano, and who taught religious training class for adults in the afternoon, came by just when the trader had added two or three purses to the things he had already piled into my hands. She called to me.

"Don't let that fellow skin you!" she warned. "He's liable to, if you don't know what to pay."

"*Haba, Baturiya!*" exclaimed the trader, reproachfully, smiling at Beverly and offering her greetings of the afternoon. I noted, however, that he had addressed Beverly, a religious teacher on the station, as "white woman"—*baturiya*. They rattled on in rapid Hausa for a short time, and I stood

---

[1] Now Mrs. Richard Brandt.

by uncomprehending, realizing anew that the school girls at Wushishi had been "talking down" to us so that we could understand a little of what they were saying.

Duly warned against being swindled, since I was such a novice, I tried to give back the purses, though I was reluctant about relinquishing the one made of exquisitely marked python skin. Instead of accepting the bags, however, the trader placed still another one, this one made from the shiny, polished belly of a crocodile, on top of the others.

Beverly laughed. "We all go through that stage," she said, recognizing me, as had the trader, for an easy victim. "Most of us find one of these baskets very handy, though." She pointed to the large basket from which the trader had pulled his stock in trade. "They make good laundry baskets."

Before she went on her way, Beverly briefed me about the price to pay for the basket, and added in deliberately rapid English, "Don't pay more than half the first price he quotes you. *Ciniki* him down hard. You won't cheat him! And another thing, don't let him see which things you are really interested in. Bargain with him on some other article, then casually ask about what you want to buy as though it doesn't really matter."

"Haven't you any ebony work better than this? This *baturiya* is not going to be here too long, and might buy something worth taking home."

The trader had probably recognized the first covetous gleam in my eyes when I looked at the elephant bookends. He placed them into her hands.

"Sometimes," said Beverly, "these things are not real ebony, but eroco wood with shoe blacking on it. I don't know much about ebony."

"Yas, ebony. Ebony, *baturiya*," said the trader, reading her meaning from her expression as much as from his understanding of her English. He seized another ebony object from his collection, took a knife and scraped the bottom of the book-end.

"*Kin gani?* Ebony."

"Yes," said Beverly, in Hausa, "but look, here you have slipped, and chipped off a piece of ear." She found more fault with the ones I wanted than with the others, and priced them all. When the trader quoted his price, she walked away.

"Tomorow we'll find another trader."

"Come into the room," she advised me, "and forget this trader."

I was torn between showing a proper respect for her advice, and my desire to have those bookends, but I withdrew with a reluctance the trader noted well. When the door was shut, he shouted another price.

"I'll reduce you three shillings!"

We waited a few minutes.

"I'll *rage* you four!"

"If you really want to do business," Beverly said, in an impatient voice, "give us your real price."

Shilling by shilling, his price came down to one-half of his first price. I bought the bookends, thanking Beverly for her demonstration of how to do business in Africa. I found, too, that I needed that demonstration, for I had to use those time-consuming tactics to buy everything from butter and meat to thatch and bricks in later days when my responsibilities stretched to such commodities.

The trader did not leave when Beverly did and he was not through with me. I bought a cushion, using Beverly's technique, and was considering the purchase of a snakeskin purse, though I did not know whether I would need such an accessory on a bush station.

The trader saw my enthusiasm wane. Like a magician, he drew out a small roll from somewhere and flung it dramatically to the porch, holding one end. It was a python skin nearly 20 feet long. Now he brought out the purse. I bargained for it, carefully.

"*Haba baturiya,*" he remonstrated sadly. "If I sold my things for that price, I could never make a living. I would not let you have it, either, *baturiya,* if you were not so friendly and I did not like you so well. And you are new in the country . . ."

At the dinner table everyone was invited to stay for a quinine bee. To evade the "bee" would be shirking a routine duty in which everyone was expected to participate. Anyway, I would have stayed just for fear I might miss something. I had been on one station too long to ignore the prospect of making new acquaintances.

The people from the bush were catching up on general mission news even while saucers were passed to all, and a generous, high tablespoonful of quinine hydrochloride was dipped into each saucer. Bowls of empty five-grain capsules had been placed in the center of the table.

"We have to fill enough capsules to last the Kano compound until the end of the rainy season. And it is high time we got it done. We have already had several storms here."

"Do you have more work during the rains?" I asked.

"It's not that," someone explained. "Later, during the heavy rains and general humidity, the gelatine capsules would be so soft that they would be hard to close; tapping would force them out of shape."

"Tap the longer end of the capsule into the quinine until it is tightly packed," said another of the older missionaries helpfully, seeing me hesitate, "then one or two light taps into the loose quinine with the empty end, and you can close the capsule. If you are not sure whether you have five grains in your capsules, you can check them on the scales."

"You ought to weigh one out of every five or six capsules, anyway," said Beverly, "to be certain that you are getting them tight enough."

The main concern was that we got *enough* quinine into a capsule. I noticed that several people were making their own special pile of capsules. They knew just how much they needed, by now, to keep malaria out of their systems. Large individuals made their capsules tighter and longer than the rest, containing as much as seven grains of quinine.

"If I'd take that kind of capsule," exclaimed a fragile little woman, looking at one of the men's stacks, "I'd have the shakes all the time."

"My ears would roar until I couldn't hear anything else," commented another.

I learned that quinine is good to paint on thumbs of babies who have the habit of sucking their thumbs. That it is very efficient remedy, far better than the time-honored washing of the mouth with soap, against rudeness or bad language in the very young of either color. I learned the reason, several hundred capsules and a blister later, when I thoughtlessly put my fingertip to my mouth.

In British territory, quinine was pronounced *quineen,* and individualism in pronunciation was frowned on. Because I had been glared down several times when I had mispronounced the subject in hand, I decided to sit back and listen. The tapping sounded like a yard of hens let loose in a shallow grain bin. Some rather interesting information was floating about, too.

Someone mentioned that the price of one of the large tins of quinine hydrochloride, such as we had on the table, was well over $500. Java, the country that produced the largest portion of the world's quinine, was making good money on its monopoly of the lifesaving drug. Quinine was so expensive that many people died for lack of it, since there was no other good antimalarial known in those days.

The malaria of Nigeria does not have regular paroxysms of chills and fever like the benign tertiary type common in the States. Almost all of the older missionaries had had ma-

laria at some time or other, and they began comparing their
varying symptoms which ranged from diarrhea to sleepless-
ness, from nausea to severe backache.

I worried audibly about being a nurse, with the lives of my
patients and fellow missionaries in my hands. There seemed
to be no specific symptoms by which to diagnose the disease.
I was confused and frightened. Nurses at home look at a chart
to see what a doctor has ordered. They are even taught *not*
to have any diagnostic ideas of their own. How would I cope
with a disease as dangerous as malaria and with symptoms
as evasive as the Nigerian type?

"If they have fever, whatever the other symptoms, give
them quinine. If it's something else, you will have eliminated
malaria, anyway."

"Usually it will be malaria, in this country."

I pondered that advice while I studied the blister on my
index finger. I tried filling capsules holding them with another finger while I remembered all the *general* diseases that
also should be diagnosed early for successful treatment, and
that could begin with fever and one of the malarial symptoms,
like nausea or diarrhea.

"How long," I asked timidly, "does it take before quinine
takes the fever down so that malaria is eliminated?"

My confusion only grew worse as different missionaries told
how long they had had a fever before it had broken. And
they knew others . . .

One of the older women, not a nurse, said, "Honey, don't
play around with malaria. When you feel tired, or nervous,
or have a headache, take extra quinine. It can so easily turn
into a malignant type. Cerebral malaria is a harsh, quick
death. Don't try too hard to diagnose carefully. Just take
extra quinine."

"And don't forget to take your quinine regularly," said
someone else. "That's where the most trouble comes in. You
go on trek and get real tired. You begin to ache. You re-

member that because your quinine was in the chop box you have not taken it for a couple or three days. So you take two, to make up for it. Next thing you know you have blackwater fever."

Blackwater fever is a deadly disease caused by the simultaneous rupture of so many millions of infected red corpuscles that they clog capillaries in the kidneys. Blackwater fever is fatal so consistently that in Dr. Stirrett's handbook on tropical diseases for the use of general mission staffs he advises, on the first sign of this disease (dark urine), the head of the station is to "pray to God—and send for the nearest doctor."

I began to see the frightening implications of a nursing career in Africa. Even in Kano people were coming to me for advice on matters that at home would be taken only to a doctor. In Kano, I could send them on to a doctor. What would I do on a bush station two or three days' journey—one way—from any other mission station, and perhaps much farther from a doctor? How I wished to return to the calm care-free routine of learning the Hausa language!

I remembered, with some comfort, that the Lord has promised wisdom to those who lack wisdom. I should certainly need to make use of His gracious provision. I slept restlessly that night. As a graduate—or rather as an expulsee from language school—I had, indeed, entered into a new phase of missionary life. Now I would see what it really means to be a missionary. How I prayed that I would be a good one!

In the morning, having renewed my resolve to be the best kind of missionary I knew how to be, I sat down at the long table in the main house, where Mr. Albert Ter Meer, our host, was soon scooping up big helpings of cereal with a large ladle. I shuddered, nausea rising in my throat. In Wushishi I had been having smaller and smaller helpings.

"Not quite so much," I gasped, when I saw a brimming ladle poised over the bowl that would be passed to me. I was

embarrassed that I was the only missionary present who seemingly had not learned to eat *kunnu*.

A very trivial matter, like an unappetizing dish, can become
strangely important. I had allowed *kunnu* to take on the
proportions of a great hardship not too graciously borne. I
had not dared to allow myself to think about four years in
even one term, for to me that represented almost 1,500 bowls
of *kunnu!*

I looked at my still-generous helping of porridge with grim
determination to eat every bit of it. The best system was
large spoonfuls, swallowed quickly. I carefully sugared my
staggeringly large portion and attacked it.

And it was good! Kano *kunnu* was made of grain ground
in a grist mill and was not sour.

Fortified with a sustaining breakfast of *kunnu,* I was almost
prepared to face the problems that nursing might hold for
me in the dim future. In Katsina, of course, I would not be
in a position of responsibility, and I certainly planned to get
as much practical help as Miss Hooge would give me for my
own use later. Perhaps the Lord would banish all my trials
and difficulties in the way that the grievous *kunnu* worry had
been so happily dissolved.

While these consoling thoughts drifted through my mind,
a boy approached me with a note. Dr. Helser wanted to see
me in his office.

I went quickly, wondering what he would want to talk to
me about. Perhaps I would be going to Katsina sooner after
all. Perhaps he would suggest that I use my time in Kano to
visit with the people and get the real Kano accent, for Kano
Hausa was the Hausa used in the Bible translation. The
Wushishi people were, many of them, of Gbari or Nupe
tribes, so they did not speak a pure Hausa at all. Of course,
I had intended to do that anyway, even without urging from
him.

I had liked Dr. Helser from the moment I had first seen

him. He was helpful and kind to us, and enthusiastic in his representation of Christ to the people of Africa. As time was to go by, my respect and admiration were to deepen, but that morning I was not elated at his proposition.

"Since you may be here about a month," he said, "I have decided to send Beverly to Miango for her holiday. You will take over her medical work in her absence."

I gulped and stammered some sort of answer. I was ashamed to admit the fears I had discussed the previous evening. I was supposedly a qualified nurse. Did I have the gumption to qualify as a missionary, or didn't I?

Beverly remained that morning to show me about her dispensary, a small cubicle partitioned off from the garage. I had visited the dispensary in Wushishi several times while work was progressing, but I was still unable to understand the quick chatter of the patients. I tried to learn everything about the Kano work that morning, but my heart sank when I contemplated taking the responsibility of the patients.

I met Dr. Helser later in the day. "Well," he inquired cheerfully, "are you eager to begin your first assignment as a missionary?"

I could not honestly say that I was. "I really don't know as much Hausa as you seem to give me credit for, Dr. Helser," I said. "Who is going to preach to them in the morning?"

"You will, of course!"

He saw my look of sheer consternation, and added, "Just read out of the Bible, if you don't think you can make any remarks."

Now, two decades later, I clearly recall that first morning with my first group of patients. There were only about fifteen or twenty people there for that first service. They sat hunched together in a circle on the ground, watching me with curiosity or impatience. I sat on a stump and read laboriously from my Hausa Bible.

A Gospel message given before clinic service begins is

routine on all mission stations of the Sudan Interior Mission. The purpose behind all medical service is primarily to draw these people, who might otherwise not be contacted for Christ, to listen to the message of His salvation.

Medicine is a wedge into needy and sinsick hearts, and it is a good one. If we can relieve people of physical suffering, they are inclined to have confidence, too, in our message. Therefore, though physical help may be secondary to the spiritual aspect of the work, it remains that the more we help the people the more confidence they will have in us—and the more patients we will have who will come to hear the Gospel. Mission medical work must not be slipshod nor haphazard.

In all, with latecomers, we may have had thirty patients that morning. I recall listening to a torrent of Hausa from patients and turning in confusion to the African who had been assisting Beverly in her work. He would simplify for me, and often as he spoke his hand would reach for a bottle on the shelf.

"Missi Pagg, she use this for that."

I have a grave suspicion that the Kano boy was in charge of the dispensary for a few mornings. But, as in my arithmetic class at Wushishi, I found there was certain terminology that must be mastered. I also had to learn British names for drugs with which I was familiar and for unfamiliar drugs that are used only in tropical countries.

Once a week, Dr. Edwin A. Harris came to the dispensary. He was the only medical doctor in the area and was trying to take care of our mission family, superintend Kano leper settlement, and oversee the work in bush dispensaries.

Dr. Harris' visits bolstered my morale, and though I must have fairly battered him with questions, I cannot recall that he was impatient with my ignorance. From him I added to a notebook of prescriptions that I had already begun to collect in Wushishi, for mixing medicines would be one phase of nursing on bush stations.

BY PRAYER was the motto Dr. Bingham, that great giant of faith, had chosen for the Sudan Interior Mission, and for many years it appeared on all mission stationery. In Kano, more than on any other station I have seen on the mission field, this motto was put into practice.

Though most stations have daily prayer together with all personnel, there was a special spirit of expectancy about those in Kano. Before we began to pray, Dr. Helser brought us up to date on prayers God had already answered, or where we could be watching God work, in answer to previous prayer. That put the prayer meeting on a practical basis and we were ready to do business before the throne, knowing that we were here as God's representatives and that He wanted advance as much as we did. I began to see, more clearly than ever before, that though our God is Lord of the infinite, He is Lord also of the infinitesimal. I had never thought of God as an efficient, far-sighted businessman. The Kano prayer meetings taught me many things.

All those who visit the model mission station at Kano should also see the station as I saw it in 1939. All that is there today, the large office, the dispensary, the eye hospital, the great stone church, the schools for the blind, for boys (begun for the waifs of the market places), the Bible school, the many fine residences, have been brought into existence *by prayer*.

I believe that these prayer meetings are also the secret of the success and great growth in the work in Northern Nigeria. Dr. Helser, the man who had the vision to pray and work toward that phenomenal growth, spearheaded and superintended the work in this vast Moslem area.

Dr. Helser's confidence that God cared greatly for His representatives, as well as for His work, did not make him presume on God's munificence. The Helsers continued to live in that same house that stood when the station was young. Newer and more commodious living quarters were to be built, but the Helsers lived in the unpretentious homeliness they had worked out with furniture made locally by African carpenters, that might even have been considered shabby in comparison with what was acquired by later arrivals. Through his hands flowed most of the funds that built Kano station as it now stands—monument to the bounty of our God.

The *main house,* as it stood in 1939, though smaller than it now is, contained the kitchen, dining and sitting rooms for guests and staff, and an apartment for the couple in charge of the house, hosts to those who came to the station as guests, or who took their meals in the main house. Besides that, at one end of what is now the dining hall—the partition has long since been removed to stretch dining space—was the small business office from which David John handled the shopping orders from isolated bush missionaries.

I remember walking into the sitting room one afternoon in search of a worth-while book. I could not find one I liked, for the Kano library was obviously a set of "culls" from libraries of people in the homeland, who had included them in one of the "missionary barrels" that are now, fortunately, out of date. While going over the titles one by one, I was startled by a wail of grief issuing from the office. Being the nurse in charge of all emergencies, I dropped my book and rushed toward the sound.

David John was on his feet, wildly waving an offending letter in the unresponsive atmosphere of the small room. It was a note from one of the out-stations.

"What in the world is the matter?" I cried.

"Look!" shouted the young man, shoving a piece of plaid material into my hands. "And she wants me to get thread to match that!"

Mr. John has long since been married and plaid sewing

thread no longer presents great problems. He, too, had much to learn.

He had been there longer than I, though, and spoke to me from his deep experience one day when I gushed enthusiastically about the wonderful people who made up our mission family. With my background, the novelty and wonder of true Christian fellowship was a source of inexpressible joy. Never, before I entered the mission, had I felt free to discuss spiritual matters with those with whom I lived or worked. This fellowship continues to be one of the great rewards of being one of Christ's servants.

"All the people in the mission are so wonderful, aren't they?" I asked.

"Well," said Mr. John, surveying me for signs of insincerity, "some of them are. But in office work you run across some pretty funny ones, sometimes."

His remark presaged some of my later experiences, well epitomized in a poem written by a member of another mission:

> To live above
> With saints we love,
> Oh, that will be glory!
> But to live below
> With the saints we know—
> That's quite a different story!

FIVE

LEPER VILLAGE

> Jesus put forth his hand, and touched him.
> —Matthew 8:3

WHAT A HAT!" I had to say something—anything. All these patients, at Ulcer Station No. 1, were watching me. I must not let these lepers know that I was horrified, revolted, by what I was seeing.

I was searching wildly for words to make conversation. I must say something light—something cheerful. I was a nurse. I must be a bulwark of strength and a source of hope to these ghastly specters of hopelessness.

"What a hat!" I said. "Did you make it yourself?"

The hat to which I referred was one with a very large, floppy brim, and it practically hid the man who was sitting at my feet, waiting for his dressing. It was obviously homemade, woven crudely of split palm fronds. It was a funny hat. So I spoke as airily as I could through a throat that hurt with the tightness of sobs choked back.

The hat tilted upward, and the man under it looked up at me, smiling for a mere second. Then, still silent, he looked down, and raised his hands slightly.

Hands? No. They were stumps. On the right side he still had a fingerless palm; the left hand was gone to the wrist.

The leper's gesture, though slight, was eloquent. How could he have made the hat? How crude, how tactless, how thoughtless could I be? I bit my tongue in exasperation at my unintentional cruelty.

This was a bad beginning. To stand there staring was to reveal my horror. To speak seemed to be worse. How would I ever be able to work among these people? I would go back to Kano—to Wushishi. I could not work here! To my inexpressible relief, Sue Hooge came out of the ulcer station carrying a sheaf of records.

"I thought," I said in English, "that leper's hands just get white, and then the fingers fall off! That's what it always sounds like when people talk about it at home!"

"It's not as simple as that," said Sue.

I was seeing the most repulsive aspect of leprosy, bared to view because all the patients had removed their dressings for inspection and treatment. Never had I seen such deep ulceration. Never had I dreamed that any disease could maim and disfigure so cruelly without bringing a speedy end. I shuddered.

I scolded myself mentally as I restrained myself, by sheer determination, from fleeing the station then and there.

Perk up, hard-boiled nurse! This is what you came out to Africa for—remember? And don't feel sorry for yourself! You're just looking at it! These people live with it all the time!

I pondered that thought. These people could smell the rotting of their own tissues and were watching, in their own bodies, what Dr. Jotcham had aptly described as "the remorseless nibblings of unhurried death."

I recalled now the eagerness with which I had watched for Katsina Leper Settlement on the previous afternoon, when Dr. and Mrs. Helser had brought me out in the station wagon in which he had brought many of these lepers to the settlement where there was asylum and some hope of improvement.

When we had arrived at last at the colony that lay six miles from the great walled city of Katsina, it appeared from the road to be nothing more than another village, except perhaps that it was not as crowded as most villages.

Set on a long hill, on the opposite side of the road and quite some distance from it, were three houses. The first, the Helsers explained as we approached, was occupied by the industrial superintendent of the colony, John Vander Schie, and his family.

"John is kept constantly busy," Dr. Helser said, "because the number of patients is increasing daily. The huts and most of the other buildings in the settlement have been built by lepers, but John must keep up with the continuous expansion with his building program."

The house in the center was a duplex, intended for a teacher and a nurse.

"Only Ruth Baxter lives in that house now," said Mrs. Helser, "since you will be living with Sue Hooge, the nurse, in the doctor's residence."

It was to that third house, the doctor's, to which we drove, and where Sue Hooge served tea for us and all those on the station. I was attracted by Ruth Baxter, a pleasant, dark-eyed young woman of unusual poise and cheerfulness.

Because everyone realized I was impatient to see the settlement, we all walked across the road—the line past which all lepers were forbidden to go. They took me first to the school, also used as chapel. Inside long benches were built of the same mud bricks that had gone into the construction of the building. The benches had no backs, of course. The windows and roof were of corrugated metal—*pan,* as it is generally called.

We paused near a small building with a large porch, deserted at the time.

"We have three ulcer stations like this," commented Sue, who was in the lead. The people come here for dressings, and every morning and afternoon they come also for their tonic or other medication and to have their temperatures taken."

On the way back toward the large stone dispensary building that was opposite the doctor's house, we paused before a monument made of native rock and cement, erected in the form of a tombstone. I read the inscription.

"This Dr. Jotcham was a very young man!" I exclaimed.

"He was my fiancé," said Ruth Baxter simply.

Only then did I learn that it had been Dr. Jotcham who had come to take the responsibility of building up the leper work when it was first turned over to the Sudan Interior Mission, and that the Entners had actually come to replace him. Though Ruth Baxter and Raymond Jotcham had been engaged and had come to Africa at the same time, Ruth had had time to go to the language school. Dr. Jotcham had been sent on to the settlement, because the leper village must not be left without a medical man in charge. They were to be married as soon as Ruth left language school.

Dr. Jotcham's organizational ability was still felt in the smooth operation of the community. Since his knowledge of the language and of the customs of the people had at first been limited, he had wisely created a council of older patients who handled the many *palavers* and were accepted as the heads of the colony.

The patients soon recognized Dr. Jotcham's sincere interest in them. On chilly nights he would throw a blanket about his shoulder, like a native *mayafi,* and go into the village just to visit his people. And they loved him for it.

When epidemic meningitis struck the community, Dr. Jotcham was one of the first to come down with the deadly disease, a terror to all of us even in these days of miracle drugs. Ruth was called to Katsina. She came before he became delirious, and she was with him when he died.

Now here, not many yards from the dispensary, on the "leper" side of the road near the people for whom he died, we bowed and thought about how young he had been and how much he had been needed! A doctor! Just through long years of training! Intelligent, resourceful, beloved, dedicated —why?

God has done it before. He has done it since. Somehow it takes the crushing-out of a magnificent young life to shake the Lord's people from lethargy and indifference. God needs *men* on mission fields. So few men are stirred by the fact that thousands of souls are dying daily and passing into a Christ-less eternity because there has been no one to bring them the Gospel. So few men are responding to our Lord's clear command that His followers must be witnesses unto every creature, to the uttermost part of the earth. When neither need nor command draws men to the task, God is left with one sad alternative, to shock men to obedience. It must tear God's heart as it breaks the heart of those who are be-reaved. Yet, for the sake of the untold millions that must be reached . . .

Jesus said while He walked on earth, "Except a corn of wheat fall into the ground and die, it abideth alone."

When God crushes out a life of great promise—a life greatly beloved—then, somehow indifference and hardness are broken and God can woo several to step into the great and previous gap. It happened after Raymond Jotcham died in Africa. It happened after five men died in Ecuador. Where will it happen next? Where is it that someone is laboring—abiding alone—where the need is beyond his strength? There —unless men step into the gap *before it lengthens*—it must happen again.

Beside that crude stone erected over a premature grave, as I wiped away tears for the young life offered in love to his Lord, and for the young woman who had raised the monu-ment and who remained to do her part alone, I rededicated my own life more wholly to Christ.

The dispensary, built of the same stone that we had seen in the monument, was divided by a wide veranda running through the center of the building. Several white-uniformed young men were in the dispensary, on the lepers' side. They were cheerful, courteous young men, and except for one, who had paralysis known as claw-hand, none of them bore any sign of disease that I could detect. Malam Kure, the efficient laboratory technician trained by Dr. Jotcham, was actually a man who had been pronounced symptom-free, though he still worked on that side. All others, however, were lepers. Sue took us through the dispensary to a small surgery.

Returning, we crossed the veranda to the "clean" side. Here were the doctor's desk, his bookcase, his files on all the patients.

"All reports filled out on the other side, for use in making these records," Sue explained, "are first submerged in a disinfectant, so that no contaminated material of any kind need be brought to this side."

Beyond the office was the drug room, with long shelves of drugs and equipment for filling prescriptions.

Next day, after the Helsers had gone, Sue told me that she would give me several hours a day for my language study.

"But would you like to see the work at the ulcer stations this morning?"

"Oh, yes!" I had exclaimed enthusiastically.

The previous day we had had little contact with the patients, for the village lay beyond the medical unit. I wanted to see the lepers. Sue took me to the nearest ulcer station and had gone inside to confer with the man who was in charge of doing the dressings. Left outside, I stared in stunned disbelief at the exposed stumps and mutilated extremities. Now I was seeing leprosy! Some people were still gingerly pulling dressings from gangrenous feet or hands. The odor, even outdoors, added to the accumulated horror of what I was seeing, made me feel faint.

I became aware that the group had ceased their cheerful chatting. They were watching me.

"What a nurse," I thought, "to stand here staring! I must

not let these people see that they are revolting to me. These are my patients."

I greeted them. They greeted me in chorus. Then they waited and all eyes on me. I must say something to win their love and confidence—but what? What could I say to these people?

It was then that I saw the hat—the funny, crude, hand-woven hat. And it was then I made that lamentable blunder. Did these people think I was making a joke of the man's disability?

Yes, I had wanted to see leprosy. Now I had seen enough, and yet I could not keep from staring at the misery about me. Here at this ulcer station were 30 or more patients, some sprawled out in the open because the seats under the wide roof of the porch were all occupied.

I knew now why there were three stations at different locations in the village. Some of these people could not hobble far on their ulcerated and mutilated feet. Some crept on all fours. Then I did some rapid calculation. If, in a settlement of 350 patients, there was need of three stations like this, did it mean that nearly one out of three was in this pitiful condition?

Actually the proportion was smaller, for the other stations served fewer people. Nor did I realize, at the moment, that the settlement had been, during those first years, more an asylum for beggars and cripples than an institution of healing. The hopelessly crippled and the outcasts had been driven from their homes or the market places to find a haven of refuge. Only after some of these disfigured people began to cast off the signs of disease did the more hopeful prospects come to the settlement. The sulfone drugs, introduced some years later, have changed the entire picture of leper work from despair to hopeful expectancy. But all these things I was to learn as time went by.

Sue explained some of those things on that first day, too. "Leprosy does not have to look like this," she said. "In countries where living standards are higher, you would not find nearly so many ulcers. Here, because of improper nutrition and lack of cleanliness, a slight scratch may break down to become an ulcer. Of course, the tissues are poorly nourished because of the neural condition."

She explained further.

"The ones who lose fingers and toes have neural leprosy. The disease runs up along a nerve, the nerve sheath thickens, and the first areas of trouble lie beyond some joint where the swollen nerve is compressed and finally cut off entirely."

"Do they have a lot of pain?" I asked. Most of the patients looked quite cheerful, though some faces were drawn and disfigured.

"A few of them certainly do have pain," said Sue, "but most of them feel only a tingling they call *majiriya*. They speak of a sensation like pebbles rolling about under their skin. Then the skin becomes anaesthetic, and slowly, as the nerve grows thicker, all sensation of the extremity is lost. And that leads to many situations that are due directly to carelessness.

"For instance," and Sue glanced along the row of patients, "Yusuful here knows that his hands are entirely without sensation. Yet instead of using his head, and the spoon provided by the settlement, he ate boiling hot *tuwo da miya*, native style, with his fingers."

I shuddered at the price the man had had to pay, was even yet paying, for his indiscretion. Sue walked down the row.

"Shaitu here did not lose her toe through carelessness. She, too, has lost all sensation in her feet. A rat chewed her toe off during the night. She did not know what had happened until morning."

Then she gestured to a man whose one thin blanket had not been enough to keep him warm. He had been sleeping, just as most other inland people do, with an open fire in the middle of his hut.

"The neighbors woke me," he had explained in the morning. "They smelled the hand burning. I must have turned in my sleep."

That had been six months ago, and the burns were nearly healed. But there was very little left of his hand. Still he was fortunate to have had neighbors whose sense of smell had not been dulled by leprosy. When the olfactory nerve is deadened, food becomes tasteless—an uninteresting means of prolonging an existence that offers little prospect for a better future.

Sue talked casually and cheerfully as we went down the line. Each patient held a treatment card which she checked, writing in any change of treatment she deemed necessary. One man held his card between his lips, for his hands were both still in the revolting process of disintegration. Sue drew my attention to his face.

"This is what they call the mask of leprosy. The facial nerves are atrophied, so the muscles sag."

Familiar with the language, Sue made a humorous remark that drew various snappy retorts from here and there. I watched this man, whose face contorted into a horrible grimace that was meant to be a smile. His lower eyelids sagged open to show blood-shot eyes. Sue expained that often eyes cannot be closed at all, so the cornea becomes dry, and opaque.

"There are thousands of blind lepers, for that reason."

I thought, as I looked at that face devoid of any expression, a face that had become more repulsive when the man had tried to smile, that the leprous mask must be the worst manifestation of the disease. We love a friend, not because of his beauty or even for his usefulness or helpfulness to us, but for the personality and character he reveals in the expression of his face. It is hard to love or understand a person hid behind a leprous mask. I smiled in compassion at this man, and his lips fell open in a ghoulish grin.

Sue was going on to the other ulcer stations, but I was glad when she suggested that I might have some unpacking to do. I went to the clean side of the dispensary and scrubbed and scrubbed my hands and arms with disinfectant, though I had touched none of the patients, nor any object handled by any of them.

"Leprosy is not really highly infectious," Sue had told me. "Ordinary cleanliness is all that is required actually, though we use greater precautions."

Leprosy, similar in many respects to tuberculosis, is seldom contracted except through close, continued contact with a person who has the infectious type of the disease. No member of the staffs of any of the Sudan Interior Mission leprosaria has ever contracted leprosy, though it would not be impossible. Sometimes the disease does appear in a person who has had very little contact—known contact—with the disease.

Next day was "needle" day. Before the sulfones gave new hope for relief, the only medication that offered even a slim hope was hydnocarpus oil, injected subcutaneously. I was to help by checking temperature charts for elevations, and the charts for the dosage tolerated by each patient. I went down toward the camp when the policeman struck the gong —a spike and a rail.

As I crossed the road, I was heralded by a shout that carried halfway to the city of Katsina. A leper, astride a donkey, waved his arms fiercely and kicked his poor beast with vicious, misshapen heels as he wheeled about and charged at me, yelling at the top of lungs as powerful as a fog horn.

I might actually have been frightened, except for the fact that the man was screaming a welcome. His mouth twisted lopsidedly in a grotesque mask. The reins of his donkey were twisted about the stump of one of his flailing arms. His feet were just heels that had been pushed back out of shape, giving the vague impression that his feet were on backward. He had been given a donkey because it was the only way he could get about.

Abu was the clown of the settlement. Though he no longer had active leprosy, he had been given a place to live in the colony with other "burned-out" cases, who were unable to make their own living.

Actually, Abu had learned his clowning in the process of making his living as a professional beggar. He had become so proficient at his trade, too, that he was often missing on Katsina market days, though leaving the colony was strictly forbidden.

We liked each other immediately, and hardly a day passed that we did not sharpen our wits at each other. Abu usually had the last word. He could shout it from a distance. A long distance.

When I arrived the line of patients had already formed, and all the latest colony gossip was being exchanged. The boys had their table out on the veranda, all set up for the day's business. Because the hydnocarpus oil absorbed slowly, all too frequently causing abscesses, the site of injection was changed each time, and all patients received their injections at the same site on a given day. On this day they would be getting their "needle" (as they called it) in the right shoulder area.

Children were first in line, and I saw them cringe from the large-gauge needle that is needed for oil injection. Poor tots, they could neither understand the fate that had made them lepers nor the blessing that hydnocarpus oil might be for them.

The truth was that the oil was very ineffective in comparison with the drugs now available for treatment of leprosy. But with the oil, and good nutrition, and proper rest, and a cheerful attitude, there was hope. Some—even a fair number —were being dismissed symptom-free, and mission settlements were having so high a percentage of cures that the government was turning over its settlements to missions.

The secret of the success of mission leper work lay not in better medication—for none was available—but in the spirit of missionary activity. The love that holds people in such a service is that divine love that God sheds abroad in hearts that are open enough to receive it. And God's love draws men to Him.

As in tuberculosis, the attitude of mind and heart are great factors in throwing off the disease. It was soon apparent that the ones who were making a comparatively quick recovery were those who had accepted Christ as their Saviour. Salvation brings joy, and peace, and hope to all—even lepers—and these were medicine for the body as well as a boon to the soul.

I read this peace in the eyes of one of the young men in white uniform who would be helping with the needles. I could see the lack of it in others.

With Sue's aid I began to read the signs of leprosy on the bodies of the patients. Areas of depigmentation, though not white as I had imagined, would show up as people pulled aside their clothes or *mayafis*. Some bodies were covered with leprous nodules, a wart-like thickening caused by the more infectious type of the disease. Many of the latter patients had faces and lips so thickened that it was impossible to guess their ages. Often the larynx was affected, so that they whispered hoarsely, bending over me when I did not hear them correctly. And many of them coughed as they spoke.

And so they filed by me, 300 or more of them, the lepers for whom I had thrown aside a promising career and my plans for working in white-tiled hospitals, well-equipped, and swarming with doctors and administrators who would take the responsibility of the orders, the finances, and the lives of the patients. I had determined, in those other days, to work only in the finest hospitals with the best staffs and equipment, and perhaps, because the finest hospitals are expensive, I should have only the wealthiest and most cultured patients. Such had been my dreams!

These dreams I had traded for a chance to sit perspiring under a tin-roofed veranda of a dispensary with a rough cement floor, where we boiled needles over a balky primus stove that had to be set into a larger drum to shield it from wind; where the only running water was that carried in a bucket by a boy who was running—and boys usually did not run with water.

I looked again at the people filing by, some of them apparently well, some limping, some creeping along, carrying treatment slips between swollen lips, a few blind, many deformed. I knew that if we should pack up to go home to our more comfortable careers, these people would have to go home too, and they would be forced to face the bitter culmination of their disease without even the meager hope we were able to hold out to them. I knew that many of them would never again hear the name of Christ.

I thought briefly of Raymond Jotcham's grave outside, then met the smiling eyes of a grateful, friendly patient and smiled back. I had no regrets. I had exchanged my own way for Christ's, and I found even then that I had chosen well.

Dan Malam, the "orderly" with the claw-hand, who had been as efficient as any in giving injections, beckoned to me when the last patient had had his oil. I found a group of the white-clad boys in the surgery.

"Musa has another patient for you to examine. He wonders if we shouldn't start injections on her today."

I looked at the grinning Moses, named after the prophet of Sinai—Musa—the youngest and most mischievous boy on the staff. He held a calabash made from a gourd covered with blemishes that looked, for all the world, like leprous nodules. Calabash—kwarya—is a feminine word, so the calabash was a kuturuwa, or female leper. She got her injection, and I got a picture.

While Sue was busy with records, I browsed about in the limited library. I was determined to learn about the many ills of the tropics while I had a sympathetic and competent co-worker like Sue to help me. I spent hours over the doctor's books on tropical medicine, and more delightful hours in the pharmacy.

Since compounding prescriptions did not require knowledge of the Hausa language, I was allowed to mix all the medicines needed on the settlement. All nurses memorize the apothecaries' and metric weights' tables, and are allowed a few periods of practical application, but very few nurses make up more than a few simple solutions.

I found this work fascinating and extremely helpful. Sue was never impatient when I spent hours checking up on the actions of the drugs I was using, or copying the British government-endorsed prescriptions into my notebook. In years to come I was to thank her for her leniency and indulgence.

Sue carried the brunt of the responsibility and, because of her generous spirit, probably carried far more than her share of the work, both in the colony and in the house. She was thoughtful, too, in letting me see any patient with unusual symptoms or a condition that I had not seen before. She discussed treatment with me.

She took me with her to the "sick line," a group of huts near the dispensary for patients that needed close observation or extra care. There was no hospital for them, so they were in the regular type of round, thatched-mud hut, sleeping on cornstalk beds covered with grass mats. There were no sheets, and often blankets were very thin because people used them during cold weather for clothing.

Sue had explained that we check charts carefully for elevations in temperature, because such patients might be coming down with leprosy reaction fever. I had looked up this fever in the thin textbook on leprosy, and knew that it must be very unpleasant.

The reaction seems, actually, a violent effort on the part of the body to throw off the infection, and if the patient is in good condition there may be improvement after leprosy reaction. However, if the patient's condition is not too good, the fever will further weaken him, the nerve sheaths will become more thickened, and more anaesthesia and deformity is often the result.

It was inevitable that sooner or later one of the patients would develop this fever, and Sue took me to visit this patient, already in the sick line.

I had felt sorry for anyone who had to sleep on the hard beds made by binding three layers of corn stalks together (the upper and lower layers, crosswise of the bed, are bound to a center layer that lies lengthwise, thus giving it firmness and rigidity). Now I looked down on a man who was alternately shaken by chills and burning with fever. His face was thickened beyond recognition. He gasped for breath, for his nasal passages, even his trachea, seemed to be congested with the reaction. His voice was entirely gone and he whispered hoarsely and haltingly, half-irrational with pain that raked his entire body. Sue gave him a bit of medicine to alleviate his suffering. Little could be done to abort or lessen the violence of the reaction, which might, in this case, be fatal.

As we stooped to get out of the hut and turned to move on down the sick line, I saw on the roof a vulture—cruel and ugly scavenger of the bush—trailing dull gray wings like a cowl, hunched over with bald head bowed in an attitude of patient waiting. I shuddered. The horrible bird seemed an evil omen.

Far more cheering was my new assignment, that of establishing a crèche for the toddlers who still were free of the disease—for leprosy is contracted, not inherited. In colonies built by the mission, newborn babies are taken from mothers immediately, before there is any contact. Such a crèche was planned also in Katsina, but because of ignorance and prej-

Small scowl, big calabash

udice we were forced to move into such a service cautiously, or we might lose women patients as well as the hope of saving babies.

By kindness and patience we must win the mothers' confidence. In the meantime we could at least begin to show them that we are kind to babies and children, and that they would be happy with us. If they would bring their babies to us for a few hours a day, we would be able to keep an eye on their general physical condition, checking their weight, treating childhood ailments before they became serious—and we would still be giving these lovely little children a chance to go through life without contracting the disease.

I accepted the assignment eagerly. Sue and I carefully inspected a supply of tiny flannel dresses that had been sent by interested women in the homeland, and sewed a few more for children a bit beyond the age the small dresses would fit. Then several times, while the new round huts were being built and whitewashed, and finished complete with the luxury of cement floors, we announced that when the white unit was finished we would prepare a great feast for all women with babies.

A feast! That would bring them! Even though food at the

leper colony was better than average bush fare, their allowance of meat was still pitifully small. We let it be known that we would serve *miyar sarki*—gravy for a king!

Enthusiastically I worked all morning setting up my small medicine cabinet, scales for weighing the babies, and equipment for giving all the youngsters a good bath with soap, a luxury most of them had never known. When everything was done, I went home to snatch an hour of Hausa study. I was almost too excited to eat my lunch.

In my eagerness, I went to the new crèche long before the policeman beat the gong that would announce the time of the feast. There was nothing to do, of course, but then, some of the mothers might be as impatient as I, for people will walk fifteen miles or more for a good meal.

It had never struck me so forcefully before how very quiet a place seems that is all prepared for a very large crowd before the people have arrived. I had so thoroughly finished all my work that there was now nothing to do but wait. I wandered about, looking at the swings, checking my equipment, opening and closing the doors of the little medicine cupboard.

Husaina, the woman who would help me with the children, strolled across the sick-line area and into my children's unit when she noticed my presence there. She, too, puttered aimlessly, without making any comments.

"I thought some of them would come before the gong," I said, half apologizing for bringing her to work before the people came, though she would not have needed to come before the gong was rung.

Husaina shrugged. Turning slightly from me, she slammed a lid rather loudly on a pot of *tuwo*. Her unresponsiveness and lack of enthusiasm were depressing.

The policeman nearest the dispensary finally beat out the gong. Another took up the cue and beat a gong at a distant part of the colony. All the people would know now that it was time for the feast. I watched for them to pour out of their huts and throng toward the crèche.

The town continued to lie quiet under the blazing mid-afternoon sun. It could have been a ghost town, as far as activity was concerned. I glanced at Husaina, with the first inkling of something amiss. She had been watching me, but now she evaded my eyes and clattered again among her pots.

Minutes dragged by. Had I prepared for this opening of the crèche less fervidly, my disappointment would have been less acute. I could not believe that the women, who seemed to like to talk and joke with me, would not come to my banquet. I waited half an hour, then asked the policeman to beat out the invitation again. An hour passed.

Kure, the Christian laboratory technician, sent his little girl, Hassana, for her helping of the feast. Two children from the sick line whose mother was probably too weak to keep them from following Hassana, straggled in a little later.

Almost sick with discouragement, I halfheartedly showed the children how to use the swings. So this was what was happening with all the games I had planned! And this was the way my crèche was opening! Well, I could bathe these two youngsters from the sick line—and Hassana just for the fun of it—and give them their bowls of delicious *tuwo da miya*.

Though I had not been able to see any sign of life anywhere in the village, many ambushed eyes had been intent on what would be going on in the crèche. When the sparkling white dresses shone out on Hassana's chubby little brown body, and covered the skinny, rib-outlined chests and bloated tummies of her two friends, Husaina set them down on a mat with their bowls of food. I crept into the medical hut to hide a few tears that insisted on betraying the bitter disappointment that I had felt.

Husaina's voice broke into my despondency, and I heard another woman answer. I peered dejectedly from my retreat.

A dozen women had arrived. They were pouring from every corner of the camp. They were bringing their babies. Every woman came!

They were two hours late, so we forgot about games, and began with baths at once. The accepted procedure in the bush is to pour water—cold water—over the head and let it run down over the body. If the baby's nose has been running, the mother takes a small twig and carefully wipes the mucus down toward the lips with a sort of winding motion. If the baby finds it hard to come up for air, after having its nostrils filled with water from the ablution, the mother blows into its face a few times, and the child catches a strangled breath from sheer reaction.

We used the shower method too, since tubs might have been the means of spreading infection, but the children enjoyed our more civilized approach. Actually, though the babies of bush women never wear diapers, the women keep them commendably clean, and, by common consent, others insist that she carefully take care of any soiling of mats or clothes, or even on the premises near the doorway of the home.

We made the mistake of putting on their little white dresses before we gave the children their *tuwo da miya,* for alas, they were never so white again! Soap is a luxury for which few of these people had the price.

While everyone was enjoying the feast, I learned what had delayed them. Word had gotten around camp that the white doctor was planning to take their babies away by force. Even for a feast, no mother would risk that. Now, as I sat with them on the new mats, I invited them to bring their children every day at the stroke of two—we would not always wait as we had today—and there would be a good nourishing dish of *tuwo da miya* for them every afternoon.

Occasionally white people came to visit the leper settlement, and one day two men came to spend the night who were on their way to French country, just north of Katsina. John Vander Schie planned to take them up to the border, and offered to take Sue and me with him. Would we go?

Of course we went. French Niger was still pioneer country. No medical work was permitted the missionaries, and the only school allowed was a religious class, unless the missionary had a teacher's certificate for the French language. Only two stations had been established in this forbidden land. Jake Eitzen and Newton Kapp looked rugged enough to take the rigors of the outlandish country.

I even crossed the dangerous boundary to pose with a French national policeman to show that I had braved the border. I am not sure that I remembered that day that it was through Mr. Eitzen's chapel address in my home town, that I had felt the first tug toward the land of Africa, and had heard the Lord say, "That's where you will serve Me!" If I remembered, little did I dream that day that the nail-scarred hand had pointed at any more definite spot than to Africa generally. Certainly I was not thinking of ever going to French West Africa. I already had learned that my next station would be in Jega, quite near the French border, but still very clearly in British Nigeria.

SIX

THE WALLS OF JEGA

> Until thy high and fenced walls come down.
> —Deuteronomy 28:52

IN THE SUDAN INTERIOR MISSION, the first year on the field is probationary. The ability to pass a language examination and to withstand twelve months of the physical and moral rigors of life in Africa had brought me to the status of full-fledged junior missionary. I knew the ropes now. From now on, everything would be easy.

My promotion involved changes about which I had mixed feelings. I had learned to love the lepers, as well as the missionaries at Katsina Leper Settlement, but I had been stationed there only temporarily to give Dr. and Mrs. Entner an opportunity to spend a few months in the mission's language school at Minna.

However, I was pleased at the prospect of going to our mission rest home in Miango, on the plateau. There I would meet more of our wonderful family of missionaries, and would hear more about work on many stations. Missionary biography would be unfolding in table conversation!

Then, too, I anticipated with growing excitement going to a pioneer bush station, Jega, in the northwest corner of Nigeria—my first stationing above a temporary basis. With my amassed experience and knowledge, I would now carve out a great missionary career!

The plateau was a long journey into Central Nigeria—

nearer the equator by several degrees latitude, but cooler by many degrees Fahrenheit because of the higher altitude. Our Miango Rest Home is over twenty wild, rock-strewn bush miles from the nearest railway stop, which is Jos, where our mission headquarters are located.

Naturally my first thought when I reached Jos, was to find out more about my new station and to get any further instructions about the great adventure on which I hoped soon to embark. After a hasty inquiry, I was directed to the office, and without delay made my way toward it. But I was waylaid.

I heard a high-pitched, eager hail. Then I saw a little old man step from the door of a tiny coop of a house. The first thing I noticed, with some amusement, was wide suspenders, conspicuous over a shirt with long and sadly rumpled sleeves. He was short and bald, with the gleam of true missionary fervor in the sharp gray eyes. Now, those eyes seemed to be probing me for something beyond my current errand, about which I informed him.

"So you're the one who's going to Jega!" he exclaimed, when I told him where I had been assigned to go. Then he kindly corrected my intonation, an aspect of the Hausa language I still considered somewhat of an unimportant detail. He reminded me that the first syllable is on a low tone, with the accent on the last, higher syllable—Jay-*gah*. His eyes caught a new luster as he spoke to me about the people of Jega and my opportunities there.

"Put the Bible into their hands," he said enthusiastically, earnestly, "and teach them to read it!"

I was very anxious to be on my way, so I nodded my agreement and made hurried excuses. Still—perhaps because the little man went into his hut to pray—I remembered. Was not that the gist of what Dr. Thomas Moody, that other veteran missionary, had told me in Salina? "Give them the Word. It won't be your eloquence or your proficiency with the language that will win them. 'The entrance of thy words giveth light.' "

But that day, on my way to the office, I was rather impatient that this little old man should detain me from my very important errand. There was not the faintest suggestion of a halo about this man's perspiring bald pate, and I did not sense at that moment that I was meeting a great missionary. I was only to comprehend, many years and heartbreaks later, that Dr. Andrew Stirrett could have delayed me with optimism and cheerful encouragement only because God had poured His own love into his heart and given him a magnificent faith in what God can do!

Like Kano, Jos office carried on a shopping service for bush missionaries, sent out mail, groceries, fresh fruits and vegetables, medicines, or building materials. The field director's office was also here.

It was to the latter office I now found my way. Jega, I was told, was way up in the hard, antagonistic, Moslem North.

"You will proceed to Jega. The Borlases have prepared a room for you in their home."

I proceeded to buy tickets—second-class for myself and third-class for Dan Boyi—to Gusau, at railway's end. This small narrow-gauge train was filthy. I had to straddle various pots and pans filled with gooey palm-oil gravy that belonged to one of the train officials—the brakeman, as I remember. There was also a live chicken under my seat, in a covered basket, that protested sharply, at intervals, its cramped quarters. My seat was right near the door of the train's unspeakably misused toilet—one that had to do for several cars, it seemed, and the stench of which was almost stifling during the many openings and closings of the door.

I spent the night in a rest house at Kaduna Junction. Next morning, I was far more comfortable in a slightly less crowded train that reached Gusau by midafternoon. Our mission had a bookstore in Gusau, but Mr. and Mrs. J. A. Trewin, who lived above it, were probably far busier with finding lorries for freight and for people who were bound for one of the growing number of bush stations beyond the railway.

The Trewins informed me that they had arranged for a lorry to take me, in the morning, the hundred miles to Sokoto Leper Settlement, where I would stay for the night. The same lorry would pick me up and take me on to Jega the next day. Mrs. Trewin also packed a fine lunch to eat on the first lap of the journey.

A lunch for a hundred-mile trip? Yes, indeed, and it was fairly late in the afternoon when I arrived at Sokoto Leper Settlement.

Lorry is the British name for *truck*, but the lorry in common use on African roads in 1940 was engine and frame only. The body, including the seat, was built on the field —of wood. A coat or blanket was placed on this seat to cushion—slightly—the painful effects of jolting over incredibly rough washboard roads.

The Negroes of the interior had learned to drive these lorries after a fashion, but they still had no comprehension of the care a motor requires. As long as the wheels kept turning, and they could hear a roar from the front end of the lorry, all was well. Only when it smoked or stalled altogether did it occur to the average of those novice drivers that a lorry needs gas, or oil, or water.

These lorries were always overloaded. When the legal weight limit of goods and passengers was reached, within city limits, the remaining passengers who had paid their fare walked out to the edge of the town, and were picked up there. Our lorry stopped at almost every village along the way, and made long halts at the five Moslem prayer periods.

At the end of two days, traveling during the heat of the most trying time of the year, jarred almost into a semi-coma of fatigue, I was no longer interested in the scenery of the

land that was now my home country. I only longed for an
end to the almost unendurable jolting.

At last, near sunset of the second day out from Gusau, the
lorry turned into a compound, and I was told that I had arrived. Someone jumped down and undid the fastenings of
the door. Dazed, I stumbled out, too tired to know how I
responded to the words of welcome from the Borlases and the
boys of the station. I have no idea how they got my belongings sorted from the other loads on the lorry. I suppose it
was Dan Boyi who managed that. Ruth Borlase, a gracious
and beautiful woman, invited me in and gave me a cool
drink. I sipped it thirstily in stolid, weary silence.

Covered with dust, my face and arms streaked with
smudges of muddy perspiration, my clothes crushed out of
any respectability, I was exhausted to a state of imbecility. I
had stumbled awkwardly even as I stepped over the door sill.

The Borlases had been for months alone on this bush station. They were eager for me to furnish them with all the
mission news. Even after I had had a refreshing bath, I was
still not able to think of an item of news from anywhere on
the field. I did respond stupidly, when prompted with questions. I was just rational enough to be conscious that neither
my appearance nor my demeanor were conducive to making a
favorable impression.

Howard and Ruth soon saw that it was hopeless to draw
any information out of me, so very early Ruth showed me to
my room, originally intended for a nursery, with apologies
about the limited ventilation. Though the only room adapt-
able for an additional occupant of the house, it was a most
uncomfortable room, narrow, with a window at one end, and
those were the stifling days of April, humid without the relief
of rain—steaming, depressing, unrelieved African heat. Naturally, I did not need to spend very much time in that room,
except during the sweltering nights, and the almost unendur-

able rest hours, which were compulsory in that climate. There
was always work to be done, and I enjoyed doing it.

There were diversions, not the least of which was our
Sarkin Kwai—chief of the eggs. He appeared a day or two
after I arrived in Jega, and draped himself, with the long-
limbed gainliness of an Ichabod Crane, on the edge of the
back veranda. Only a person of genius could ever have found
his way into the picturesque rags that hung—precariously
intact—on his body. But then, Sarkin Kwai was bright
enough, probably, not to undress for the night. The various
knottings and stitchings were cumulative. His baths were
undoubtedly postponed, too, until time and stress should
finally weaken any hope of retying the last verminous shreds.

These tatters were the robes of his position, and Sarkin
Kwai wore them casually and from choice. Howard had given
him clothes. Sarkin Kwai had sold them. How could he,
with such respectable attire, continue to extort a living from
prosperous Moslems who hoped to find favor with Allah by
alms to the destitute?

He had discovered that professional beggars did not find
favor with Howard, so he had elected himself chief of eggs.
His deal was to supply us with eggs, at two *aninis* each, guaranteed to be fresh. It is probable that he begged them in the
town, and it is very certain that he was given many an egg of
doubtful age. One hatched in our pantry, a fact indicative
of Jega's climate as well as our egg situation. Other eggs did
not hatch, but they were far more objectionable.

One day Sarkin Kwai begged from Howard all the rotten
oranges in an order we had received from Kano which had
been too long on the road. Though we regretted the condition of the fruit, so rare in Jega anyway, the oranges were
entirely inedible. We wondered what Sarkin Kwai would
do with them.

Later that day we found out. Sarkin Kwai came to show
Howard a *tukuci* from our chief, a rather important digni-

tary. A *tukuci* is a tip given to the messenger who has delivered a gift for another. The *tukuci* is always brought to the
donor to see, for he evaluates the appreciation or gratitude
his gift rated by the value of the *tukuci*. Howard protested,
"But I didn't send the chief anything!"

"Oh! But I took him the oranges as a gift from you."

Everyone treated Sarkin Kwai's eccentricities with amused
indulgence for, said he, "Everybody knows I'm not very
bright."

Like Shakespeare's astute "fools," Sarkin Kwai was not
afraid to speak the truth.

"You ought to learn Hausa," he advised me that first day.

I had passed my official Hausa examination not too long
since, and with a gratifying rating. I said, somewhat indig-
nantly, "But what am I talking right now?"

"That's just *Kananci*."

He was right. Kano Hausa (*Kananci*), the accepted dialect
used in the Hausa Bible, was different in many respects from
the local *Sakwatanci* patois. Sarkin Kwai bluntly brought to
my attention that one is never through with language study.

Ruth Borlase took me into the town, and introduced me to
the people to whose compounds she now had free entry.
Nearly every compound in Jega was enclosed by a high mud
wall. It was illegal, she explained, to enter any compound
without permission or invitation.

All this was new to me. Wushishi was then in largely pagan
territory, with only a few walled compounds. Almost all
homes had been accessible. In the leper colony, of course, we
came and went at will. Now I was to learn how formidable
were the walls of Islam.

A compound has only one entrance—the *zaure*—a thatched
or mud-roof building built right into the wall. No grown
man outside the immediate family ever presumes to go beyond the *zaure* unless his host invites him to do so.

The *zaure* opens on a court where horses and donkeys are

tethered. A wall separates this part of the compound from the inner court, where the family lives. The inner door of a *zaure* and the entrance into the private court are situated so that no one sitting in the *zaure* can catch even a glimpse of the women inside. The women dare not venture from the inner court. They are *kuble*—locked in—not by a key, but by a vicious religious custom.

A chief's compound or the compound of a wealthy man may have a building between the outer and inner courts. Through some it is necessary to be led, or to feel our way, since the passages are tortuous and completely dark.

The men we glimpsed in the *zaures* were almost invariably antagonistic Mohammedans, and the women, locked into the inner courts of the compounds, did not even have a chance of knowing that anyone passed by outside their walls, far less give us the necessary invitation to enter.

Ruth told me how when they first came to Jega a newly built station, she and Laura Best, another young missionary, had spent days wearily trudging to and fro between those high mud walls, praying for an opening. They could hear sharp voices raised in anger or pain, and the laughter and crying of children. They could hear the women pounding their grain, and their weird, sad chanting in a minor key. The women inside those walls were lost, without any way of ever learning of the Saviour unless someone could make her way in to tell them of Him. Outside, helpless, were these two women who longed to bring them that Gospel message. Would they ever be able to reach them?

This is the challenge and the heartbreak of work in strictly Moslem districts.

Months went by, and the two women never ceased to go into the town, though often their slogging through heavy sand, beaten by the relentless tropical sun, seemed but a futile gesture. Men whom they passed withdrew even from their shadow!

Finally, through the openings medicine made for them, they had entered a few compounds, and they had seized any opportunity to find such an opening. One by one, slowly the number had increased. But hundreds of compounds were still closed.

Life in Jega began to become routine, most of it a very lonely routine. Every day, right after breakfast, I would go to the dispensary for my service and take care of the few patients. Most of them were from distant villages, for it was common knowledge that the chief of Jega had issued an order that his own townspeople were not to go to the "infidel" for medicine.

What made his decree most annoying to me was that he recognized the value of our treatment or medications. When he himself, or some member of his own family, needed care he demanded that I go to his compound to treat them, though my visit was carefully supervised, a guard following me about as I worked among the women, lest I talk to his wives about Christ.

Ruth and I went into town together at first, but as my medical work increased, she found that she lost a couple of the coolest hours of the morning by waiting for me, so we often went into town separately—at least in the morning.

Witnessing in Moslem compounds takes the patience of Job, for during a first visit, no matter how entrance permission was obtained, the man of the house would either remain openly hovering within hearing distance or would go back to his *zaure*, keeping watch from there. He would check with his wives, or older children, too, when I had left, as to what I had said. If I had mentioned the name of Christ during the first visit, it was quite probable that the compound would thereafter be closed to me.

So I spoke of the children, of the work of the women, talking about their small world within the four walls, beyond which many of them might never pass except in death. The

women welcomed any break in the monotony of their existence—unless it involved a beating from their men.

A woman might even be interested in the Gospel, or yearn-
ing for its message of peace of heart, but she was forced to be
extremely careful even when her husband's suspicions had
been allayed. A rival wife was ever watchful of some way to
get her *kishiya* into disfavor with their husband. So we needed to be very cautious, sometimes entering a compound five
or six times before we dared to speak of our Lord. Gradually
the head of the family would grow less vigilant, and all the
women more eager to have our visits repeated.

I had found several compounds where I was welcomed
eargerly. I had learned to spin cotton thread—after a fashion
—and by doing so I found a real point of contact with the
women who spent most of their leisure time spinning thread
for their homespun cloths.

My spinning was more of a source of entertainment for
them than any real help, and one woman laughed when I
showed her what I had done.

"*Hanjin 'kuda!*" she said.

Though my thread was like the "intestines of a fly," as she
had succinctly described it, the women were flattered that I
should share their humble toil. The first person I led to faith
in Christ in Jega was the woman who taught me to spin.

In one or two homes, the women did fancy weaving, working bright-colored designs, in tapestry effect, into the long
narrow *goyo* cloth of magenta-dyed cotton. Each design had
a symbolic meaning, often religious in character. These cloths
were worn only by the wealthier women, or kept for holiday
occasions like their big *salla* day, and were used to hold a
heavier child securely on a mother's back.

Accepted by the people, I began to learn more of their
intimate affairs. I was invited to "throw henna"— the con-
gratulatory gesture for a young bride-to-be. I threw my little
handful of henna into a pot set at the doorway for the con-

venience of guests and well-wishers, and murmured some
sort of rhyme, repeating it after my hostess. The henna
would be used to stain the young bride's hands and feet, and
to soften them, in preparation for the wedding.

My eyes had to become accustomed to the darkness before
I could see the bride, who was hunched up in the farthest
corner of a windowless hut, with an indigo cloth over her
head and face. This, I learned, is accepted custom for happy
brides in Africa!

The retreat to darkness by Hausa brides seems an interesting custom to people who think of weddings as occasions of
light, and music, and happiness. A marriage in Hausa territory means, at best, the end of freedom, the inside of dark or
even hostile walls. It may mean a form of slavery to a brutal
husband to whom the girl is but chattel property, or to an
uwardida (first wife) who exercises her right of authority by
tyrannical cruelty bred of jealousy.

I personally knew a chief whose harem contained far more
than the Moslem quota of four wives. Once, while riding
through the town, he happened to see a comely young girl
playing with her friends. He asked someone who she was.
Next day, not even waiting for the week of "wailing" that is
customary, the chief had her in his harem.

In Zabarma compounds, babies are often paid for in in-
fancy by a friend who has a son. Other children may be
married off for their dowry. This I learned on one of Jega's
streets, in a manner that has burned itself indelibly into my
memory. Ruth and I had rounded a bend in the path between two high-walled compounds. There in a open space
a woman was beating a little girl about eleven years old. The
child cowered against a wall, whimpering, but submitted
resignedly to the abuse. As we approached, the woman gave
a few more brutal blows to the bare, bruised back of the
child.

The angry woman repeated our question. "What's the

matter? Well, matter enough. This scamp"—and she cuffed the girl's head to accent the word—"has run away from her husband two times, and I'm beating her until she goes back of her own accord."

The child said nothing for herself. She looked frightened and hopeless and somehow old. A little girl turns to her home when she is in trouble. This child had come home. Her own mother was beating her, driving her from the only refuge a child knows. Her father had spent the money paid him for her. Since the marriage price could not be refunded, she would be driven back again and again.

Why did the little girl stand there, taking the fierce lashing, cowering, but unmoved? Was it worse, then, in the home of her husband? Poor little girl! *Poor little girl? Yes, but multiply this little girl by hundreds and thousands, and hide her behind high mud walls; set her to pounding grain with her thin little arms—to bearing children before she has reached womanhood. This is heathendom. This is Islam.*

So the bride seeks a dark corner and drapes a new-dyed indigo cloth over her face. To her it is a custom, and she performs it even if her heart does not beat with excitement or happiness. But surely the custom began in darkness and grief and terror.

Ruth had shown me that I could make friends of the youngsters by giving them used Christmas cards. I had quite a few of these, so it was a common thing for me to have a dozen or more naked children tagging me about the town. They did occasionally invite me into their homes, but not often.

Inside a compound, however, I could often have a service with women who had been warned not to let me preach to them, by asking if the children would like to see my pictures. The children usually answered that question themselves with whoops of pleasure. And, of course, the women—to whom I was talking as much as I was talking to the children—listened eagerly to the story of the pictures. I learned those days the

wonderful truth that every Bible picture holds the seed of
a Gospel story.

I discovered by sheer accident that those cards could become tickets into new compounds! One day, I had acquired
a large train of children who were demanding pictures. I did
not want to give away too many cards, for my supply was
running low, so I said, "From now on, I won't give them
away unless we have a service first."

Moslem law prohibits a service in a market place, in a
street, in the vicinity of a mosque, or any place, practically,
besides our own church or a private home, and the latter only
with the host's permission. So it had to be somebody's home.

One of the children shouted, "Why, then, come to our
house," and he headed a shrill-lunged pack through a *zaure*
and into a compound I had never entered before. Children
are allowed to enter women's quarters quite freely, so nothing was amiss. They were all shouting that we were going to
have a service and that they would all get pictures.

It worked, too. Since it was just something to amuse the
youngsters, I was permitted entrance and a service *the first
time I entered the compound!* That, of course, was a major
triumph. On days like that, knowing how difficult it had
always been to get a new opening, I would go home light-
footed in spite of midday heat, fairly singing, "A new compound! Another new compound opened today!"

Church services on the mission compound were very poorly
attended. Houseboys came because we expected them to do
so. Sarkin Kwai came occasionally, when he chose to, since
his claim to deficient mental capacities cancelled danger of
persecution.

Three boys in their early teens came a few times. They
were the incorrigibles of the town and came probably to
demonstrate their defiance of adult control.

One Sunday, to strengthen an illustration in his sermon,

Howard turned to one of the boys with the question, "You used to be a thief, didn't you?"

The boy's bosom friend spoke up loudly, and somewhat indignant, "He still is!" That spoiled Howard's illustration, but it set him right about current history.

Since fear of persecution as well as personal antagonism kept people from coming to us, we arranged for a service in an open Zabarma compound. Our Sunday school was collected as we strolled leisurely through the large community market place. The result was quite a contrast to the well-washed and carefully dressed Sunday school pupils of our own land. Most of the urchins in the market had never worn clothes at all.

Pictures, we learned, when used among people who have not learned to interpret them, may be distracting. While we told a story, someone would discover what the colored designs meant.

"Look, it's a person!"

We might be at a point where we desired most attention, when the African, still studying the picture, would ejaculate, "Even fingernails!"

So we left the pictures at home. Even so, I recall that when I was the one to tell the story, I was invariably hoarse from trying to outshout the general commotion, which might include fist fights, cursing, shouted greetings, or snickering naturally ensuing from a hundred children packed down solid on the bare earth.

Illiterates memorize easily. We taught them the Word, and they loved to sing. One chorus, to the tune of "In My Father's House," was especially popular because of its easy repetition. In the Hausa translation, each stanza ends with "With Jesus the Saviour."

I learned one day that through that song we were changing in young minds the Moslem concept of Jesus as *one* of the prophets (though Mohammed is *the* prophet). If I asked almost any child in that town of 8,000 who Jesus is, I would almost invariably receive the answer, "Jesus is the Saviour."

"If I can teach these children songs," I decided, "they will not realize that they are learning Gospel truths, nor will their parents. And the message will reach the people inside the compounds, too." So I began singing short Gospel choruses with the children, and in compounds where I visited. I hoped that soon even the women would be singing them instead of their dismal chants.

Everyone thought the singing was great fun and soon joined in with varying interpretations from their limited five-pitch vocal scale. The harmony was far from soothing, but the fact that the message of salvation was being hid in these hearts far outweighed my aversion to discord.

I could sing in any compound. The delighted women were happily unaware that, as a singer, I would get very little attention—favorable attention, that is—in my homeland. If I sang in a compound, I was sure that I would be welcome to come again—and again. So I sang on, with the women now joining in for a phrase or two.

Our musical endeavors were interrupted one day, by a sharp "Hsst!" from a blank compound wall. Then I saw, above the top of the wall, a woman's hands and the top of her head. Evidently the women in the next compound had piled up a couple of the wooden mortars in which they pound their grain, and while one kept watch on the *zaure,* the other had clambered to this favorable vantage point to see what was going on.

When she saw me singing with the children she must have concluded that I was not dangerous, though some locked-in women shrink from white people. Also, knowledge of us must surely have been carried from compound to compound by the old women who distribute the local gossip, as well as the housekeeping supplies they vend.

"Come and *wasa* in our compound, too." It was a cautious stage whisper.

The word *wasa* showed that she considered me in a class with professional beggars or transient entertainers who live on the tips they receive for their performances. It was no time to be offended, however. Here was another new compound!

"But I don't know where the door to your compound is!" I called back, also in a whisper.

My hesitation was not due to reluctance. Compounds are built with common walls which give not the slightest indication, at times, as to where one compound ends and another begins, and the shapes of those compounds, behind the outside wall, are often quite unexpected.

"We'll send someone to bring you in here."

Presently a little girl came, announcing that she was to take the *baturiya* to *wasa* in their home. Had I gone out to find the compound of those women, I would surely have stumbled into the wrong one, for we passed by two *zaures*, I believe, before we arrived at the right one.

I was always welcomed into the compound of the harlots, and I had freedom there to have services. One of these women was especially friendly, and I was almost sorry when she said she was going to be married to a rather important man, Zigge, who owned several trucks.

"Look," she cried, pointing to one of the few two-storied houses in Jega, "I will be in a wonderful home."

I was not happy. She would be locked away now and she had not yet accepted Christ. I felt that she was near.

"I may never get to see you again," I said sadly.

"Oh, but you will! I've even talked to Zigge about you! He says you can come to see me as much as you like. I'll send someone after you."

She was as good as her word, and she sent a little girl who took me into one of those secluded, dark compounds with a long, dark passage between inner and outer courts. And there were two women inside this compound, Tuni and Halima, who would never have heard of Christ but for this marriage.

The marriage had been a mistake, but it lasted long enough for me to have been in the compound many times. Tuni was not well, and my treatment made a great difference in her life. I was always greeted with joy, and it became my favorite place to visit. Tuni and Halima were a striking contrast to the loud, blustery woman who had entered to share their home by way of their husband's unfaithfulness and who always demonstrated a sort of personal proprietorship toward me when I came to see them.

Then one day, when I came through that dark central passage that led to their inner court, calling, *"Salama! Salama!*[1]*"* there was no answering call of welcome. I sensed immediately that all was not well inside. Finally, when I came to the door of the inner court, I knew that something was wrong.

Both Tuni and Halima were there in the little hallway they were permitted to enter. They neither smiled nor answered my greeting. In quick concern, I asked them what was wrong.

I cannot recall the name of the harlot-wife, but they told me, stiffly, that she was gone. That did not sound so dreadful to me, but something was bothering them. Surely they could not be mourning the dismissal—for it had been that—of this rather objectionable person from their home.

They stood there. They answered my questions in monosyllables, giving information sadly. They did not even make a move toward their open court. That meant I was no longer welcome here. It was time for me to be grief-stricken.

"Does that mean that you don't want me to come in and see you now?" I said, indeed sad.

_____
[1]Peace

"Do you mean," gasped Tuni, "that you would *want* to visit us, even after *she* is gone?" Bless their hearts, they thought I was enamored of the woman who was sent away because she had been generally troublesome, but who had let it be known, often enough, that she thought I had come as her personal guest.

I loved my work with the women and children of Jega, so I was not too resentful that the chief was hindering my medical work. Naturally, I did not even dream, in those days, what a great opening a dispensary can make for the Gospel! I knew that the women were happy to see me, and some were receiving the Word of life. The walls of Jega —some of them—had lost their formidable aspect.

SEVEN

FURLOUGH

> Ye are my witnesses, saith the Lord. . . . Woe to
> them that are at ease in Zion.—Isaiah 43:10; Amos
> 6:1
> Blow the trumpet in Zion, sanctify a fast, call a
> solemn assembly: gather the people, sanctify the
> congregation, assemble the elders, gather the chil-
> dren. . . . Put ye in the sickle, for the harvest is ripe.
> . . . The whole land is . . . desolate, because no man
> layeth it to heart.—Joel 2:15, 16; 3:13; Jeremiah
> 12:11

IN MARCH, 1943, when I was taken to Kano to await passage
home, I knew that death lurked in the air and in the water
between Africa and the States. I knew that some of our
number had already been in grave danger. I knew that God
does not always prevent death from striking His children.
Three of our missionaries had been fatally wounded by Ital-
ian bombs in the Anglo-Egyptian Sudan. And God had given
me what I was convinced was a word of warning and preparation: "For me to live is Christ, and to die is gain."

To die is gain. I had enough time to examine this com-
forting thought while I was in Jega. By the time I got to
Kano, on the first lap of my trip, I had a deep calm and quiet,
peaceful anticipation of an entrance to everlasting joy and
rest. Later at home, my Little Sis exclaimed, "You constantly
speak of Heaven, and when you do, it seems so wonderfully
real!"

Perhaps everyone would be blessed by the experience of

122

seeing Heaven's gates almost within reach, and pondering on a meeting with a loving heavenly Father, and the prospect of the exchange, once for all, of beauty for ashes, the oil of joy for mourning, the garment of praise for the spirit of heaviness that so often presses down upon earth-bound souls.

I was to remain in Kano until some way of travel opened up for me. Another of our missionaries was waiting to go home. Bernetha Odell had not completed a term; she was being invalided home because of a serious heart condition. No steamer schedules were available, of course. We must be ready at all times to pack our things in a few minutes.

Bernetha's heart condition provided both of us with transportation. When the local commander of the United States Air Force contingent heard of an American citizen in a rather serious physical condition in need of passage home, he offered her space on one of the United States military planes, *if there would be space not needed for Air Force personnel.* Another stipulation was that a nurse must accompany Bernetha. Thus I was included in the offer.

I busied myself in getting the doctor's orders for any foreseeable emergency. No one knew just how Bernetha would react to high altitude. I had to have emergency equipment and medication ready for instant use. We lived, for several days, right out of our suitcases. Then came the exciting moment when we were given twenty minutes to be at the airfield.

"Of course you realize, don't you, "warned the officer at the Air Force Headquarters, "that you have no priority whatever, since we cannot give you a place needed for military personnel? You may be set down anywhere, and you can have no complaint, even if you remain there for months. Is that clear?"

It was clear. Dr. Helser had given us letters of credit and other instructions of what to do in case of delay anywhere enroute to America. Our first stop was in Accra, seaport of the Gold Coast.

The man who checked our papers there exclaimed wonderingly, "These are very unusual documents, to say the least. Do you realize that you have no kind of priority whatsoever? I don't see any chance of your leaving Accra within six weeks. It may be that many months."

Then he looked up sharply to see our reaction. Neither of us showed any great concern, but I noticed that he studied us as carefully as he had studied our irregular papers.

Bernetha's face was puffy, and the authenticity of her heart condition was quite obvious. I was almost gruesomely thin, and a depressing shade of yellow from my heavy dosages of atabrine. Neither of us looked very substantial.

The weeks we would probably be spending in Accra did not promise to be too interesting, as we would be required to be within call at all times. We got a bit of exercise, that first night, washing our things and rigging up lines in our room. The coastal air was very damp. We would have to wash something every day, so that we would never again have as much as we had that evening.

Not long after we had made this resolution, we had a telephone call. "Be ready," said a voice, "to leave the hotel at four-thirty tomorrow morning. We will pick you up."

We had to pack our wash into our luggage wet, for the muggy night had not removed much moisture. We worried a little about overweight charges because both of us had taken with us our full weight allowance of personal things, many of which our friends were soon to insist that we discard.

When we landed in Natal, Brazil, our papers evoked the customary comments about no priority.

"We may have a good chance to get acquainted," said a young officer significantly. "We are taking you to generals' quarters—and you may be there a long time!" He explained that our luggage would be brought as soon as the plane was unloaded.

There was nothing lavish about the accommodations for generals, but the rooms were spacious and airy. A woman and her little girl already occupied one room in these barracks. For Bernetha and me, a delay was only an inconvenience, but for this woman, delay had probably robbed her of a chance to live. Since the previous November, when she had been told she had a malignancy that must have immediate surgery, she had been trying to get passage from India to the States, and finally she had come this far by way of Africa.

"*We* have nothing to complain about," Bernetha whispered to me, when we went back to our room.

The large building where meals were served was not many yards behind our barracks. We had a good meal, walked around a little, then remembered our bags. We went to investigate, with an uneasy feeling that we might have waited too long. We became actively concerned when our bags were not in the department where baggage should be claimed. We were sent to another office. From there, we were sent on.

"No one seems to be eager to see us make a scene," laughed Bernetha, when our predicament became all too obvious. "Let's surprise them, and not make one."

The first words of the captain in charge of the storage shed we now approached confirmed our fears.

"Do you really need those bags?" He was breaking it gently.

"We haven't a thing to wear!" I mourned, in spite of myself.

The officer looked at me with the experienced air of someone who has heard that wail before. He did not even look sympathetic.

"We left your bags in the plane," he said.

I grinned feebly. "It's just as well to know the worst."

Turning to Bernetha, I added, "And you know the worst? The damp clothes we packed into the bags at Accra!"

The plight of our wardrobe, future as well as present, was tragic to a comic degree.

"Of course," sighed Bernetha. "There must be Indian blankets . . ."

The officer interrupted us, just as we were at the door. "We are putting you back on that plane, you know. Can you get by until tomorrow, then? It will save us moving a lot of other luggage."

We raced, with our good news, back to generals' quarters. Our neighbor was busy packing; she, too, had been notified. Next morning we ate our breakfast with one eye on our watches. The captain had promised transportation to the plane. We were back at our barracks several minutes before the time he had specified.

But no army vehicle appeared. After waiting several minutes, we began to wonder if we had missed our transportation. If so, we were in serious trouble. We were too far from the airfield ever to reach it before flying time if we walked.

Across the road we could hear, rather than see, that someone was working with machinery of some kind. I walked to the fence behind which I had heard the rattling of metal. In the early morning dusk, I could just make out the outlines of two men.

"Is there a car here," I asked, "that could take us to the airfield? Our plane takes off in ten minutes."

The man nearest me came to the fence. He spread his hands eloquently, and spoke a few words in Spanish. I tried, desperately, to make him understand. I had to report failure to the other two women, who were now anxiously waiting at the edge of the road.

Our friend's life depended now on a car. In this emergency, we prayed God to send a car. Time swept on. Six minutes before the plane would leave the field, we saw the headlights of an approaching car. I stood right in the middle of the road and flagged. An army truck ground to a halt.

"Do you, by any chance, understand English?" I challenged shrilly anxious as I squinted into the dark cab of the truck.

"I most certainly do!" replied the unseen driver, with an exquisite Oxford accent.

"Would you take us to the airfield?" I cried, relief stilling slightly the furious pounding of my heart. "Our plane is due to leave in a few minutes. They must have forgotten to get us."

"It will give me great pleasure!" replied the man with the cultured voice, maneuvering the truck into a quick turn. We were all breathing thanksgiving to God, who had sent deliverance in the very nick of time. We had a bare six minutes before the scheduled take-off; it would take all of that time to reach the plane. We might still be too late, but now we had a chance of making it.

We were not standing with folded hands, of course. Each one seized some of the luggage, for we could not wait for this soldier to lift it on for us. We would have to throw it onto the truck, and scramble on somehow, just as soon as the truck had come to a stop.

But the truck did not stop! With a roar and grinding of gears, the soldier called back in his precise accent, "I'll be right back with a proper conveyance!"

I could have wept. Had I failed to communicate the urgency of our predicament? Any American would have shouted, "Jump right in. We'll make it—or bust!" Courtesy and too high a respect for social amenities can become disconcerting.

Helpless beyond words we watched the red rear light of that perfectly good truck fade into the distance, and finally disappear. Each second that passed was like an hour. We heard a plane gunned to a roar; we saw its lights as it lifted into the indigo sky.

Our British friend returned, and with a more sedate vehicle. He knew how to drive it too, and probably thought that he was giving us an exciting time as we fairly hurtled through the night. He will never know that anything, after tense moments of dismay, would have been anticlimax. We slid to a stop, beside our plane, with a loud shriek of brakes, just before the landing ladder had been withdrawn.

Before midnight that same day, we circled above a city outlined against the black velvet of the ocean like a coronet of flashing jewels. We had left Africa one day and arrived in America the next! People were spending small fortunes those days for that kind of priority flying and not getting it. But a greater power than wealth had planned our flight schedule.

It was almost difficult for me to comprehend that we had actually come home safely. Had the Lord not warned me of imminent death? I began to re-examine the portion of Scripture that I was convinced God had given me for my trip. I turned to it again, in Philippians 1:21: "For me to live is Christ, and to die is gain."

I began to ponder that—because my attention had been fixed on the glory of the last phrase—I had hardly seen the first seven words. I recalled, then, the little pamphlet, Dr. Trumbull's testimony,[1] that I had been carrying about with me.

> There is only one life that wins; and that is the life
> of Jesus Christ. Every man may have that life; every
> man may live that life.

"God's message to me, then, is not death, but life, a more abundant life—the *Christ-life*." As this truth broke in on me, I determined to use this furlough searching for this deeper aspect of a Christian's life. I further dedicated myself to this

---

[1] *The Life That Wins*, printed by *Sunday School Times*.

quest as I reread the paragraphs that were still not clear to me, but were opening the doors slowly to a vision of the "heavenlies," so often spoken of in the Word.

Do you wonder that Paul could say with tingling joy and exultation, "To me to live is Christ"? He did not say, as I had mistakenly been supposing I must say, "To me to live is to be Christlike," nor, "To me to live is to have Christ's health," nor, "To me to live is to serve Christ." No; he plunged through and beyond all that in the bold, glorious, mysterious claim, "To me to live *is* Christ."

And that is how I know for myself that there is a life that wins: that it is the life of Jesus Christ: and that it may be our life for the asking, if we let Him—in absolute, unconditional surrender of ourselves to Him, our wills to His will, making Him the Master of our lives as well as our Saviour—enter in, occupy us, overwhelm us with Himself, yea, fill us with Himself "unto all the fullness of God."

It meant a revolutionized, fundamentally changed life, within and without. If any man be *in Christ,* you know, there is a new creation.

How plainly Dr. Trumbull had written it all out, but I was still vaguely fumbling! Perhaps because, as a missionary, I was asked so often to speak in the various churches I visited, and so heard fewer sermons, or perhaps because so few men in the pulpit proclaim this glorious truth, I heard little to help me find the glory that is to be had in the heavenly position of oneness with Christ.

But God had not given me a vain challenge. The phrases *in Christ, through Christ,* and *by Christ Jesus,* in the epistles, began to glow with a glory that I wanted to know personally. And then the Lord brought into my hands the works of saints who walked in this glory—F. B. Meyer, A. B. Simpson, Andrew Murray, L. E. Maxwell, F. J. Huegel, more of Dr. and Mrs. Howard Taylor's writings, and many others.

The knowledge that this life in Christ is possible—that, indeed, it is the *normal* Christian life—gave me a great dissatisfaction with my own Christian experience.

Much later, when I discovered that in his book, *Come Hither,* DeVern Fromke has made a masterful and orderly compilation of these great truths from the writings of some of the world's greatest saints, I wrote to him for several copies. In his letter to me, he touched on the secret of my failure to attain the heights I longed to experience.

> It takes a *prepared* heart before the utter necessity of this aspect of Calvary truth dawns and then becomes a living revelation in a life. But such is constantly happening in many who have been going through the defeat-failure pathway to resurrection *union* in Him.

I was still trying to meet the divine challenges in my own strength, and though I was not content, I did not realize how far short of the goal my efforts left me!

So I came home with a spiritual hunger that few people guessed was there. They recognized, by the way my clothes hung on my gaunt frame, that I had had some physical hardships, though my thinness was probably due more to the fact that I had never in eighteen months been able to throw off my low fever.

Soon after I got back to Kansas, I visited the wonderful people of Salina who had so faithfully sent in my support. The hospitality of this group of Christians, now organized into the Salina Bible Church, was as hearty as their support of missions. They now showered me with beautiful things to wear, lovelier than I had ever had before. The Salina people seemed never to have even heard about the proverbial "missionary barrel"!

I spent the following summer as camp nurse at a Bible conference, where I met Mrs. H. F. Sugden, wife of one of the conference speakers. When she spoke, in glowing terms, of their wonderful church in Jackson, Michigan, I knew that both she and her husband were heart and soul in their work, and that the people sensed their interest and love.

A day or so later, I was invited to eat at the Sugdens' table. Mrs. Sugden's eyes sparkled as her husband told me, "We have been talking to your mission's deputation secretary. He says we can have you as our missionary by providing your service support!"

I was nearly overcome with delight! I had heard enough about the church in Jackson to know that they would be wonderful people. I needed to have my service support supplied, for the general or allowance support does not nor can it cover the expenses of transportation to and from the field, free medical care and drugs, and the various services that are given all missionaries.

When, later, I was in the home of the Sugdens, in Jackson, I learned to know more about the people of Ganson Street Baptist Church. They not only wanted to take on my service support, but they were going to supply me with food for my next term. Never again would I be starved for fruits and vegetables!

It was humbling that God should be showering His bounties on me as though I were a favored child. Who else had two such splendid groups of Christians to stand back of him as he went to the field? What more could I want? What more could anyone do for me?

The people of Jackson found something else that they could do.

One day, Pastor Sugden burst into the front door, and came up to my upstairs room three steps at a time.

"Martha," he cried, breathless with excitement and unselfish joy, "I've just come from church board meeting. We are going to build you a house in Africa!"

Such boundless liberality was more than I could take in. I was so overcome that, for once in my life, I was speechless. I just stared dumbly at Dr. Sugden. Did I manage to say that

I appreciated the church's thoughtfulness? I have always had the uneasy feeling that I gave him the impression that I was not very grateful.

I was to have another surprise. One day I met a woman in one of the halls of the church who introduced herself, talked a little to me about her position as missionary president, and then, as she started to move down the hall, she asked, "Is there any little thing we could do?"

Missionaries are constantly meeting people who exclaim, soulfully, "I wish there were something we could do here at home!" I had learned, the hard way, that most of these enthusiastic exclamations are just polite talk. I had even offended some of these people by suggesting things that *can* be done here in the homeland to make a missionary's work more effective.

So, since I had grown to eye such offers as polite but rather fruitless gestures, I said lightly, "Well, if you happen to have some pieces of material in your scrap bag, you could make a baby dress or so. Even if you have to use two different pieces to do it. Our babies won't care!"

She asked me, with no undue interest I thought, about the style I wanted. I explained that our people hardly know how to use buttons, so simple ties or drawstrings would be preferable. To excuse my desire for baby dresses, I mentioned that babies are always the last of the family to have clothes, and that during the harmattan season the men usually wear the family blanket against the cold of the morning and evening. Then I forgot all about it.

I had learned, to my bewilderment and sorrow, that people were actually not very interested in hearing about my people and their needs. As long as I spoke of my own personal problems, people could understand. Somehow, I had been unable to invoke in many people any real interest in *the work* I was doing in Africa.

"Tell me all about Africa!" my own uncle had exclaimed.

Then he went to sleep while I showed him a small album of my pictures. Such things hurt!

I had publicly shown some slides loaned me by Sue Hooge, who had had them made by a deputation secretary of the mission. People said, "You should not show such things. It makes us sick."

"But these are the people we work with day by day," I protested at first. "How can we show you our work without showing you our people?"

"Well, they should have more clothes on, in the first place. Your pictures are shocking."

I grew tired of explaining that many of the pictures already were spoiled by unnatural poses, because women had been asked to adjust their cloths before the picture was taken. I grew impatient that people should not be able to look for a few minutes on Africa as it is when missionaries are sent to live there for years!

Finally, I spoke without using pictures. Even then, in one church where I had done so, the pastor's wife came to me and said, "You missionaries take your work too seriously."

I have spoken to many missionaries on furlough. Invariably the thing that strikes them first—and hardest—when they reach home is the superficial interests that seem of vital importance to Christians. We are astounded at the way people fritter their precious time away, quite heedless, it seems, of the reality of eternity.

Are we missionaries on furlough partly to blame for this complete oblivion to the worth of a lost soul? Perhaps because we see people so occupied with tangibles, we hesitate to present the real purpose of missions—of our own work—for fear we will offend. People want to be entertained. If we learn how to achieve this art, the contributions toward our work are quite gratifying. So we polish up our best stories.

A missionary looks at luxurious home furnishings and fancy little-used gadgets in terms of how many orphans such a thing might support, or how long it would keep a young Christian in Bible school. Do we lift the curtain to the spiritual abyss from which these orphans are saved even as they are fed and clothed? Or do we let the people think of orphans as just so many meals and dresses provided for so many happy children? Do we portray a Bible-taught national as someone we have taken under our wing to soften his life and our own task, or as the key to evangelization of his own people in our generation?

I have looked speculatively down a long line of well-fed young people at a Bible conference snack bar, ordering malts and sodas just to be sociable, and have estimated how long I could run my dispensary on the proceeds of just that one evening's ice cream and pop. So sinful a waste did my prejudiced mind hold this practice that I suppose I patronized soda fountains only two or tree times during my whole furlough, unless the luxury was pressed on me by others.

But did I truly show these same people, in my opportunities to talk of my work, the *eternal* aspect of that work? Did I make it clear that every pill, every spoonful of medicine, every bandage applied, formed a wedge into hearts that might never hear of *eternal* life had they not been drawn to receive help for their physical life? Something is terribly wrong with our perspective!

The people in America spend 10 times as much money for soda pop, and 12 times as much for Christmas toys as they do for missions. They spend 15 times as much money for jewelry, and 10 times as much on cosmetics and beauty treatments, as they spend for missions. They spend more for dog food, by 45 million dollars, every year, than they do for missions.

I have come to see that buying toys or ice cream or dog food is not sin. The sin lies in permitting Christians to remain victims of a warped sense of values that is impoverishing their own lives and robbing them of a great inheritance. Thousands of Christians would become God's enthusiastic stewards if we called their attention to the multiplying eternal dividends on investments made on shares in Christ's everlasting kingdom—with accumulating compensations beginning at once. We sin when we pocket people's contributions to "our work" without letting them enjoy the fruits of what *they* have done!

As missionaries, we have acknowledged Christ's marching orders to take the world for the cause of His kingdom. We have His word that every Christian is a soldier. No Christian is spiritually under a 4F rating; no Christian can claim honorable discharge from this desperate warfare. A Christian not in battle is AWOL. We have our Captain's warning that, if we fail in our warfare, souls will be taken into eternal bondage by Satan, ruthless master of fearful strategy.

In warfare, it is treason to be aware of the approach or infiltration of an enemy without sounding a clear warning. On the battlefield it is cowardice to note such advance without counterattack. Is it not sin then—for us, who have seen with our eyes the swift advance of Islam's forces—to tell clever little yarns carefully calculated to get the laughs, or the tears, at just the right places, so that we become known as entertaining speakers?

It is sin to allow earnest young Christians to plan mediocre lives around a materialistic ideal without challenging them to battle. We sin if we do not offer to lead the charge! God has sent us into a stirring conflict, one that should stir response in the blood of every Christian. We carry the banner of One who has already conquered, and God holds us responsible for advance!

The two churches that supported me demonstrated what happens when Christians get just a glimpse of these realities, and of the fact that the primary justification for congregational organization is that of forming and training an orderly and unified force that is able, intelligently and co-operatively, to obey Christ's command to witness for Him "both in Jerusalem, and in all Judea, and in Samaria, and unto the uttermost part of the earth" (Acts 1:8).

Locally, wherever there was an avenue of witness, they pressed into that opening, through their homes and their businesses, in visual aid classes for children and rallies keyed for youth, they visited those confined in hospitals or in prison cells, they took servicemen into their homes, and they formed servicemen's clubs so that they might introduce these lonely men to the Friend that would stand by them in the time of their need.

They reached beyond their own community by supporting Bible camps and Bible conferences. They supported a radio witness. That small group of vital Christians, pastored by Nye J. Langmade, who met in the Odd Fellows' Hall in Salina, wanted an even greater outreach. Africa, surely, was in the "uttermost part of the world"! I was their first missionary, taken on in faith before these people had a church or a church organization! As their representative, it was my responsibility to inform them of what they were accomplishing in my field of service by their prayers and by their liberality.

In their letters—and in our discussions when I came back on furlough—these people mentioned my patients and my converts by name, because they had repeated those names before the Lord in intercession. They had helped fill my bottles in the dispensary; they had sent sulfa drugs and penicillin to counteract the myriad infections; they knew about trachoma blindness, meningitis epidemics, and the ulcers of yaws, and of leprosy. They asked intelligent questions, because they had an active interest in the problems of treating these patients. Women in these churches had rolled literally miles of bandages; they were not displeased when I showed them my movie of a bandage parade of over a hundred ulcer patients filing by on one morning.

Perhaps I became more scrupulously careful of how I spent the Lord's supply because I knew that, to send money to me, one woman had given up her long-cherished and carefully hoarded fund for a new bedroom suite to replace a sagging and dilapidated old one. I learned to accept such money gladly, knowing that what is placed into God's hands or into His service is never lost. Someday, in Heaven, we will be allowed to see a bedroom suite that glitters with the jewels of our Lord's remembrance of a sacrifice made for His sake and the Gospel's. And gifts of sacrifice are backed by prayer. Money for missions is hard to come by, but earnest, definite prayer is far scarcer than money!

I feel sorry, deeply sorry, for those unfortunate missionaries who may get a very full and regular income from a board into whose coffers come enough indifferent and impersonal nickels and dimes to make up the whole of their salaries, donations from congregations that neither know nor care, except in a casual sense of having done a religious rite or duty. I feel sorry for the people who gave the dimes or nickels, for they never have the joy of knowing what they accomplished, nor have they much incentive to definite, effectual prayer.

I have attended a fine fundamental church where letters from missionaries supported by the general funds of the denomination's constituency were read before a group of elderly women. When missionaries, supported by the denomination, appeared to tell of their work, they were allowed to show their pictures and give their "reports" at midweek services for the older adult group. Young people—the group in which might have been found prospective missionaries—complained that they never got to see any of the missionaries. Yet the young pastor of that church was sincerely and deeply disturbed because the denominational census showed that the number of missionary applicants from his area was less than that from smaller churches, where complete congregation participation meant that the youth of the church got to hear an occasional challenge in missionary services.

Seminaries and Bible institutes are surely aware of the staggering statistics of inequality in the distribution of God's laborers. How long will it be before they send out pastors trained to challenge young people with the need and the joy of working in the Lord's harvest fields?

How long will they turn out pastors who relegate to the women's missionary society of their own church all the information and activity that pertains to missions—and in which lies the challenge to service? How long will the Lord be robbed of the red-blooded young men who might go to those fields if they ever heard of the harvest, not only white, but lost—lost for want of young, strong reapers!

How long will it be before the remedy will be taught by the very institutions that teach the well-grounded scriptural truth that building up mission churches is primarily a *man's* work, that training national pastors is *man's* work, that trekking to frontier areas is *man's* work? How long will it be before they send out pastors who know that to provide men for missions, *men* must be informed, *men* must be challenged, and *men* must be set to work! Until the whole system of mission presentation in churches is changed, every mission's cry will continue to be, "And God sought for a man, and behold—*women!*"

Some few churches are pioneering the way. I have attended a church where a regular part of the midweek educational program for even the children included a comprehensive study of all the mission fields supported by that church. Across the country have risen a few, a rare few, churches where the men's mission society is as active as the women's.

Like women, the men inform themselves of mission needs that they are qualified to fill. Deliberately, with premeditated strategy, the older men call on the energy or ingenuity of young men of the church to help. While these young people work with hammer and saw, or with screw driver and precision instruments, they are hearing and discussing situations and events that challenge their interest and their sense of responsibility. In such a group, it is no longer so conclusive that the out-going packing boxes—so painstakingly constructed to be suitable for use as furniture out on the field—will be taken out by a woman!

In Ganson Street Baptist Church,[2] individual Sunday school classes had missionary projects—big projects. The Crusaders class furnished a roof for my house. It was the Sunday school in Salina Bible Church that made the heavy contributions for mission support. Why? Because letters from missionaries were read in the general assembly of the Sunday school and in individual classes. Because each of these churches had a "Missionary Sunday" each month.

I attended my first missionary conference in Salina during this first furlough. For eight days, missionaries from five or six foreign and home fields presented their work every afternoon and evening. On the two Sundays, every Sunday school department cancelled its regular class study, and a missionary spoke of some phase of missionary life that appealed to that particular age group. A missionary talked to the Sunday school assembly; the morning service consisted of two missionary messages. The evening services, throughout the period included pictures, a five-minute "field flash" from another missionary, and a message by a third missionary, representing another field.

Each afternoon two messages and a field-flash were given. Missionaries, like other speakers, are stimulated by eager interest in their audience. To protect our own interests and to keep within the schedule, we solemnly warned each other that any missionary that talked overtime would be "hung up by the thumbs."

---

[2]Jackson, Mich.

Missionaries were not moved from one home to another for the night, but for meals they were placed in pairs or in groups in the homes of different members of the church. The food was so good that we missionaries were forced to make a plea for one light meal during the day.

We missionaries appreciated the opportunity to discuss with other missionaries the differing field problems. Methods of combating illiteracy, polygamy, and the persecutions of Christians could be compared by missionaries from South America, China, or Africa. The informality of the home atmosphere encouraged us to share a few experiences that would get a good laugh at some of our mistakes.

"I never knew how interesting missionaries can be," said one hostess, "until I got several of you together at my table. I learned more about missionary life, and the difficulties of the work that you do, at that mealtime, than I had ever known before."

At a Salina missionary conference during my second furlough, I heard Patrick Arnold, of West Indies Mission, say that an electric shock—such as results from shorting the current of a car motor—would neutralize the venom of scorpions and relieve pain. During the following term in Africa, dozens of people walked miles to take advantage of the almost immediate relief gained from this simple expedient, which was far more effective than injections of novocaine locally, or morphine—which we had tried when some of the missionaries had writhed with the pain for hours after a scorpion's sting.

Nor were the statistics of these conferences dull. At the time when the membership of Salina Bible Church was around 150, the last Sunday of the missionary conference recorded 253 people in Sunday school. The *Sunday school offering* that day was $881.45, and when the offering from the morning service was added to that of the Sunday school, I calculated, as I looked at the board on which the figures appeared, that the *average* donation that morning, including the cradle roll, had been around six dollars. By the year of that conference, however, Salina Bible Church had been supporting about ten missionaries, at least in part.

No high-pressure pep talks were used to pry money from reluctant audiences. These people were hearing of projects of which they *wanted* to be a part.

"If any of you have heard that message, and don't feel that you want to share in that work, then you'd better just keep your money."

Such was the succinct comment that preceded the offering at an afternoon meeting. Clyde Smith, who was the layman in charge of the meeting, was the man who had printed my letters and those of several other missionaries, addressing and sending them out as well, entirely without any cost to us. And this was only one of his many activities toward making the Gospel known.

"We just stood and looked at each other, wondering where the money could be coming from," said one of the deacons who had helped to count the offering after one of the meetings.

The church was made up, almost entirely, of working people—farmers, clerks, businessmen, teachers, housekeepers. The secret was that every aspect of that church's program was permeated with the responsibility and challenge of Christ's great commission.

This was not "giving until it hurts"! It was the hilarious giving of the Macedonian churches.

> Somehow, in most difficult circumstances, their joy and the fact of being down to their last penny themselves, produced a magnificent concern for other people. I can guarantee that they were willing to give to the limit of their means, yes, and beyond their means, without the slightest urging from me or anyone else. (II Cor. 8:2, 3, J. B. Phillip's translation.)

At the end of my furlough, when it was time to pack, I had
a far more complete outfit than I had had for the first term.
My dresses and uniforms were again sewed by the women of
Salina Bible Church, though many new friends had lavishly
supplied more than I would have expected. Ganson Street
Baptist Church, of Jackson, sent cases of a fine variety of
tinned fruits and vegetables, a pressure cooker large enough
to sterilize all the dressings I would need, with bandages
packed around all to make the boxes solid and tight.

Not all that I packed, during those days, could be classed
as necessities. Among the treasures upon which I lavished
special care was a gift from the Jackson people. When I had
received their Christmas check of $50.00, I had written to
Mrs. Sugden that I would soon be having some dental work
done, and that this provision would just about cover these
dental expenses. Mrs. Sugden's strenuous objection arrived
a few days later.

"You will not spend our Christmas present to have pain!
We want you to get yourself something that you want, but
feel you can't afford."

I did not have to think long to know what I really wanted.
I recalled, only too well, the aching loneliness of a bush station. In carefully calculated extravagance, I spent the entire
sum on phonograph records.

But those were not the only records that I was taking. During the missionary conference in Salina, I was house guest of
the Clyde Smiths, together with Agnes Harder, another of
our Sudan Interior Mission missionaries. One day our host
brought in huge stacks of records from his religious bookstore.

"Both of us will be working this morning. You can while
away your time playing these," he said, then added, "and keep
the ten you like best!"

All morning, we gleefully played those records, making two
stacks, the ones we just had to have, and the ones we might
possibly do without. The only unpleasant element of that

delightful morning was the painful process of eliminating records from the choice piles that had grown too high!

Now at the end of my furlough, when I was nearly through with my packing, another box arrived from Jackson, Michigan. This one came as a surprise. It contained baby dresses —ninety-nine of them.

Amid all this bounty and with all these tokens of God's care and direction—if this were good missionary biography— the rest of the chapters in this book would reveal the unfolding of magnificent vision and great faith. Since this record is not fiction, nor good missionary biography, it must continue to be nothing but an account of the faithfulness of God.

EIGHT

AND AGAIN—*KANO!*

The Pharisees also asked him how he had received his sight.—John 9:15

A BLIZZARD WAS HOWLING through the windowed canyons of New York City and a great war was still raging throughout the world when at last I was ready to return to the field. Travel was more perilous than ever and transportation increasingly difficult to obtain. Women and children were being refused permission to travel by air or by sea. Some of our men were on the field without their wives and families.

On February 19, 1945, Ida Trapp and I were sent to an office in downtown New York to apply for passage to Nigeria. Ahead of us in the U. S. Transport Service office were three other women of imposing dignity. It was impossible not to hear their list of highly impressive credentials and the well-presented project that was impelling these women to apply for transportation—just where Ida and I wished to go.

My heart continued to sink steadily while the woman at the desk mildly but emphatically explained to these important dowagers that she could not give them priority to travel. In fact she told them she could not give them a permit of any kind.

"You are here where it is safe. Stay here."

Over a chorus of protests, her voice was firm. Women could not travel during the war.

I looked at Ida. "That lets us out!" I whispered. "We might as well go home."

Had we come all the way to New York for this? There seemed no point of making an application for two insignificant missionaries' passages. If women who were officials of nationally recognized organizations could not get permits, our own prospect looked hopeless. But the woman at the desk turned to us, while the disappointed dignitaries were being shown out.

"I could not help hearing," I stammered. "We want to go to Africa too."

"And what do you want in Africa?"

"Both of us are nurses—medical missionaries."

My terse statement was more apologetic than convincing persuasiveness. Already defeated, I did not even think to use, as a talking point, the tremendous medical work that Ida had built up in Biliri, Nigeria.

During her first term, Ida had been delivering around a thousand babies a year. This was but one phase of a general dispensary service that included several leprosy segregation villages besides her thriving and heavy inpatient work. Ida's record would not have helped my own cause much, for my very limited experience in tropical practice in Jega and Katsina was insignificant in comparison to hers. All I had was my nursing degree.

But that was all that was necessary. Our intention to resume medical activities qualified us for priority certificates. Ten minutes later we left the office with instructions to leave at once. We were promised that we would be placed on the first plane that had available seats.

I had come to Africa at the beginning of my first term during the coolest part of the year. This time, we were just approaching that oppressive season that is most debilitating and trying. Acclimatization is always somewhat difficult. Our sudden transition from winter in New York to equatorial heat was a real physical and even a psychological shock. Both of us secretly wondered if we could finish another term in this land!

After three days and two nights I arrived in Kano, where the sun looked like a bleary eye as it tried to pierce the veil of red Sahara dust that the harmattan winds hang over the continent during the winter months.

During the harmattan season, planes that did not fly entirely by instrument were grounded by the heavy pall that rose miles into the atmosphere. We could not see from one side of the mission compound to the other. Everything we touched—books, clothes, bedding, our own skin—had a harsh, gritty feel, and our hands were soon chapped from frequent washing. The air that carried the dust was so dry that after one day my nose was bleeding and my throat raw and sore.

Kano was my favorite station and I found that I would be staying there until my loads arrived. I had been told, even in New York, that I would not be going back to Jega, but to French Niger, the very land to which the nail-scarred hand had pointed when I was first called into mission service.

At the time I had heard that message in Tabor chapel, all medical work had been prohibited by the government. Now after decades of applications repeatedly presented and as repeatedly refused, a large government dispensary had been turned over to our mission. I would be working in that first dispensary!

Faithful is He who calls—even to the impossible—for He will also bring it to pass! Though we follow His bidding as blind ones, He leads unerringly, for He knows the end from the beginning. How fascinating it is to see some of His foresighted leadings unfold through circumstances of varying origin!

Like a vastly intricate and patient game of chess, God maneuvers people and circumstances into His eternal design. As with the knights, the moves can seldom be in an obvious straight line. What strategy and perseverance were needed to take just one self-willed nurse who had no intention of being a missionary, point her to medical work in a field where medical work is impossible—and then get her there!

His obvious moves were with the kings and rooks when He put men in government circles into a sequence of events that brought about, at last, an opening of medical work, into which He could slip that nurse. How many quiet, seemingly inconsequential moves must He make to bring two nurses together in Brooklyn, New York, for a casual, twenty-minute conversation? What incidents and emotions and agents must He use to move one of those nurses from the Niger medical work into the greater pattern of her own destiny, while the second nurse, half a world away—just the one to whom God had revealed this field as *her* destiny—was chosen to fill the vacancy in Niger medical work?

How does God synchronize all these separate moves and all the separate destinies? How does He erase the impossibles until they look like mere coincidences? I have no answer for that. All I know is that such things make it tremendously exciting to be in the service of an omniscient and omnipotent God.

I believe part of the pleasures of eternity will be in retracing the complex patterns made up of accidents and co-incidences—even supposed calamities—to work out the design of greatest possible blessing, a design that was always clear to God.

Going to French Niger did not sound like a light undertaking. Our work there had developed from the very depth of a need that drew a few courageous souls across the French boundary. At the time of which I write, we had missionaries on only two stations in Niger—Tsibiri and Zinder.

In Zinder, where once the French had built a walled citadel for the Foreign Legion, the Sudan Interior Mission had

established the only mission station in 200,000 square miles!
Two people manned that station!

Tsibiri, nearer our Nigerian field, with two couples and
two single women, also had a parish of many hundreds of
thousands of people. One of those missionaries, Dr. D. M.
Osborne, a New Zealander, had been incarcerated in a con-
centration camp as a spy during the Vichy regime.

In those days, no mail or written message of any kind had
been permitted to reach the missionaries. I had been in Kano
once, when Dan Nana, a Hausa Christian whom I was later
to know well, had slipped through the lines, his mind
crammed with messages to our mission family and with questions from the news-hungry isolated missionaries who valiantly kept at their labors for Christ. He had to memorize all the
information that he carried back across that formidable
border.

The Vichy forces had withdrawn by now, but mail was
still slow. We were currently enjoying a love affair that was
glowing between Ruth Butts, in Tsibiri, and Jim Jacobson,
in Nigeria. In spite of the fact that it took some of their
letters six months to cross that high though invisible boundary barrier, they had arranged, not only an engagement, but
were making plans for a more or less formal wedding. They
managed it successfully, but their love had to weather many
tests before the day--and the veil—arrived.

My house, the one provided by the people of Ganson Street
Church, would be built in Tsibiri, but I was warned that it
would have to be more modest than mission houses for that
price in Nigeria. Legal exchange of our money differed
vastly from black market—or actual—value demanded for
wages or anything we would buy in Niger. Building materials, unobtainable in Niger, would have to be sent from Kano
—lumber, cement, nails, hinges, locks—with the added price
of exorbitant customs rates. Even laborers would have to be
sent from Kano to Tsibiri, over 200 miles.

I looked forward to going to this new station, but I was glad to hear that I would be staying in Kano long enough for me to learn a bit about eye work, for much of our general dispensary work is treatment of eye disorders. I would remain until Dr. and Mrs. M. D. Hursh, both of whom worked in the Eye Hospital, had had a month's holiday in Miango, and later, while Delta Bond, the only white nurse, took her vacation.

Delta is the kind of person everyone loves. Vivacious, and radiating with good will and sparkling humor, she made me feel at home immediately, for I lived with Delta in a house just across the street from the Eye Hospital. Both of us love to talk, and if she had a slight edge on me, it was not a very sharp one. We did not have much opportunity to tire each other, for we managed to be very busy at the hospital.

Besides, Delta was spending every spare minute studying Hausa. She had been on the field nine months, but she was getting no practice in speaking the Hausa used in the home, and her language examination loomed darkly and frighteningly on her horizon. After I had learned the rudiments of the hospital work, she was to take time out for concentrated language study.

The best place to learn the language is to go to a bush place where no one understands English, and where people have not become adept at translating Hausa words used with English idiom and sentence structure. Delta and Mrs. E. Bingham, a new missionary from England, cycled out to a village six miles from Kano. They were as excited about their first trek as we had been on the way to Babban Zaure.

After one day out Delta cycled back, fairly bursting with excitement and comment, carrying a long list of things to be added to their already amusingly large trekking outfit. The harmattan season was nearly over, and real heat was beginning. Delta had never experienced this sultry season, and a crowded native hut is none too comfortable when the wind blows like a blast from an overheated oven.

"O-ooh!" wailed Delta, in mock despair. "I'll never live through it!"

Older missionaries always get a bit of fun out of initiation of newer workers, so it was only natural to hear Dr. Helser say, "Oh, but this is still the cold season. Wait until it gets hot!"

Of course, it did get really hot. By the last week in April the weather became a table topic. Someone reminded newer missionaries to wear helmets very faithfully because out in the sun the temperature could go to 150 degrees.

The heat of April presages the violent rainstorms that break the heat. When I learned that nothing had been done as yet about my house in Niger, I asked that the building be delayed until the end of the rains. I was informed that builders had already been sent to Niger, but they were busy at some other project. My house would have to be built now, for it would save the cost of transportation of all the Nigerian carpenters and masons.

This distressing logic ground my spirit between panic and faith. I had seen an early wind-driven rain destroy a house in a few minutes on the Sokoto Leper Settlement. The sun-dried brick walls had been complete, nearly ready for the roof, when an unseasonal storm had swept down, melting the walls into clumps of mud. Everything had had to be rebuilt, right from the cement foundation. If my house melted once —such a fine house as this promised to be—what would happen to me?

Days slipped away; the rainy season was approaching relentlessly. No news either of good or ill came from Niger.

Life in Kano was far too absorbing to permit me to spend all of my time worrying about what was going on in Niger. And there was work to do.

The Eye Hospital sprawled like a giant *T*, beautifully

Blind beggar

contrasted against an avenue lined with flame-of-the-forest trees.

The hospital was still new, and eye diseases and infections have spread and prevailed in Africa for generations. There are some 85,000 blind people in Nigeria alone. Market places of cities and villages are lined with blind beggars. Now the people were finding relief from pain and hope for sight, and they flocked to the Eye Hospital in increasing numbers. People came from hundreds of miles. Blind! Alone! On foot!

Five mornings a week these people gathered at the clinic entrance. After a brief Gospel message, they formed a queue that passed the admission desk. Here Laura Hursh made out a card for new patients, or found the patient's card in the file that was, even then, bulging with accurate records. Patients were sent to take their places in the rows of seats at the right; the cards were taken to one of two treatment alcoves at the left and lined up on the treatment tables in the order of the patients' arrival. One alcove was reserved for treatment of noninfectious conditions. Most of our patients were victims of infections, and the two benches on either side of the treatment table in that alcove were always lined with patients.

Pam, a huge, hulking African orderly in white uniform,

checked and recorded all new patients' vision before they ever entered either treatment area, and rechecked them periodically after treatment had been started. Delta and I checked the cards to give all routine medications. Dr. Hursh saw all new or complicated patients and prescribed treatment.

Dr. M. D. Hursh is an ophthalmologist, who could be both wealthy and famous in America with far less effort than he was putting into his work in Kano, where he dedicated all his talents and skill to give nearly free care to the poor of Africa.

I kept wishing, as I watched Dr. Hursh move about quietly and efficiently, that all new missionary nurses—and doctors— could work with this man who had brought orderliness and superb organization into missionary medicine and surgery.

Dr. Hursh did not have ideal equipment, but he had built equipment necessary to do superior work. God has promised to supply all needs of His laborers. Dr. Hursh needed expensive instruments to do eye surgery. He had them. And we treated them with due care.

Though Dr. Hursh never raised his voice, I must not give the false impression that treatment areas were sepulchrally silent places. Our waiting room was large, but 80[1] people who had been squeezed tightly into long benches (and who couldn't read a *Silence please!* sign if there had been one) had to speak quite loudly to carry on 30 or 40 simultaneous conversations. Babies swarmed back and forth on all fours, adding to the shrieking uproar of other babies who were getting silver nitrate drops put into their eyes.

---

[1]In 1945, our patients seldom numbered much above 125 at the clinics, and rarely did we operate on more than 10 or 15 patients in a week. When I was compiling material for this book, in 1957, I wrote for up-to-date figures. Dr. Hursh supplied the following statistics:

Figures for 1956: There were 17,796 different outpatients who made a total of 78,413 visits, or a daily average of 280. The total number of operations was 3,737. At the end of 1956, the highest number of patients was 400, but the top number, so far, in 1957, was 513 at the daily eye clinic. The average number of operations a week is 72, and our highest runs around 100. We have had (with two doctors and three nurses) as many as 40 in one day.

"Any information I give you will be outdated before it is printed," wrote Dr. Hursh, "for the work continues its phenomenal growth."

One day Dr. Hursh looked at a new patient whose cornea protruded from between the lids. They were quite opaque.

"I can't do anything for him except relieve his pain," he said, in English.

The patient, not understanding Dr. Hursh's remark, said trustingly, "I will stay with you while you fix my eyes."

"No," Dr. Hursh replied. "You can go home, and come for medicine in the mornings."

"My home is far," said the patient in a weary tone, so hopeless that Dr. Hursh, who knows all distances seem far to the blind, asked how far he had come.

"I have been twenty-seven days on the road. Yalwa is my town."

Dr. Hursh was amazed. Yalwa, it seems, is over a hundred miles from Kano. "Who brought you?" he asked the blind man.

"No one but God. I felt my way along the road with my stick all the way."

Yet for all his great effort, for him our medical work had come too late. We saw scores whom we could not help physically. A few remained to enter the school for the blind, where the textbook was a portion of God's Word.

For me, it seemed more heart-breaking that we had come in time for some, but they had not come to us in time. At the beginning of the rainy season, the "eye fly" spreads an epidemic of acute conjunctivitis (pink eye). It usually takes one sleepless night to bring the ones with *good* sense. But Islam breeds stoical submission to the "will of Allah." Many, even of the local people, came after the disease had done irremedial damage.

Babies, bound on their mothers' backs, often with their hands pinned down, are the special target of the eye flies, for here they spread their evil germs undisturbed. Often the mother, too busy to bother with the child, comes only when the baby is totally blind, with the iris prolapsed through a blistered or ulcerated cornea. Occasionally the whole cornea bulges out to form what is known as staphyloma. Often the lids were so swollen that when we tried to open the eye for examination or medication, the lid would invert itself painfully, though still completely hiding his eye.

It is no small task to put into such an angry eye a medication that everyone concedes stings excruciatingly and which the young patient may already have experienced. But even for that we had a system. Pam would sit down beside the mother with a towel in his lap. With his huge hands he would hold the child's head firmly against his knees, while the mother pinned down flailing limbs and body. Our task then, was to be quick about what we had to do, before the whole bench was overturned in the heat of conflict.

Many patients came to the clinic whose eyes had been scarred by an infection that had not harmed the internal structure of the eye. If the scarring did not cover the entire cornea, though it covered the pupils of both eyes, these people could see nothing, but were conscious of light. For these people there was a remedy, for Dr. Hursh made hundreds of false pupils, somewhat off center, but still giving a gratifying degree of sight.

Trachoma causes more blindness in Africa, I believe, than any other disease. The infection attacks mainly the lids, at first, causing them to become rough. As time goes on, the disease causes scarring that draws the lids inward. Then the eyelashes sweep the eyeball, causing excruciating pain. To get some relief, the patients pluck their lashes. The torture recommences, with a vengeance, when the lashes come back in, sharp and stiff, to scrape the cornea like a brush. Gradually the cornea clouds and becomes opaque with pannus, a curtainlike network of fine blood vessels. Plastic surgery of the lids, with proper treatment of the disease before surgery, raises that curtain again, if the damage has not gone too far, and the cornea may become fairly clear. A large part of our surgery was lid plastics done for these trachoma patients.

To draw lashes from scraping the eye, Dr. Hursh removed a shuttle-shaped piece of skin carefully estimated to draw the lashes out to normal position, but not enough to leave the cornea exposed to air.

Native medicine men have also found a way to relieve this agonizing condition by picking up some of the skin of the upper lid and tying it off. The tissues, robbed of blood, slough off, scar, and draw up the eyelid. Sometimes the results are entirely satisfactory. More often the lid is puckered, with some lashes still on the eye, and worse, admitting enough air to dry the cornea, causing blindness.

Without anaesthetic, one cannot imagine the process of "tying" to be pleasant. I remember one of our patients who came to us expecting the same kind of torture.

Dr. Hursh warned her, as he was about to insert the needle to inject the local anaesthetic, that it would hurt a little. The woman on the table laughed.

"A *little*?" she said. She had heard, from others who had had their lids "tied" by the *malams*. She knew the worst.

The injection completed, Dr. Hursh paused, as usual, while the anaesthetizing agent was taking effect, to ask God's blessing on the operation. Although our patient was a Moslem, she inserted so many requests for blessing on the doctor that he remarked—aside in English—that he was not quite sure who had done the praying.

By this time, the anaesthetic had taken effect, and Dr. Hursh proceeded with the lid plastic operation. The woman braced herself for the pain. But she also wanted a thorough job.

"Tie it tight," she kept telling Dr. Hursh. "Don't be so gentle. Tie it tighter!"

Much of our surgical work was the removal of cataracts. This delicate operation requires good light, as well as a skilled and steady hand. With a section of tin, and a few other odds and ends from his workshop, Stan Myers had rigged a light that was focused on the site of operation, shading the eyes of those who worked. How he made it adjustable remains one of the secrets of those who perform mechanical miracles.

The operation for cataracts fascinated me because it seems the most rewarding of all forms of medical or surgical help. The patient is led to the surgery, usually almost entirely blind. A few days later the bandages are removed, and the patient exclaims, almost incredulously, "I see light! O Likita! I see your face!"

Most rewarding of all, however, were those quiet moments with the patients when a light more blessed than sunshine penetrated the heart. Of those who found Christ, while I was in Kano, none had a clearer, more definite testimony than the educated daughter of a southern chieftain. Agbami had come to have one of her eyes removed. but with her one good eye she had been reading our Christian magazines, which she carefully concealed from her Mohammedan visitors.

Seeing her interest in reading, I brought her a wonderfully simple exposition of Gospel truths in the little book, *Great Lessons for God's Lambs,* written by my pastor, H. F. Sugden, of the Jackson Church.

Any literature is prized by English-reading Africans. An hour later I found the book in the possession of Godfrey, one of our hospital nurses. Agbami managed to get the book back though, and in discussing it later, I asked her if she believed its message. Though she had been brought up a Mohammedan, she was ready, then and there, to take Christ as her Saviour.

It sounds easy and simple, but the conversion of a Mohammedan is not a simple and easy decision. The first result of turning to Christ is ostracism by the family, who often will not so much as eat with one who has turned "infidel." Property may be confiscated and treated as though the Christian were dead—without heirs! Sometimes the believer soon is literally dead. Dogon Yaro, evangelist of Kano, has been near death from poison several times. Abba Moussa, evangelist working in Zinder, dared buy no food openly for himself, for he too had been repeatedly poisoned. Wives often leave Christian husbands, so that they are almost compelled to buy their food in the market places.

We received word that my house had been roofed before the rains, but rains had been so torrential that the roads to Tsibiri would soon be impassable. So urgent was the tone of the letter from Niger that Delta Bond was recalled from her much-needed holiday in Miango, and I was sent on my way toward the hardest—and most rewarding—sphere of service of my life.

NINE

BRIM OF SAHARA

> Got any rivers you think are uncrossable?
> Got any mountains you can't tunnel through?
> God specializes in things thought impossible,
> And He can do what no other one can do.
> —My Tsibiri Theme Song

IT WAS AUGUST when Mr. D. M. Osborne's urgent letter warned us that the *malka* season of steady, torrential rains was imminent, and that meant that Niger's dry-season roads would become completely impassable. It was imperative that I reached Tsibiri then, and not after the rains had ended, because Mrs. Osborne, who was in charge of the medical work, was expecting a baby.

Even before Delta arrived in Kano, our office was trying to make arrangements with a lorry bound for French country, but there seemed to be very little traffic going beyond Katsina. Then Dr. Hursh found a solution. One of his patients that afternon was a French customs officer, who had come in to buy glasses and who would be returning to Maradi the next day. Tsibiri was only eight miles from Maradi. Dr. Hursh had already made arrangements for me to go with him.

Shaking hands with the *douanier* was the extent of my ability to communicate with him, for though I was going into Niger territory to work, I knew no French except for a few words that have crept into the English vocabulary. I would be working with the natives and entirely in the Hausa ver-

nacular, so I had not been too distressed at my inability to
speak the language of those in power. Even now, before I
had reached Niger, I began to understand why it would
become necessary to learn French.

Although I had been ready to leave soon after sunrise, I
waited in vain throughout the morning for the Frenchman
and his lorry. At noon it had still not appeared. When it did
come some time in the early afternoon, the *douanier,* who
knew no more English than I knew French, was unable to
furnish any reason for the delay. Knowing how little was
obtainable in French canteens, he may have been held up
shopping for some very important items on his shopping list.
Just as probable was the solution that, as so often, the delay
was caused by the driver who had loaded the lorry at leisure
while he bargained with passengers about their fees.

Two girls, Jessie Massie[1] and "Bernie" Thompson, were
"manning" the station in Katsina, where the Sudan Interior
Mission had established a bookshop. The *douanier* took me
to the mission station about supper time, and by eloquent
gestures at the lorry and at his watch I knew I was to be
ready early next morning, when he would pick me up.

Later that evening, however, missionaries from the leper
settlement, where I had spent a happy six months of my previous term, came in for a visit. They invited me to go out to
the settlement with them. As much as that appealed to me, I
declined.

"I'll be leaving first thing in the morning."

"That's what you think," said Bob Smith. "There's a
washout near Jibiya bridge. You won't get through that tomorrow morning!"

"But I must!" I exclaimed. "We've come through some
bad roads today. We can get through another washout."

After my friends had explained the seriousness of the washout near Jibiya bridge, I began to wonder if I was already too

---

[1]Mrs. William Magill.

late to get into Niger during the rains. Mr. Osborne had warned us to avoid just such a catastrophe, for that would leave the dispensary in Tsibiri without a nurse for weeks, and might mean a withdrawal of the hard-won permit to continue medical work in that territory. This, I recognized, was a situation in which God would certainly take a hand, for His work was directly involved. Silently I asked Him to make a way where apparently there was none.

We felt it only fair to warn the Frenchman at whose order the lorry would be starting north next morning. He seemed amused at our earnest pantomime of rains and rivers, but he still pointed at his watch. We would start early next morning. We finally found a French-speaking Englishman in Katsina, who explained to the *douanier* that his heavy lorry could not possibly get through the stream bed near Jibiya.

The *douanier*, whose position probably hung in the balance, was undeterred by these warnings.

"He says he'll get a lighter lorry," said our interpreter.

The lighter lorry that the customs man had found belonged to a Lebanese, who spoke both French and English. Mr. Abed had probably been offered enough money to risk whatever hazards the road offered. In the city of Katsina road blocks had been erected, prohibiting northbound traffic. Mr. Abed casually drove his truck around most of these signs and over a few less substantial ones. To a policeman who attempted to stop him, Mr. Abed offered a ride to the border. If anyone could get us to French Niger, the *douanier* had certainly found the right man to do so.

The road from Katsina was poor, but not dangerous. At Jibiya, however, we found a line of lorries drawn up at the side of the road, covered with tarpaulins. Passengers had scattered and the drivers were passing their time by organizing a few serious card games. A few onlookers bent tensely over the shoulders of the players. Nobody was even considering a crossing of the deep washout that made entrance to the bridge entirely out of the question.

Mr. Abed stopped his truck and walked toward the largest group of men who were lounging about on the sand. By various gestures these men made, it was quite apparent that they were telling Mr. Abed to join them. However, perhaps by dint of offering a larger reward than the stakes in the game, the men reluctantly got to their feet and sauntered toward the right of the bridge where the bank led down to the swift-running current at a less dangerous angle than elsewhere.

Mr. Abed and the lad he had brought with him as flunky waded into the stream to find the shallowest route. He came back, determination written on his face. I had noted that the river, though fairly swift, was not too deep, and it looked far less dangerous to me than climbing the opposite bank by lorry. I told him that I wanted to wade the river. The Frenchman made the same decision.

There were a few very tense moments in the middle of the stream when it seemed that the lorry would bog down and remain there for the duration of the wet season. Mr. Abed, however, was an able leader and had the added persuasion of whatever cash was needed to get the lorry through to the other side. To the accompaniment of a great deal of grunting and shouting and some genuine shoving, the lorry finally pulled through the stream and started up the steep slope of the bank. That ascent did not take nearly as long as the crossing had done, but it was far more frightening. I was very glad I had not remained inside.

At last we were on the other side. The French border lay near Jibiya, and Maradi was only 52 miles farther into Niger. The Englishman who had talked with us the day before had been an official of the Nigerian road system, and he had mentioned nothing more of much consequence beyond the bridge.

The road in French territory was far worse than the road

to Jibiya. We detoured some spots, shot through some others
with the same casual daring that had marked Mr. Abed's
contempt of hindrances all along the way. Sometimes we
were jounced and jolted roughly, a few other times we seemed
to keep our balance only because everyone held his breath.
Once Mr. Abed did slow down while his Nigerian boy found
the road for us, feeling for holes, where the road was covered
by an expanse of water nearly a mile wide.

Every mile brought us nearer Maradi. We had only 13
more miles to go when we plowed over a slight rise on which
was built a small village. Below us lay a literal lake, miles
wide.

Mr. Abed shouted at his boy, who tumbled down from the
back of the truck.

"Where's the road?" shouted Mr. Abed, in Hausa, to the
villagers, who had begun to collect.

"Don't send that boy into that water," said a man in a
tone of authority.

"How deep is it?"

"Deep enough to swallow you up. Your car too."

Mr. Abed contented himself by shoving a long stick into
the water as gauge, then sitting down for an hour or more to
estimate how rapidly the water was falling. It became clear
that no one would drive a car here for many days. To go
forward was impossible. To return to Katsina was almost
out of the question.

Mr. Abed was still in charge of the situation. He took us
safely back over all those precarious roads to the near side of
the Jibiya bridge. In Jibiya, he told us, he had a friend,
another man from Lebanon, who would give us supper. This
man, who owned a canteen in Jibiya, took us back into his
one-room house where he served us a hastily prepared chicken
dinner.

For four days, I was marooned with these three men, one
a Frenchman, to whom I could not speak at all, our driver,

who spoke both English and French, as well as Hausa and
his own language, and our Lebanese host who spoke to his
"brother" in one language, to me in Hausa, and to the
Frenchman (like myself) only through Mr. Abed, who acted
as interpreter.

Each day we tried vainly to find some way around the
flood. While we were not on the road, my quarters were the
onion storeroom of the canteen. I had my loads with me and
whiled away spare moments writing letters and reading a
magazine I had not found time to look into while I had been
rushing about in Kano. Naturally I carried my Bible. I had
even brought a French Gospel of John, thinking that I might
be able to learn a little French by comparing passages.

One day when I had brought my magazine to the house so
that I could read while I waited, the Frenchman spread his
hands in a gesture of frustration, and spoke to Mr. Abed, our
driver.

"He says he wishes he had something to read, to make his
time pass too."

When circumstances seem to lead into a dead end, though
we have trusted God to make a way, we are prone to ask,
"Why?" God's reasons are often hidden. As I watched the
French *douanier,* who admitted he had never read the Bible
or any part of it, poring over the Gospel, I wondered if God
had had to maneuver this situation because there would
otherwise have been no other way for this man to find the
Word of Life. And perhaps, too, the man might never have
been willing to look into a Gospel of John except for just
this very set of circumstances.

On the fourth day, Mr. Abed took me back to Katsina. I
reached Katsina just in time to receive a note brought from
Niger by a messenger who had found a way across the floods.

"Be in Jibiya tomorrow with head loads," said the note.

Jibiya! I had just come from Jibiya. It was the place I
had spent four fruitless days. But the letter from Tsibiri had

a solution to flooded roads. Mr. R. G. de la Haye, one of the
Tsibiri missionaries, would meet me in Jibiya with a horse
and carriers. We would ride the fifty miles by a winding
hill route, through the bush, and so dodge the flooded roads.

Though we followed the hills, we had to ford many swollen
streams. Neither I nor my horse was accustomed to this kind
of riding, and he approached the steep, slippery inclines and
the muddy, eddying streams that concealed our path with a
good bit of snorting and protest.

Ray de la Haye told me that the present flood was the
worst in the recorded history of the area—or in the memory
of the oldest people. Those were hard miles, too, fighting to
get our horses down steep banks, into streams, crossing wet
guinea cornfields that were surely 15 feet tall. The stalks
that lashed at us were usually wet with dew or a scattered
shower.

By the end of the first day—I walked the last few miles—
I was so tried that I did not wait for the boys to set up my
army cot. I just slumped down on a native mat a bit out of
the public eye. We had come only 15 miles, about one-third
of the way.

The next day we started out in a heavy drizzle. Most of
our paths that day seemed to lead us through dripping guinea
cornfields. Not only is it uncomfortable to be constantly
drenched, but even the best guide can become lost. Once
we took the wrong path, and made a great loop in our trail
that lengthened our trek by at least an hour. Our destination
was Jiritawa, and that was 20 miles—five miles farther than
we had done the previous day. Near Jiritawa was an aban-
doned² mission station, where Ray said there was still a bed
and a stove.

Perhaps because the terrain was less trying, or because both
my horse and I had lost some of the fear of the steep and

²Abandoned for lack of personnel. *Jiritawa* means *the waiting ones*, and at
the time this book goes to print, the people of Jiritawa continue to wait for
the day when messengers of the Gospel will reoccupy this area for Christ.

slippery descents into rivers and spent less time hesitating, we reached Jiritawa fairly early in the afternoon, and though we had come farther I was not nearly as tired.

It was still early enough for us to ride on to Maradi, which was only five miles from Jiritawa. We had no mission station there, but Maradi was on the road. Ray would send one of our carriers on to Tsibiri, to the mission station. When Mr. Osborne heard that we were on the road near Maradi, he said he would come in his car and we would reach our destination a whole day ahead of the planned schedule.

Riding five miles did not sound much harder than putting order into the depressing devastation of the Jiritawa house, which did not give much promise of rest during the night if it should happen to rain. Sleeping in a real bed, with the knowledge that the trek had been completed, sounded heavenly in comparison to another night in a low-thatched hut, which also would probably leak during the rain. Ray did not have to talk long to persuade me to undertake the ride.

On the way to Maradi, Ray and I talked about the Model-A touring car that was the only car serving our mission family north of the Nigerian border. Both the old Ford and its driver had become widely notorious for speed and endurance. But, though all one heard was not conducive to overconfidence, even a hair-raising ride on the dilapidated jitney sounded much less wearing than another long eight miles on horseback.

Just before we reached Maradi, near sunset, it began to rain. During the rest of our travels we had taken a drenching as a matter of course. This time I viewed it as a major catastrophe, especially after Ray reminded me that in French territory, because of the quality of the dry-season roads, it is illegal to drive on the road during a rain and for 12 hours afterward!

Ray further informed me that to arrive at the point of road that had meant the least riding for us, we had by-passed the government rest house by several miles. He felt, under the circumstances, our wisest action would be to ride on to Tsibiri. And Tsibiri was still eight miles away—eight long, dark, wet miles.

Although I did not accept his proposal with enthusiasm, I did not doubt his judgment. All that had kept me cheerful in the saddle had been the prospect of early release. Eight miles is quite a long ride to contemplate.

To encourage me, the men kept telling me that Tsibiri was just beyond a certain swell of sand. We would come to a rise, and I would look eagerly for the light.

"Not this swell—the one you see there, ahead!"

Eight miles of swells, slogging wearily through sand and slushy mud! Eight miles—but at the end lay Tsibiri!

By the time I had dismounted after having ridden the distance originally scheduled for two days, I was hardly aware of the eager and gracious hospitality of all who lived on the station. Daylight did little to make me bask in the triumph of my attainment.

I had come from *Farin Gida,* the gleaming ivory compound of Kano. I had sent ahead the floor plan of one of the houses of Kano, a house that had a fine corrugated metal ceiling as well as roof, a house in which Juanita Kluve had brought out the richness of her solid eroco doors and other woodwork by varnishing them. I had noted all the details of her house, so that I could make mine just like hers. I had bought the varnish for the woodwork, and I had sent ahead the locks for the doors, so that I could have knobs instead of padlocks.

Even the sunlight brought out more potently the glaring difference in architecture. Because the bricks of Tsibiri were made almost entirely of sand and would melt in the rain, every building on Tsibiri station including my own was swabbed on the outside with a heavy and odoriferous coating of sticky tar.

Perhaps a corrugated pan roof does not suggest the apex of

luxury to those who live in civilization, but pan does protect from the elements. Even now, my mud roof was leaking literal rivers of lye solution (for ashes are added to roof materials to make them more weatherproof). Two of the precious glass windows, of the three that I had in the house, had broken sections because no fastenings for them had been brought from Nigeria, and they had not been available locally, so the windows had been allowed to slam back and forth in the storms.

Inside, every floor had a broad and uneven strip of tar near all the walls, and a liberal spattering here and there in the center of the cement floor. A generous swabbing of tar also adorned the lower few inches of wall above the ant coursing.

I had brought cement-paint all the way from the United States, because I had determined that my nice new house would look as clean and as fresh as I could make it. It is impossible to sweep a tarred surface until it has collected enough dust and litter to coat the sticky tar surface.

Though the tar seemed to do little to impede either the appetites or the activities of white ants, the odor that pervaded the house was repellent to human beings. But of course, that would have been true anyway because of the amount of tar on the outer surface of the building.

In true French country tradition, too, all the woodwork in the house, including inbuilt bookcases, doors and window frames, had been generously treated with a mixture of peanut oil into which tar had been mixed. As long as that house would stand, I would never be able to use the varnish that I had so hopefully brought from Kano.

This was the house for which I had eagerly planned and for which my friends had made many beautiful contributions. I had planned a front room of rose and soft green, and draperies, scatter rugs—even vases carried that color scheme. Friends from a farm bureau unit, to which I had once belonged, had given me dishes in shell pink and gold. All these had been planned for my house—my beautiful new house!

Had I planned less, and expected less, my disappointment would not have been as acute. As it was, I developed a lively antipathy to this new country and everything connected with it. Everything that touched my life seemed blemished with the hardness of the desert. To return, unescorted, the same way I had come, seemed less difficult than to stay and face the problems that confronted me.

My discontent blinded me to the fact that I still had the best house in Tsibiri by far, for all the other buildings were so poor that heavy and hideous buttresses had been built against the outer walls to keep them from crumbling under the weight of the much-patching of mud roofs. Not one of those other houses had even one glass window, and they were dreary indeed when shutters had to be closed against the frequent storms.

I had lost sight completely of the text God had chosen for me, and which I had so piously quoted during my furlough, "For me to live is *Christ!*" I was still sadly involved with tangibles.

I suppose I had sensed this preoccupation with "things" as being something for which I must be wary, for I recall asking God, before my lovely outfit was sent across the war-infested Atlantic, that He would keep me from setting my heart on these "things," lest He would have to take them away. For I knew that in those days, more than one missionary had lost an entire outfit in transit.

God had kept my "things" for me, but He also saw my absorption with the purely mundane. To have lost my outfit at sea would not have provided the lesson I badly needed to learn, for I half expected some such mishap and my carnal defenses were up. I could have taken such loss philosophically. But God had allowed the "spoiling of my goods" to come where I had not expected it, so that He could teach me

in His patient, longsuffering way to let my life and my desires
be centered only in Christ.

In me He found a pupil very slow to grasp His meaning. I
might have found quick comfort in a busy schedule, and a
knowledge that I was needed. He saw fit, to make my lesson
more thorough, to forestall even that solace.

The massive government-built dispensary, in which I was
to work, languished damply on an island of very small cir-
cumference, for flood waters lapped at its very foundation.
The three mud huts that had been the hospital unit had been
broken down and piled about the dispensary to save the main
building. Two inpatients, the ones who had no other refuge
to flee to, wandered disconsolately about the building and
slept in the drafty open veranda. The work of Tsibiri did
not promise to be any more attractive than its ugly buildings.

The people who sent that $50.00 Christmas gift and in-
sisted that I buy myself some future enjoyment can never
dream of the comfort there was in the music I had brought
with me. One evening Mary Louise Schneider and I took
my portable phonograph, also a gift, out to the porch where
it was cooler than indoors. Halima, wife of our young evangelist, Dan Nana, joined us with her little tom-tom. I daresay
that this was one of the rare times when Beethoven's magnificent Fifth Symphony has been accompanied by the intricate
rhythm of a native drum in the dark hands of an African
woman.

Gradually, my attention was taken from the harshness of
life near the desert and drawn to the fact that the people in
this area are more approachable than they were in Northern
Nigeria. The flood had helped, for it had pushed its in-
quisitive fingers even into the few mud-walled compounds
in Tsibiri. Most of the women had far more freedom than
the locked-in women of Jega. More than half of my patients
were women who were bringing their babies to me for medical care.

Down the hill, to the west and beyond the dispensary, lay the town. *Tsibiri* means island and suggests that in some other wet seasons the water had encircled the town. This year, however, Tsibiri almost became the bed of a lake. Who had ever heard of such a flood right under the borders of the Sahara?

The flood had come swiftly, creeping up silently in the night, licking at the walls which softened quickly and succumbed to the weight of sodden mud roofs. The residents tried to build a dyke to save the town, keeping just about a half-inch ahead of the water for some time. Then, when it collapsed, the exodus that had already begun became a panic rush for the hills.

The water pushed determinedly through the town, leaving half the homes in crumbling ruins, and crept toward the dispensary. All night the people at the mission worked to save the dispensary, breaking down the three huts of the hospital unit to pile about the foundation of the larger building. The inpatients slept in the open veranda until they were driven later, when the scourge of mosquitoes became unbearable, to the chapel on the hill. Thirty to fifty patients waded to the dispensary every morning.

As the flash-flood waters subsided in the town, the people gradually moved back to the sites they had been wont to call *home*. Some found their huts livable after walls were mended; others found their homes in heaps of soft mud. These were forced, against their inclinations, to remain in their temporary shelters on the hill. Others built grass huts among the wreckage, trying vainly to continue life where it had been interrupted by the deluge. Doubtless, they would have lived right among those ruins, building up a new life, possible vicitms to another such flood, if the French government had not taken things very firmly in hand.

The announcement that French authorities were demanding them to move their town was so incomprehensible an order that many rebuilt their walls. Tsibiri had always been here. Tsibiri would always be here.

The commandant of Maradi sent surveyors out to mark off the site for the new Tsibiri—a town such as these people had never dreamed of. The usual village is just a maze of walled compounds set down at random or at the whim of the house-builder. If a path crosses a good plot, he just builds, and traffic finds some new though more devious route to its destination; and the maze grows more complex as children and children's children crowd compounds near the parental plot.

The new Tsibiri got its pattern from the great *Etoile* of Paris, where twelve streets and boulevards (including the celebrated Champs Elysees) radiate from the historic Arch of Triumph. In Tsibiri, the chief's compound lay at the center of the wheel, with a few spokes eliminated in front of it to provide for a large market place. Every homeowner would be required to plant trees provided by the government to make shady avenues for the wide streets. The compounds as planned were so roomy that the sun would have a chance to purify the litter, I thought. I was happy at the prospect of more healthful living conditions, but others, knowing that during the rains only grass huts can be erected, were worried about fire.

Because it was a thing never before heard of, the people's reaction to the mapping of a new town was not so much in-credulous wonder as utter indifference. They continued to carry bricks to the valley to rebuild their fallen walls. A few of the more progressive people, and some, like our Christians who were urged by those who comprehended the situation, staked out the boundaries of the sites they preferred.

Mr. Osborne, head of the mission station, heard that the Christians were enthusiastically planning to build together in a cluster. He called the elder Christians together.

"You are the salt of the earth," he said to the men. "Scatter your homes among the people, so that your testimony reaches the whole town."

As for us, we staked out the site for a church in the new town. Then interest in the new town grew, for the Moslem leaders protested against our having the plot.

Mosquitoes had been multiplying in hundreds of thousands of pools. Someone had loaned me a mosquito net, before my boxes arrived, and during after-sunset hours, our only recourse was to get into bed. There I wrote many letters and studied my medical books until they were dogeared from wear, searching the diagnoses of the many weird and violent diseases that were quickly rampant—the pestilence that follows floods.

I looked at one baby that was brought to me with fever. Every inch of her body was covered with tiny elevations, some of which were scratched and blood-encrusted. The skin manifestations were not flat like smallpox (though I was to see smallpox with as heavy a rash during the year—a fatal case). This rash was definitely a more pronounced breaking out than measles. I asked Kulungu, the man who helped me at the dispensary, whether there was another childhood disease prevalent in that area that could be diagnosed by skin signs.

The mother laughed. "Those are mosquito bites!" she said.

Of course. When I began noticing, most of the babies had welts just like this. Some women had blankets or cloths and could protect their babies a bit. The poorest people had to lie quietly by, while babies tossed and cried restlessly throughout the hours of darkness. Desert nights are cold too. We, who were accustomed to a cooler climate used more than one blanket to keep warm. Now, forced from their homes to nearly open-grass shelters, the people suffered with the cold. It was not uncommon to hear Christians pray, "Lord, take us through this season!"

Suddenly, in early January, 1946, the entire population

(some 30,000) was electrified with the formal government announcement that the coming Friday was absolutely the deadline for the old Tsibiri. Soldiers would be sent into town to enforce obedience to the edict to move to the hill. They would break down the homes of any who had not moved from the valley. Roofs would be burned.

I never expect to see a more entertaining and picturesque drama than the turblent confusion that flowed between the two towns on that Thursday—the dead Tsibiri—the "island" that had been a lake—and the new Tsibiri, built on so high a hill that it would never again really be a *tsibiri*.

Men and boys were carrying on their heads threshed grain that had been stored in mat *cikarofas*, or grain that had been stored in bundles. Some shouted at donkeys laden with the family's food. A donkey indiscreet enough to stop and bray his greetings at a passing acquaintance was soundly thumped by even the most easy-going of masters. This was no day for loitering.

Every member of a family was busy. Women carried heavy mortars chipped out of solid trunks of hardwood trees. Children, in various stages of growth, staggered or danced under whatever article of personal property had been placed on their heads. Lambs were worn about the neck, like protesting scarfs, toddlers carried their allotment of squawking and flailing chickens. Girls balanced the blackened cooking pots, or the narrow-necked *tulus* that had been foresightedly filled with water from the germ-and-frog-infested ponds nearest the hill. They were sadly aware that, from now on, they would have to carry their water far, and up a rather steep incline. Smaller girls carried calabashes and baskets, cotton, and the equipment for ginning and spinning it. Young boys were ingaged in more than one losing tug-of-war with unwilling goats, which, finally persuaded, augmented the screaming pandemonium by rushing headlong through the crush, often directly in the path of people who dared not dodge for fear of disturbing the balance of heavy loads on their heads.

Weaving in and out of the ebb and flow of the traffic were village roofs that looked, from a distance, like huge six-legged turtles. The six legs, at second glance were six men with the weight of the roof on their heads. We saw one roof, a smaller one, suitable for a granary, approaching us, looking like an ambulatory toadstool which had to tilt every once in awhile to see where it was. One man struggled up the hill with that one.

This roof transfer was strictly illegal. The French officials wanted a brand-new town, one that would be viewed with favor by the governor who would be coming to see it. But Hausa people are resourceful. One roll of new thatch over and old roof is much easier than a brand-new roof!

On the hill, men were busy making holes and sticking in posts to mark the edges of hastily chosen compound sites. No post-hole diggers are needed in Tsibiri, for the town rests on the crest of a huge sand dune. As deep as the hand can reach—and much farther, well-diggers discover to the peril of their lives—there is nothing but fine sand. No pebbles large enough for a fish bowl can be found anywhere near.

Visualize the uproar and activity of a town a-building. Experienced, the men were astute enough to know that, whatever the emergency, two wives cannot be expected to live under one roof. So for as many wives as a man had he erected a house. Sticks, tamped into hand-dug holes, were quickly planted in circles. Then with adequate heaving and grunting, roofs rescued from the old town, or newly made, were mounted to the top of these poles. Around these supporting poles a *zana* mat, woven from tough elephant grass, was deftly fastened, and the new home was ready.

I did not expect very many patients at the dispensary, but my number of inpatients had grown steadily.

Kulungu was back in time to give a short message before

the dispensary opened. He had not had much time to prepare, but Kulungu could think fast and had a ready tongue (quite evident when a quick alibi was needed, and he needed one far too often). His theme had a timely application.

"Folks," he said, "you know our present situation right now. We expected to keep on living exactly as we always had. Yet today we must leave our homes. If we have not provided a home on the hill, we will probably sleep out in the bush with the hyenas. That is the way with life. We expect to keep on living exactly as we always have. But someday we will have to move. If you are a believer, God has provided you a place in Heaven, but if not, you'll have to move to the 'house of fire.' "

In the local idiom, Kulungu's illustration was apt and forceful, as were many of the illustrations used by the Christians who took their turns coming down the hill to give a testimony or a message at our preclinic service.

Umaru, a recently converted Moslem who at that time worked as our yard boy and who, still unable to read well, stumbled painfully through a verse or two of Scripture, had a heart-warming testimony of a life that had dipped into the dregs of evil, and a new life and peace that "make it possible to lie down at night and sleep, unafraid of the inescapable day of reckoning that awaits all mortals."[3]

In one of his short messages, Umaru used a startling illustration—one that might not be considered in good taste in a preclinic service in the West—but Umaru was speaking to the Gobirs of Tsibiri. Umaru spoke of the new birth, a term that has puzzled many a learned person since Nicodemus asked Jesus to explain Himself.[4] Umaru was speaking to simple illiterates, yet he made the term as clear as a titled expositor could make it.

"You women who are about to give birth to a child,"

---

[3]Hebrews 9:27
[4]John 3:4

Umaru said—and there were women who smiled without self-consciousness or embarrassment that he should so address them—"do you say that your child has life?"

Any woman who had experienced the last months of pregnancy knew what Umaru was talking about, and there was a general hum of assent. Yes, without any doubt, the infant moved and lived.

"Yet if that movement ceased before you came to birth," continued Umaru, "and the baby did not breathe after it was born, would you not say that the infant had never lived?"

Again there was general assent.

"You who say you are alive and think you are but are moving about in the darkness of your ignorance and sin are as this unborn babe. God says the unregenerate man is 'dead while he liveth!' Only when God fills you with the breath of His Spirit—a new life that is eternal life—can you know what it means to experience light and life. If you do not know this life that is gained through salvation by Christ—if you have never been born again—you have never really lived!"

TEN

HOW PINCHES THE SHOE!

> There was an old woman,
>   Who lived in a shoe,
> She had so many children
>   She didn't know what to do.
> And Old Mother Hubbard
>   Was grieved when she found
> She hadn't a T-bone
>   To feed her pet hound.
>
> But these two old women
>   Have nothing on me,
> For I've run out of space
>   For my big family.
> They double up gladly
>   With two on a bed,
> But tonight told me sadly
>   They hadn't been fed.

MY SHOE WAS A BIT TIGHT as soon as I reached Niger. The inpatient huts of the dispensary compound had been sacrificed to the flood. Gambo, a querulous paralytic who had been living on the premises for a long time, had been sleeping in the chapel on the hill. As soon as the water subsided, a very small emergency hut was built for him.

Humbly, without protest of any kind, a Tuareg shared that hut with Gambo, even waiting on the helpless man at night. I was too busy with the epidemic of dysentery among the refugees on the hill to be amazed that this fair-skinned member of that proud race of Sahara tribesmen should condescend

177

to minister to a Negro, who repaid him with neither gratitude nor money.

During those months when the strike tied up my medical supplies and the flood prevented delivery of orders from Nigerian drug companies, the people came in increasing numbers. My scant supply of drugs was better than the best that the villagers had, so they kept coming.

One day at tea I was discussing with the other missionaries the possibility of building another grass hut, for that morning a woman had come from a long distance. We hesitated about putting her into the chapel, since she had a huge draining abscess and I did not have sufficient dressing materials to take care of her respectably. Even as we talked, someone came in to report that people from another village were bringing a woman to stay with me because she had been badly burned.

I let the group decide on a place to put this second woman, as well as the first, while I walked down the hill toward the dispensary, wondering how I could stretch my dressings and medications for large body burns and still have enough for the patient who was already taking far too many dressings. I had not reached the edge of our own compound when a woman called to me.

"I have come to stay here while I get medicine."

By the message brought to me at the tea table, I had anticipated an emergency, with a woman being carried in. I greeted the woman joyously.

"Are you the woman with burns?" I asked. My relief on seeing a patient able to walk and without a huge body burn made me want to laugh.

My relief was short-lived. This woman described her ailment—one of the common diseases of the tropics. As I entered the dispensary grounds, I saw that the "burn" patient had been put down outside. The men who had carried her were hovering around her in somber solicitude.

Kulungu, who did not know about the woman with burns, met me at the door of the dispensary.

"I'm glad you have come early," he said. "I have a little girl out on the veranda. Her parents brought her not long after our clinic closed this morning. They have been four days on the way."

Since the patient on the veranda was not an emergency case, I did not even go to look at her, but got Kulungu busy getting out dressings while I went to see the woman who had been burned.

This patient, I discovered, had been carried a long distance and was in a state of near-shock. It took me a long time to do her dressings. Then I turned to the woman who had come for medical treatment. Kulungu reminded me about the little girl on the dispensary veranda.

"They are Buzus," said Kulungu.

My heart picked up a beat! Buzus! These were the darkskinned, indigo-robed nomads of the Sahara, serfs of the paleskinned Tuaregs. I had seen them from a distance, with their camels, but they had remained gravely aloof and somewhat mysterious—the veiled men of the desert.

The Sudan Interior Mission had made repeated applications to the French government to open work in Tahoua, one of the nearest large oases, in order to make contact with these people. The reply had always been, "The natives of this area are too dangerous."

Naturally I had watched them as their caravans had wound by the dispensary. I had noticed the symbol of the cross on the pommels of their lavishly ornate saddles and on the hilts of their leather-sheathed swords. All men in these caravans were veiled. The Tuaregs, I had been told, wore white veils; the Buzus—Negroes once conquered as slaves—wore veils dyed with the native indigo. Both spoke the Tuareg language, tongue of the master race.

Sophie de la Haye had shown me her collection of Agadez

crosses, beaten-silver ornaments worn by the desert women. We had wondered about the origin of the Tuaregs, who were pale of skin. We often conjectured about the origin of the emblem of the cross which was upon all their possessions. They were Mohammedans, who follow the sign of the crescent and despite the cross of Christ. Still we knew that the Gospel of the cross had reached Africa before it ever reached Europe. Was this the last visible sign of a truth that had once left its imprint on every tangible phase of their lives? Had the indifference and lack of zeal engulfed the truth, allowing all but the symbol to be lost in the dense shadow of the dark continent? Or had the Gospel message been stilled by the dripping sword of Mohammed?

I made my way to the veranda to see my first Buzu patient, a tense little bundle crouched under an indigo-dyed cloth that had been drawn up over her like a dark shroud. When I gingerly lifted a corner of the cloth that covered her face, all thought of the romance of camel caravans, veiled nomads, or history of symbols, was driven from my mind.

Frightened black eyes gazed at me in mute apprehension; the shrunken skin lay in wizened folds over a face wasted with suffering and drawn now in fear. A more pitiful sight would be difficult to imagine. From the crown of Yar Dangi's head—and that means throughout her matted and unkempt hair—to the soles of her feet, this little eleven-year-old girl was covered with ulcerations, large and small, that exuded a serous discharge. From day to day, from week to week, these exudations had dried into scabs that had crusted, especially under her chin and in her hair, to over an inch in thickness.

It had required special grace to take care of the woman already on the hill, whose cavernous abscess continued to drain large amounts of heavy, odorous pus onto dressings I had to wash, because I had no cellucotton or other absorbent disposable materials with which to work. Untreated native cotton, I had discovered to my chagrin, is worthless as a dressing. Fortunately, I had brought rubber gloves in my head loads.

But now I needed more than gloves and more than the grace to use them gently and the added grace to keep the nausea and revulsion from showing in my face. I needed wisdom. I had not the slightest idea what terrible disease caused the little girl's symptoms, for I had never read or heard of anything like what I was seeing.

As I stooped to begin the careful soaking of those crusted ulcers, I challenged God silently with one of His promises that I was to claim countless times in those wonderful and rewarding days ahead: *If any of you lack wisdom . . . ask of God, that giveth to all men liberally, and upbraideth not; and it shall be given* (James 1:5).

Far more painful than this repulsive external manifestation of her disease was the complicating arthritic condition that had drawn up limbs and made her a helpless huddle of misery. Yar Dangi could not feed herself; she could not sit up. Every slightest move of any part of her body caused her to cry out with pain, yet I had to apply dressings to those ulcers. When at last I was through, after hours of gentle soaking and swabbing, my patient was whimpering with pain and relief—and I was exhausted. Yar Dangi looked like a veritable mummy, swathed from head to foot in bandages.

"What could cause a thing like that?" I gasped to Kulungu, when I had gone back into the dispensary.

"It's *kabba*," he said.

Kabba was a new word for me, as there were many new words in the Gobir dialect. But I had gathered from previous descriptions of patients with that disease that it was a certain stage of syphilis, mistakenly considered as a separate disease. I was wrong, but by God's grace my misunderstanding still led me to give the right medication for yaws, a nonvenereal disease related to syphilis. How important it was that God guide me to decide on the right treatment for this one

individual patient, I could not then know. I saw only this
little girl who was very ill, and who had come to me for help.

But Yar Dangi's parents had brought her from far to the
north. Knowing the lumbering gait of a camel, one could
understand that every moment of that long trail had been
slow torture. I could visualize the villagers looking at that
drawn face and emaciated and ulcerated body; it takes little
imagination to hear the eloquent, stoical click made far back
in the throat, that expresses better than words, "Too bad.
She can never make it. Why disturb the child?"

Given a drug that is specific for yaws, the disease cleared up
almost incredibly fast. In one month, Yar Dangi wore no
bandages and she was able to stand on her feet and take a
few cautious steps. She was feeding herself. And she had
gained some weight.

When the course of injections was completed, Yar Dangi
went home. Her parents must have returned by the same
route on which some weeks before they had been forced
so often to stop to give Yar Dangi relief from the pain of the
camel's motion. They must have stopped again at each place
to advertise what the white man's medicine can do. I think
God arranged this advertising campaign. And advertising
pays! The North just seemed to move in on us. In the next
few months, hundreds of Tuaregs and Buzus came, some from
oases as far as 250 miles away. So though missionaries were
prohibited from going into Tuareg country with the Gospel,
God was drawing these people from hundreds of towns and
villages to visit us.

I copied a government map of our *cercle*, and then checked
in red all the towns from which I had patients. Many of my
patients came from hundreds of miles off the edge of my map,
though I had a record of over 300 towns or villages when at
last my medical work became so heavy that I had to give up
my time-consuming hobby.

When Tuaregs came into Hausa country they entered hostile territory, for the Gobirs hate the people who a generation ago raided their villages for slaves and carried them into the oblivion of the North. My desert patients found no welcome in Gobir homes. This circumstance, again, God used to the extension of His kingdom, for the strangers from the North accepted gratefully the inadequate accommodations that we had to offer. They lived right on our dispensary compound.

Much later curiosity drew me to make a trek into the forbidden North. Everywhere in this supposedly dangerous territory I was welcomed as a friend and given kind treatment. By that trek I learned that the Lord's arrangement of bringing patients to live right on my compound was much more effective for giving out the Gospel than trekking could be. On trek, people come as curiosity leads them. Many may hear only one of several services held in one place. In two weeks' trekking, I had services in perhaps a dozen villages and towns, and only in four or five places did we remain more than one night. So even those who were interested could attend only a very limited number of services.

In Tsibiri, on the other hand, we never gave out medicine in the morning without first presenting the Gospel. But even better, we gathered our family every afternoon for an informal visit. We could lead our patients to chat about our faith; we taught them Scripture portions; we answered questions. We were able to approach the inpatients individually too. Many of these people remained for a month. A few remained as long as six months. All this time they were absorbing the simple tenets of the Christian faith under the most favorable conditions.

Kindness and the relief that medical work brings are powerful wedges into the hearts of even those who suffer in stoical silence. Those who daily watched us doing in love menial and distasteful tasks that they would hesitate to do for their most dearly beloved relatives recognized in our service the grace of our God.

"*Ikon Allah!*" Many exclaimed thus, attributing the power for our service to the living God. The numbers grew, too, as more went home to tell of the "House of Christ" at Tsibiri. Patients began to come three at a time. Even before Yar Dangi did my advertising for me, we began work on the mud walls of four huts.

One night I came down the hill to see a patient who was quite ill. Outside, near the corner of the building, I nearly stumbled over the body of a thin little Fulani boy who was being treated for a rheumatic condition. Had the others driven him out? He was of another tribe and spoke another language.

"My dear child," I said, "couldn't you find a place on the veranda?"

"That's all right," said the boy, doubling up against the harmattan wind that penetrated the threadbare shirt, his only covering. "I'm used to sleeping outside."

I strode into the veranda, bent on making room for the boy. Open as it was, it still offered a degree of shelter from the wind. The veranda was crowded with sleeping patients.

I used to keep my tithes very carefully for "nothing but active evangelism," priding myself on being a very careful steward of the Lord's money. I believe many of God's most faithful servants have the same prejudice I had against investing money dedicated to God in anything as silently inactive as a building. As I stood over this sick little boy, hunched together against the sharp, cold harmattan, God changed my mind about a few items of investments for eternity.

And God sent me more and more money to invest. In Jega I had had only a few gifts during the entire term; now money came in to rebuild my medical huts; in fact, we decided to build six of them. While those walls were going up, we hired our ambulatory Buzu patients, or their relatives, to make the roofs. Even while these walls were going up, the patients were far too many for six huts, and they could not wait for them. Before the roofs were ready to set on the walls, people, desperate with the cold, found a refuge against the chilling harmattan.

With a bundle of sticks, or a pile of mud bricks, they propped up those roofs just enough for a person to squirm underneath. One day when I started my phonograph in the afternoon to gather my people, I was amazed and saddened to see that those roofs were literally swarming with sick humanity.

Children were in their element. Sliding in and out from beneath a roof was no hardship for them, and they squirmed out while I stood there watching. The young mother who had a small baby chucked it out first and wriggled out after it. She had to be very careful, of course, for she had a very angry and painful ulcer on her leg.

And there was Jari, who had not walked for months. She had been brought on a donkey from Kurfi, a village not very far from Jibiya, just that day. I did not stay to watch how she would manipulate that 15-inch entry into her hospital ward; I ran for my camera.

She had drawn herself out as far as her waist when I returned. I could not help her out since she was edging herself

Children wriggled in and out of the "hospital" easily.
For Jari it was not so easy.

forward very carefully, gingerly pulling her swollen and ulcerated leg after her. I aimed my camera, and took her picture.

Jari laughed about that moment later after she knew me
better. When she saw me rushing out of the dispensary with
this strange black thing, and then pointing it right at her,
she thought instantly of the white man's *bindiga* with which
he shoots elephants or lions.

"Yau ajalina ya iso!" she thought, in typical fatalistic and
colorful idiom. We might express her thoughts weakly by
saying, "This is it! This is doomsday for me!"

But Jari didn't whimper, nor did she cringe. I did not
even guess that she was terrified. She was plucky, too, in
getting about, though she could not walk. She made light of
her handicap and her pain, and crept about on all fours quite
cheerfully. As the pain decreased she became quite nimble.
She began to call herself my "little goat." Jari soon infected
us all with her cheerful good humor and organized us into a
family, tying us together with the bonds of her own loyalty
and wit.

Desert nights are bitterly cold in the dry season, for during
those months there may be a fluctuation of 50 degrees from
noon to midnight. In March, when it was coldest, my mother
sent me $50.00 for my birthday. I wrote her about the pa-
tient so seriously ill that I went down to see him late one
night, not too long before she sent the gift. To reach the sick
man I had to step over huddled forms of the people sleeping
on the dispensary veranda. I counted them. There were 16,
all of them too sick to sleep out in that cold—one near death.
I could think of no better way to use my birthday gift than
to build a place for those people to sleep.

With them in mind, I contracted with a local builder for
an L-shaped *shigifa*. Within the straight walls of a *shigifa*, I
felt, beds could be placed with less loss of space than in round
huts. Together, the contractor and I measured off the area
for the building. We took a cornstalk bed, put it down, then

leaving just enough space for a patient to sit on the bed with his feet between beds we put down the bed again, thus measuring off the 18-bed hospital that I was planning. I could have done this mathematically, but my builder had to be shown what I had in mind.

An American contractor would have discouraged me. My African contractor did not build that hostel for $50.00, but let me think he would. My policy was never to get into debt. If God saw a need, He could provide before the money was due just as easily as He could provide afterward. God had seen the need and He had provided enough to get us by while the rest of His provision was still in the mails.

Though we now had patients in eight round huts and more in a two-room *shigifa* (built with Mother's Christmas Gift—and intended for a resident evangelist), before the new building had a roof on it over 60 patients crowded into it for shelter from the wind. The work has grown. We have had over a hundred residents on the dispensary compound, including the people, of course, who came to cook and care for patients who were too ill to fend for themselves. Most of our patients were ambulatory, but many came to me with very serious conditions. Often, very often, I looked up from my well-thumbed medical books over which I mulled under my mosquito net, and admitted, "Lord, I don't know what's wrong with this patient. Show me how to help him."

And God was there. My knowledge and wisdom often failed, but in answer to an urgent plea, offered silently even while I worked, He often "made manifest the savor of his knowledge" by giving me an idea that worked, or getting the patient to mention the one symptom that was the clue I needed for diagnosis, or—when my ministrations failed—by putting His hand on the patient for nothing less than a miracle. Those Africans were illiterate, but they were intelligent enough to know whether they were feeling better. I kept telling God that I would keep making the Gospel my main purpose if He would keep bringing the people. You can be sure that God did not fail on His end of the partnership!

By the end of the harmattan season, in those blistering days of April and early May, though the Buzus and Tuaregs migrated back to the north and inpatients were fewer, the numbers at the dispensary still increased. Whereas before the inpatients had suffered from the cold, now the patients from distant villages were suffering from the heat. I began my medical work an hour or more earlier when I discovered that unless they received their treatments early, people from ten miles or so away had to wait until evening to go home, for the sand got so hot that it burned even their heavily calloused feet.

By the time we were ready to begin our work, the wide verandas were crowded with patients. Often as I looked over that great crowd, knowing that many missionaries in Moslem areas seldom if ever have such a great audience, I bowed in humble gratitude for God's sending me to serve Him in French West Africa. I knew, also, that almost without fail there would be at least one present who had never before heard the Gospel of everlasting life through faith in Christ, and probably there were some who would never hear it again. How important that the Gospel be told clearly and simply! It was a great opportunity—and a great responsibility.

In this again I had encouragement. I knew that someone had been in the Throne-room in behalf of me and of these people. The very friends who were sending the funds that kept my medicine bottles full of first-rate drugs, the very people who had wound literal miles of bandages for me, were beginning to write in their letters, "We are praying daily." God would not fail to honor their prayers.

After the short service, the people filed in, holding their treatment cards on split grass stalks so that their fingers would not make them too dirty to read. I sat behind a low mud wall, two feet in height, that protected me from too

much physical contact with their soiled clothing and infectious skin lesions. The broad window behind me (since
it had neither screen nor glass) was almost always filled with
young rascals whose numbers were far down the line and who
liked this ringside view of the proceedings. They scattered
before a broom or a dipper of water, but swarmed right back
to breathe down my neck.

By this time, I had two boys working for me. Arzika had
been our garden boy, but he was intelligent, quick at his
work, and, most important, he was cheerful and kind to the
patients. The dressing boy was not always the same, for it
took a very strong stomach to spend every morning leaning
over the ulcers and burns that made up one-third to nearly
one-half of our cases. Kulungu had gone back to farming.

While at the Katsina Leper Settlement, I had learned, from
British medical charts, the clever trick of making concentrated stock solutions of common prescriptions. These con-
centrates saved me hours of time over the apothecaries' scales,
and could be diluted in such proportions that every one of
the routine prescriptions had exactly the same dosage. This
is a wise precaution against error in dosage when half-literate
Africans dispense the drugs. I had to give all but the routine
drugs myself until Arzika gradually learned to read all directions without error. I could never trust Kulungu to do so.

To doctors and nurses who think it incredible that I should
have seen and intelligently cared for 200 to 250 patients a day,
and others who might be skeptical of such rush treatment, let
me hasten to explain the difference between clinics at home,
where a patient goes off with a prescription that may last two
months, and a dispensary in Africa, where patients are almost
invariably illiterate. In British territory it was law that no
patient be given in his hand more medicine than he could
safely take all at once. This was French territory, but the
rule was a wise one, and I adhered to its principles.

Obviously, patients with acute illnesses often had to come

to the dispensary every day, but many of them could be checked into the record book with a quick question about whether or not they were getting the desired results from the treatment. Ulcer patients and those with simple conjunctivitis were also usually sent right by without undue delay.

The French government medical service had evolved a marvelously simplified record system that was quite ample for all but the very ill patients, on whom I kept a file. It was that minority of new patients, and those who were not improving, or who needed daily careful checking, who took most of my time.

When it was necessary to give several doses of medicine during the day, I carefully pointed to the sun's position as I gave the Arabic word for the Moslem prayer-time when each dose must be taken. Often I had Arzika repeat the directions as he laid the medicine into their hands. All medicine that could be given in the dispensary, we personally measured and gave to the patients ourselves. This added to our work and increased the noise, for many of our patients were children.

For the many diarrheal diseases, I often prescribed chalk and bismuth powders to be taken several times a day. All these powders, carefully measured or weighed to be correct for different ages, had to be prepared in advance, or we would have been all day taking care of a few patients. If carbarsone or sulfa were added, especially for babies, those tablets were crushed and put into the powders, so that the mother would not be confused by too many separate directions.

Generally, I took physical histories while patients stood in line. For more personal confidences or for examinations that required a prone position, I had an examining room that had been renamed derisively *the jail*. From that *jail* came some of my best advertising.

With 150 patients or more standing in line, I had come to the conclusion that it was not fair to the people waiting that

I should spend ten or more minutes searching for the record number of a patient who had forgotten or lost his treatment card. At first I let them waste a lot of my time with their glib alibis and fell for their stories of thefts of clothing, burned roofs, and rats with a strange and unnatural appetite for dispensary cards. However, when thefts and fires became the general order of the day, I became very harsh and listened to all calamity stories with calm indifference.

"I'm so sorry," I would say. "If you'll wait in the examining room until I have taken care of people that got numbers at the same time you did, I'll find your record number for you, and write up a new card."

Often I knew someone's card was missing by suppressed chuckles and gleeful jeers of anticipation from down the waiting line, or by a chorus of helpful suggestions of untried and highly original alibis. When I pointed to the *jail*, the whole line would break into cheers for another victim. The victim would grin and jeer back, and watch, from his point of vantage, the hundreds of patients receiving treatment. With plenty of leisure to get a good estimate of our daily business, his report brought us even more.

Old Goshi, a wizened little woman who had come to stay with Halima, a girl crippled by a rheumatic condition, was known to all for wittiness, a ready tongue, and her huge enjoyment of the discomfiture of those bound for the *kasso*. One day she misplaced her card. That was the day of vengeance for many an unfortunate jailbird. When she took her position in *jail*, a literal "boo!" rose from the queue of people, many of whom she had tormented. This was the only time I have heard Hausa people boo anyone. It seemed to imply amused derision of someone beloved.

The *jail* was also a mild torture chamber. Since many of our patients had yaws, they received three injections a week. At first, I did all the injections myself, but as my own work grew I decided that Arzika must learn to do the routine

yaws injections, if not the more complicated graduated dosages given for some of the other diseases. He had already
learned to wash and sterilize the syringes and needles.

Arzika was not too badly disturbed when I announced that
this new duty would be given him, for it increased his self-
esteem as well as his prestige with the patients. After the outpatients had gone for the day, I checked with him, as I often
did, his method of washing the equipment and the length of
sterilization time. He readily learned to read the simpler
dosages in cubic centimeters. I asked him to prepare 0.5 c.c.
of sterile water as he would for an injection.

"You can practice while there is no crowd to harass you."

"Where's the patient?" he quipped.

I bared my arm. Then he began to shake.

"*You?*" he quavered.

"Certainly," I said. "If you are going to learn to do injections, you are going to learn your technique on me. Then
I will not be afraid to have you use the needle on others."

Somehow even a black man has a peculiar idea that slipshod methods will not have ill results when applied to black
people. Though Arzika trembled while I watched him
through his first injections, he gave thousands of injections to
natives thereafter, through very badly neglected and unclean
skin; but I can remember only one needle abscess—and that
might just as easily have occurred had I inserted the needle.

Arzika was not the only one who trembled occasionally.
Time and again it became necessary to lance deep abscesses.
Ainhum is a fairly common disease that lays a constricting
band below the skin around a toe, until even bones are absorbed and the toe is a swollen ball of pain—excruciatingly
painful when it brushes against a stalk of grass. A few longi-
tudinal cuts sometimes alleviate this condition if done in
time; but when the bone is atrophied, nothing brings relief
but amputation, which becomes a very simple and painless
procedure with a quick-freeze anaesthetic. However, though

flesh and bone have been crowded out, blood vessels have not. The biggest problem was to prevent a hemorrhage after the amputation.

Less pleasant was the snipping away of gangrenous tissue, especially when it was a tiny baby's foot that had gotten into a fire, or a few fingers of a man's hand, burned so severely because he was a leper. But all of us will always remember Halima.

It had been a busy morning and it was far past time to go up the hill for lunch. Mary Louise, who ate with me, would be famished. I closed my records with relief that the rush of another morning was over. I rose to go.

As my heavy homemade chair scraped the cement, it nearly struck a woman who was crouched on the floor, somewhat behind my chair.

"Haven't you been treated?" I asked.

"She came too late to get a number," said one of the boys.

The woman was a picture of abject misery. Never had I seen a more repulsive human being than this Buzu. Her face was swollen and misshapen with the nodules of leprosy. Both of her hands were gangrenous and crusted with a nauseous pus that seeped from deep abscesses in her forearms. Without the use of her hands, she had been unable to take care of her matted and unkempt hair, or even to tie a *kalabi* about her head. Her tattered cloth was unspeakably filthy, stiff with the dribblings of the decay that she bore about in her own tissues. Around her clung the stench of carrion, and her face wore the hopeless aspect of one who had experienced, day by day, the fearful nudgings of a death she could neither hurry nor escape.

Now she lifted her numb, festering hands in a gesture of suppliance that was without much hope. "I have just now come," she said, in the harsh whisper peculiar to lepers, and added, "on a donkey."

My heart sank. If she had come on a donkey, she expected

to stay. I could not have asked any of my patients to share a room with her—because of the odor—even if she had not had leprosy. I could not keep a leper on the compound with my other patients. She must have interpreted my dismayed expression as unwillingness to help her at all.

"Don Allah!" she pleaded, literally groveling at my feet. ("For God's sake have mercy.")

"We will take care of your hands now, and give you medicine," I said gently, to reassure her. "But you will have to find some other place to stay." I tried to say the inhospitable words kindly.

"If you'll only take care of my hand, I'll go away. I'll only come in the mornings for medicine. Only help me. I'll find a place."

Halima was still imploring, as one who has been driven from place to place without pity. She reminded me of a stray dog that has been kicked or beaten wherever he goes and whose worst crime is that he is alive. Halima's whole cringing attitude bespoke a fear that she could not dare to believe that we would really help her.

"We never refuse to help anyone who comes to us, Halima," I said reassuringly, "And we will be glad to help you."

My words were belied by the ulcer dresser's unexpected action, for he was a fine lad. He refused to touch her. He came to me, looking embarrassed but determined.

"I just can't do it," he said.

He had never refused to treat any other patient, and the new ulcers that he dressed every day were no bouquet of roses. I did not argue with him. There are some things beyond which the most willing soul rebels. My own stomach turned over when I thought of the dinner that Mary Louise was trying to keep hot for me on the hill. I knew she would soon grow concerned if I did not come home. So I asked Arzika, the head dispenser, to take care of her. He, too, for the first time told me he could not do what I asked.

All this the cowering woman was forced to hear. Her last hope gone, she slumped to the floor and crouched there, her despairing face bent over her knees in abject hopelessness. I called to her, but she did not stir.

She looked up in amazed incredulity when I touched her, and told her to come with me to the treatment table. Would I, a white woman, do what the boys could not do? She could not believe that.

I tried to make up, with gentleness and kindness, the hurt she had suffered from the boys' attitude, while I drained the pus from her festering and lifeless hands, washing away the decomposing, gangrenous tissue the odor of which made all other human beings shrink from her in revulsion.

That afternoon she was on the dispensary compound, sitting apart from the others. I did not scold. I did not ask her why she was there. I knew the reason. She expected to be driven away from here too, as she had been driven from the town, for I had explained to her, that noon, that the government would not allow me to keep her in any of my huts.

A grass hut is quickly made, and it can be burned after a patient with an infectious disease has used it. I sent for my yard boy.

When I took her to the solitary grass hut, erected out in the bush some distance from my dispensary compound, her gratitude was pathetic. For many days we saw her only when she came for her dressings; then she would dissappear, returning only at night to sleep in her little hut. I presume she spent the days begging the coins that at first were probably thrown at her from a distance. But as the abscesses cleared, as the sloughing flesh was trimmed away, she became less obnoxious to herself and others. No one protested—for Halima remained at a discreet distance—on the day she joined us for our afternoon "family" gathering around the phonograph and the Word of God.

Little by little, Halima lost that hunted look. Finally

came the day when she smiled. A happier day came not much later when she accepted the Saviour who not only changes the heart and life but who has promised that this mortal body—even a disease-ravaged one like Halima's—will be raised perfect and incorruptible. When you see Halima she will have exchanged disfiguration for beauty, her beggar's calabash for a golden chalice of praise, her grass hut for a mansion.

There was something strikingly beautiful about her smile, even in those days, and we learned to love Halima. Her hardships had taught her humility and deep gratitude. We soon began to find her meek, gentle spirit and quick flashing smile an inspiration in times of weariness and stress. Even in worship, she set us an example.

One Sunday Halima came to our church service on the hill a bit later than the other patients who had already settled comfortably on their mats. I motioned for her to sit down near me. When the usher passed the small grass kwando for the offering, he took my money, ignoring the patients, for they usually were so poor that asking an offering would be embarrassment for them, and, of course, many of them were not Christians.

Halima looked up at me. She pointed to a Nigerian penny, which was strung by its central perforation on a strip of material that was part of the homespun cloth she wore. Then she pointed at the reteating back of the usher.

I beckoned him back, praising the Lord for her unsolicited gesture of devotion. Then watched as her scarred, lifeless hands with the shortened, numb fingers—and but few of them —shook with eagerness as Halima struggled to untie the knot that held the perforated coin before the usher got back to her.

She flashed me a bright smile as she put her offering into the basket, and I remembered Jesus' blessing on a widow who had cast two mites into the temple treasury. Which, I wondered, in the books of Heaven, is the greater gift—two mites or a Nigerian penny worth two French francs? I wished I could see the books. I wondered about one more thing. Would Halima have lunch that day?

She gave the only coin on her cloth.

As Halima shamed me by her devotion on that Sunday, so Mazhgo, an old Tuareg woman, shamed me by her sincerity on another day.

Certainly I praised God for sending me many patients, patients whom I could in turn introduce to Him. But there were days when the work seemed a bit too heavy and the patients almost too many, when the heat of May drained the body of natural energy and threatened to drive me into a spiritual torpor. On a day like that, it is hard for a missionary to keep her halo on straight.

For this need God called my attention to His Word: *The heathen shall know that I am the Lord, saith the Lord God, when I shall be sanctified in you before their eyes.*

On one of those hot days, Arzika came to say, "The numbers are all distributed, and there are still patients without numbers. What shall we do?"

A record-breaking crowd on a day of thermometer-breaking heat! The stress of trying to get through that throng of patients might have been less trying in a cool, quiet doctor's office, with patients fingering the proverbially outdated magazines. But in Tsibiri, my line of waiting patients whiled away their time by holding shouted conversations across the room. Ten of them would talk to me at once, punching me when necessary to gain my attention.

The friendly boys who used the window as a ringside seat on the bedlam being staged inside blocked off all my air. Patients arrogantly demanded to be taken out of turn because they were local dignitaries or suffered from self-importance. What grieved me most was that some of the most troublesome of these were Tsibiri Christians, or their relatives, who were indignant that they could not have the immediate treatment that we gave Bible school students who had to be dismissed from their classes for their visits to the dispensary.

Hard to bear, too, was the indifference of a mother to her own child's sufferings and the nausea that clings for hours after some horrible spectacle of neglect must be cared for, the stench of new ulcer patients, the vapid stare of ignorance, the worshipful confidence of patients who are hopelessly ill or who need surgery which they can never have, because there is no surgeon for hundreds of miles—and my knowledge of the relief surgery could bring if there were more doctors—all these things add up to a crushing and fatiguing load. And always there was the heat—harsh, suffocating, devitalizing heat.

How easy to shout an angry demand for silence, to scold the negligent mother, to snap at the boys in the window and the boys who helped me with the work! How timely the Lord's reminder that what I did that day would be lasting and eternal in its effect! Not the medicine I prescribed, but the patience I displayed in trying to elicit the symptoms from people who had no idea what I was driving at. Not the mat that I gave to an inpatient, but the degree of compassion I had shown a stranger who had come for help. Not the preaching I did with my still-ineffectual Hausa, but the smile I wore when my stomach revolted at what disease can do to human flesh.

It was after such a morning as this that Mazhgo came up to the house, following me from the dispensary, saying that she wanted to talk to me. I expected a detailed account of her symptoms, for she had many, and more frustrating, I knew I could do little for her. I did not think she had long to live. But what could I do? I put her off until after tea. I told her to wait in the shade of a tree on the compound.

After tea, pressing duties drew me quickly down the hill.

I needed to make up prescriptions, mix ointments, check in-patients—Mazhgo was forgotten.

She followed me down the hill. *"Maijinya."*

"Yes, Mazhgo!"

"You *have* to tell me about your Way, *Maijinya*," she said, using my native name, and not reproaching me for forgetting her. "I cannot understand Hausa well—and they preach so fast!"

Here was a woman on the brink of eternity, and she had had to pursue me with her anxiety to be shown the way to Heaven! *Oh, let me never be too busy to see my people's greatest need!*

What if she had not followed me down the hill? She might have been offended. She might have gone away!

Was there a pressing task then? Ah, yes! The one from which I had run away. I dropped everything and sat down in the dispensary, native style, and carefully told Mazhgo how she could be saved. She accepted the Lord whom she had been seeking, right then and there. I asked her to thank the Lord for this salvation.

"You must tell me how."

"You must speak what is in your heart—and God understands any language."

So Mazhgo poured out her heart in her mother dialect, and I joined her, in my heart, with an English *amen.* Then I prayed aloud, in Hausa, for God to keep her and make her His witness. As the medley of languages rose in the incense of prayer, I knew they had been translated into the language of Heaven.

The heat and fatigue, the harrying pressure of being a medical missionary under the skirts of the Sahara were forgotten in the thought: She might have gone away. *But she didn't!*

Mazhgo. Remember the name. I think you will know her.

ELEVEN

CUPBOARD OF N'WALA

_____

About that time there was again an immense
crowd, and they found themselves with nothing to
eat. So He called His disciples and said to them,
"My heart yearns over the people, for this is now the
third day they have remained with me, and they
have nothing to eat. If I were to send them home
hungry, they would faint on the way, some of them
having come a great distance."

His disciples answered, "Where can we possibly
get bread here in this remote place to satisfy such a
crowd?"

"How many loaves have you?" He asked.

They answered, "Seven."—Mark 8:1-5, Weymouth

N'WALA," SAID JARI, "is the name of Maijinya's village."
Nobody argued. Jari had spoken. So be it.

Jari ruled us with a ready tongue and with her sharp sense
of humor, and we loved her. As she laughed away the pain
and humiliation of her own circumstances by referring to
herself as the "Nanny Goat," so she also lightened our own
problems, not by ignoring or belitting them, but by setting
them in a place of honor.

Jari was unique. Even while she made her way from place
to place on all fours—never say *crept!*—she became queen of
the compound. She wielded her authority with subtlety, by
relegating ostensible honors and power to others.

"*Maijinya* has many people here," she announced one day.
"We must name her town. We will call it N'Wala."

Abdu, *Galadima* of N'Wala.

Since she and all other patients knew me only as *Maijinya*, the Hausa word for one who ministers, or *nurse*, the name of the town, N'Wala, had nothing to do with my own name, *Wall*. The selection of name is noteworthy since it was made in all sincerity, not in rancor or discontent, and it means, "Let me settle here comfortably where I won't be crowded."

Jari had light-heartedly forgotten that when she had come, there had been no place for her but under a half-finished roof and even that had been wretchedly crowded.

By common consent, I was chief of the town. Abdu, a young man who had a large ulcer, she quickly named the *galadima*, because of his seniority as a resident patient. He protested, with a reflection of her own wit, that Sarkin Ragga

—king of rags—would be a more appropriate title than that
of prime minister. He demonstrated his logic by holding up
the tatters of his homespun *taguwa*.

No mother is prouder of the first steps of her first-born than
I was when, after months of treatment, Jari walked. All
stooped over and leaning on a stick like a lovable gnome, she
now walked all over the compound, keeping the "family"
well in hand.

Makau was another who learned to walk after being bed-
fast for six years. He had been on my compound for that
many months before he took his first painful steps. Makau
was a man from the Fulani tribe, the nomadic cattle people
with aquiline noses, long, silky hair, and with skin nearly
as light as that of the Tuaregs.

Makau had been placed into one of the temporary grass
huts built because of the housing emergency. There he had
lain, day after day, suffering great distress from a rheumatic
condition, while the harmattan winds howled through the
zana mat walls of his shelter. Meanwhile, I prayed for wisdom
to discover what was crippling Makau.

Because of Makau and others who could not leave their
beds, I usually brought my phonograph out to an open area
in the middle of the cluster of hospital huts. I often sat on
a low stool, or right on one of the mats the patients would
quickly bring from their beds. The fine Gospel records in
Hausa not only attracted my family together, but by repeating the six records so often the people were memorizing the
message of salvation. Our family gatherings were completely
informal; quips and questions were the order of procedure.
We had a good time.

One day, when we were about ready to disperse, I became
aware that I had lost the family's attention. All eyes were
fixed beyond and above me. I turned. Makau was standing
behind me, leaning heavily on a staff. Though his face was
set stoicly against pain and haggard, he was literally beaming.

"How wonderful, Makau!" I exclaimed. I was delighted. I had never seen him out of his hut before. "I only wish you would have come to join us a little sooner."

"I started getting up before you came out," he answered, "when the boy brought out the gramaphone box. I'm just not very fast!"

But he was proud. He had gotten up, unassisted, from the low cornstalk bed. And he had walked a few steps.

After that, Makau, tall and gaunt,[1] his face aged and drawn with suffering, stood in the background of every meeting. At length he could even sit down. But long before that time came, Makau had accepted Christ as his Saviour.

I had about a dozen others on the compound whom I affectionately called my cripples. All but a few of them could get around—like Makau and Jari—somehow. Jari later shared a hut, and doubtless waited on one of my patients who could not move from her cornstalk bed. While Kimba was there, for many months, we always had our afternoon meetings outside her hut.

African bush people have no chairs in their homes. When Kimba's arthritic condition had made it impossible for her to work, she had sat with her legs doubled up under her. Now she could not straighten out her legs at all.

One day I expressed my sympathy to Kimba. I wondered if just propping her up on a chair would ease her knees.

"Oh, Maijinya, don't feel sorry for me now! I'm so much better!" she answered. "For all those months and years, day and night, I could only sit and lean my head forward against the wall. My back is so much better now that I can lie down."

And on what was she grateful to lie down? Not an inner-

---

[1] Years later, a tall robust young Fulani brought a relative to the dispensary for treatment. "Do you know me?" asked the tall man.

By that time, I had seen tens of thousands of patients in Tsibiri. It was impossible, of course, to know all of them, though all expected me to recognize them. Hadn't I always known their names when I looked at their treatment cards? I shook my head.

"I'm Makau—the cripple!" he said, enjoying my amazement.

spring mattress, but a hard, unyielding cornstalk bed, ridged
and rigid, about as thick and wide as a door, and usually
shorter than the person who used it for a bed. Mats made of
woven palm strips were placed on the "bed."

Sheets? If I had even been indiscreet enough to furnish
sheets to my patients, I should have had the surest way of
getting rid of both the sheets and the patients. During those
days, any cloth could only be obtained by bartering with
peanuts, for France was suffering a wartime shortage of oil.
No matter how ill my patients would have been, they could
not have passed up the opportunity of that much cloth! Anyway, sheets are a luxury undreamed-of in their homes, and
far beyond my means to supply.

I did try to supply one item of comfort. My patients complained bitterly about *tsutsa*—a kind of grublike parasite that
preys on sleeping human beings if they are in contact with
the ground. I learned that if the bed is raised from the floor
only a few inches, the *tsutsa* do not bother. In homes I had
often seen that beds can easily be raised by letting three pairs
of forked stakes support three sturdy poles across which a bed
is laid. I decided that my sick people deserved—in a white
woman's hospital—freedom from at least those vermin not
brought to the premises by the patient.

My kindness was gratefully received until the next cold
season when, one by one, the bed posts were used to rekindle
dying fires. Worse, the roofs were sadly depleted of thatch
because my cripples found it convenient to use as kindling.
My boys showed me a defense against that form of sabotage.
They tied thorn bushes along the edge of all roofs!

One evening, just as the sun was setting, a Buzu led a camel
right to the dispensary veranda and barked at the ugly beast
to kneel. I knew I had another patient, so I went outside to
welcome the woman who was slumped over the high pommel
of the saddle. The Buzu grunted gruffly to the woman to dis-

mount. She tried to step from the kneeling camel and collapsed in a heap.

"You must be very tired," I said, helping her up.

"Four days I have been on this camel," she sighed.

Ma'inna was the first—and the last—Fulani that I have ever
seen on a camel. No great friendship exists between the Buzus
and the Fulanis. Ma'inna's arrangement had been one of necessity rather than amicability, and the Buzu, I soon learned,
had taken nearly all of the sick woman's money. He had left
her six shillings (about $1.25 at the current exchange). This
sum was to furnish her food while she was to be healed of a
disease of several years' duration.

Her confidence in my ability to effect an immediate cure
was flattering, but I knew it was misplaced. My policy, like
that of most dispensaries, was to furnish drugs and dressings,
nothing else. Our term "hospital unit" was an ambitious
term for a shelter for resident patients. Every patient who
used our inpatient quarters was expected to bring with him
his grain and someone to pound that grain, cook his food,
and take care of his normal needs. My small staff did well to
do medications and treatments. I provided most of the cornstalk beds and mats, the earthen cooking and water pots, and
mortars and pestles used to pound grain (for they are too
heavy to bring from distant villages).

"I am in your hands," she said.

"On my hands, you mean," thought I. I was vexed because
she had provided herself with so little money that I could not
send her home, for she would surely be stranded somewhere
along the way. Yet could I allow her to stay? On what would
she live?

"I have no one to care for me but you," she said.

I knew Ma'inna spoke the truth. In Mohammedan lands,
many a woman is only cared for as long as she can earn money
or serve in some other way. When she becomes helpless, she
is cast off. However, I definitely could not be held responsi-

ble for her. I would have to send this Buzu back, demanding grain. Probably my word, as a *baturiya*, would bring results. It had to. I would make my message very stern.

Already the Buza was slapping his camel; it hitched itself to its knees, then lumbered to its feet.

"I have a message that you must take back to Ma'inna's home," I commenced importantly.

"Sorry, Maijinya," said the man, politely enough. "But I'm not going that way. They hired me because I happened to pass by their town. I am going north." His interest in this woman was finished.

Ma'inna was not just a patient. She was a problem. I knew I could not afford to keep her. Still, I could not imagine Jesus turning a sick and hungry person from His door, and was N'Wala not part of the House of Christ—so named by the people? I was Christ's representative. Anyway, she was here. I could not send her home.

Our allowances were still none too good, for though the war had brought money to people in the homeland, they retained the memory of the lean years, and the joyful sharing with missionaries was not yet. Besides, our exchange from British to French money was impoverishing. I could not provide for Ma'inna, keep up my dispensary expenses—and eat.

I suppose when I went up the hill I looked as though I had already gone without a meal or two, and was facing the prospect of death by starvation a bit glumly. Someone took a look at my face, and struck up the Tsibiri theme song—

> Got any rivers you think are uncrossable?
> Got any mountains you can't tunnel through?
> God specializes in things thought impossible,
> And He can do what no other one can do!

All right. It will have to be God's problem. I supposed that I could put her care into His hands with the same trust that Ma'inna had in me—who was but a foreign woman to her. Didn't I know God better than she knew me?

Ma'inna stayed. She ate. I ate. And, as I could report, joyfully, some time later she became a Christian.

Another Fulani Christian! Another witness for Christ in a tribe that because of its nomadic character then had no missionary witness assigned to reach it. Fulanis were being reached only through market services (where such services are allowed) in the trade language of the areas in which the Fulanis happened to herd their cattle. A few were reached by occasional personal contacts, but many women did not understand much of the trade language beyond the *ciniki* involved in selling their milk and butter.

Fulanis make good missionaries. They wander from place to place. They meet many of their tribesmen who in turn will wander hither and yon. Fulanis had demonstrated their missionary capabilities by their diligent propagation of Islam. They had brought the false doctrines of Mohammedanism from the North and by their very nomadic habits, they had already spread the evil into all corners of central Africa, from whence it was flooding, like a tidal wave, down into equatorial and southern reaches of the continent. It was time that Fulanis also carried the message of Christ.

Curiosity, or reports roving Fulanis carried to her family *ruga* that Ma'inna was doing quite well, brought a half-dozen others from Bulumbukut to have treatment for ulcers and other chronic ailments. Through them, Ma'inna's needs were soon supplied. For God there had been no problem, only for me who had not learned to trust.

When the Fulanis went their way to Bulumbukut—a town I could never locate on the map either by name or by description of the area—I put them down in my prayer list (where they have remained ever since, though they may long ago have wandered from the scene) as the Christians in *Bulumbukut!* Seven of them.

God keep them! They had no little knowledge of His way, but He has knowledge of theirs. They accepted the redemption through the blood of Christ, according to the riches of His grace. He will keep them in whatever unknown places they wander seeking pasture for their flocks. *And may they gossip the Gospel of Christ wherever they go!*

It became a fad for women to come in groups, usually with an older woman who acted as chaperon to the younger ones. I was happy with the arrangement, since they took care of each other's needs. Later in my term I extended each end-wall of the large L-shaped *shigifa* to make a rectangular enclosed court for women patients, which was intended to give them the same sense of privacy that they would have in their own compounds.

Though I had built a small *shigifa* on the dispensary compound hoping for a resident evangelist who, among other things, could teach illiterate Christians to read, I never was able to get an evangelist—they were needed more elsewhere. It grieved me that Christians must be sent away without the ability to learn more of the *Way* than the little we could teach them in those few days or weeks they remained on our dispensary compound. Our time for this most important objective was limited, though Rita Salls and later Alberta Simms, who joined the Tsibiri staff soon, realized the importance of instructing the "family" in all they needed to know. These two missionaries spoke to the patients individually, and answered many of their questions about personnal problems relating to Christianity.

We diligently applied old Dr. Thomas Moody's advice to make God's Word our primary approach. I had learned to use Wordless Books in helping my Little Sis with child evangelism classes in Los Angeles during my furlough.

Ah, yes, Little Sis, who had so resented my letter of joyous testimony before I left for my first term in Africa that she did not write to me for months, told me many years later that

it had been *that very letter* that had drawn her to a reconse-
cration of her life to her Lord. Four years later, when I was
on furlough she was in charge of child evangelism in one Los
Angeles district, and has quite probably won more souls for
Christ than I have done. It was she who put into my hands
a marvelous tool that works as well for illiterates as it does
for preschool children.

A Wordless Book is exactly what its name implies. By
means of colored pages, black, red, white, and gold, the simple Gospel truth can be "read" by people who have never
learned any alphabet. And I could "read" it, also, to hold
a message slanted exactly for my audience.

We allowed the patients to earn one of these booklets by
learning to "read" it. We had no intention of allowing the
message of the book to be garbled because of insufficient
understanding. We wanted the people not only to take home
a souvenir of N'Wala, but a clear Gospel message as well. So
they had to repeat all the verses word-perfect.

I was lenient with Jari, who was old, when she repeated the
second verse from the red page: *Repent ye therefore, and be
converted, that your sins may be blotted out.* She made a
mistake. To quote correctly, she should have used the word
juyo (to be turned), but she said *birkito* (turn-about-face
toward speaker). All the patients, who "knew better,"
laughed at Jari.

I wasn't so sure. I wondered if Jari hadn't used the word
that the translators had missed! She got her book—and used
it. Months after she had gone home, walking, people kept
coming from Kurfi.

"Jari sent us. And she sends you greetings from your
Nanny Goat."

"Did Jari tell you about anything else besides our medicine?"

"Oh, yes! Jari told us about the *Way.* She read us the
book."

One day a woman came back to the inpatient department who had been there the previous year. When I brought out the Wordless Book at our afternoon gathering, she reached for it. I had not much time to sit patiently prompting her on all the verses connected with the Wordless Book message, so I said, "You listen this time. Tomorrow, when your memory has been refreshed, you may say them."

She insisted, however. So, reluctantly, I handed her the book. She said all the verses, in proper order, without a mistake. Nothing could have made me much happier, for the strategy of the Wordless Book was working. Nobody can repeat anything from memory after a year unless it has been well-learned, and more—unless the memorized material is frequently reviewed. This woman had been witnessing!

Not only did this little book give the people an opening for the Gospel as soon as they reached their own home towns, but by its order of colors prompted my people to "keep the story straight" by suggesting the verses in the order they had always been recited.

Though I expected the Wordless Book to do so much, I was very stingy—in proportion to the smallness of my faith—for I cut those Wordless Books in three so that my supply would reach farther. That meant that each patient got only a strip about an inch wide. They still worked hard to get the books. In fact, even the social life of N'Wala was built around the stingy scraps of these little books.

In other villages the accepted social pattern is drumming, dancing, and all the evils that accompany these openly sensual practices, including *bori*, which is nothing less than voluntary submission to demon possession.

My patients of N'Wala gathered socially as they would have done in their own villages. An inverted calabash makes a fairly effective drum, and I heard short bursts of such drumming from time to time. Making rhythm is an integral part of African life—women pat the intricate beat of the tom-

tom into the very blood of their children as they hold them in their arms.

The rhythm of N'Wala was of a new and heart-warming kind, for my family would gather, on those nights cold with the sting of the desert, about bonfires the youngsters built from brush they had brought in, and would drill each other and newcomers on the Gospel message, chanting in typical African rhythm the Scripture passages used in connection with the Wordless Book. I often found them there when I came down the hill to see a patient who needed special attention.

By describing so many of my *cripples,* I may have given the false impression that all of my resident patients were afflicted with some chronic disease. Most of them were, but considering my own limitations of training and knowledge, far too many of my patients came with acute and serious conditions. Of the ten doctors who were in charge of the French medical services of Maradi during my first two years in Tsibiri, the first one—who was there only a few months—cared most for his patients, and many people who are alive today have him to thank for it.

During the dry season that followed the flood, an epidemic of meningitis raged throughout all that region. The French doctor alerted me to the fact that a few cases had already been seen in some of the villages. Every case I saw, he wrote, must be reported, and patients with active meningitis should be sent to Maradi hospital. He enforced isolation of the family and other contacts by police control. They would move to grass huts in a location a mile from the town. I was held responsible for their prophylactic treatment.

I was careful to check temperatures of my clinic patients those days, and when there was fever I carefully tested reflexes and looked for any sign of rigidity. My precaution added greatly to the time I must spend on each of my patients, so I quickly slipped the "routine" conjunctivitis and ulcer patients by the desk with as little time spent as possible. Among these patients was Hassan, who reported a mild conjunctivitis. I told him about hot fomentations while I quickly wrote out his card and handed it to him. He took it, started down the line, then, as countless of my patients did, delayed my proceeding to the next patient with an afterthought. "I have a headache too."

A headache frequently accompanies conjunctivitis. I quickly added an aspirin to the order on the card and turned to the next patient. At the end of the morning, I was relieved that so far the meningitis epidemic had not reached us.

Next morning, before breakfast, Kulungu came to report. "They are bringing Hassan. He has the evil disease!" The name of the disease, like *death,* was a word not spoken. Neither did Kulungu have to speak the word! Hassan had had one of the symptoms twenty hours earlier—and I had given him *one aspirin!*

I raced down the hill, breakfast forgotten. Hassan was quite delirious, and it was only by God's mercy that the 20-hour delay was not fatal. Some children, in that dread and unforgettable scourge that swept the land, got up to play outside in the morning. By noon their bodies were being measured for graveclothes.

Sulfa drugs were still very much in the experimental stage, but fortunately I had a form that could be injected intramuscularly, for Hassan— and many others—were beyond the stage where they would co-operatively swallow even powdered sulfa tablets. Even while I was giving Hassan his injection, his older brother was brought in on the back of a donkey. He came in, staggering drunkenly between two men, with death in his eyes, it seemed to me, and on his ashen face. Meningitis is not a pleasant disease to see.

I sent a messenger to the doctor, as he had instructed me to do, for he had an ambulance of sorts. I waited for him. By the time I had seen my clinic patients that day, I had four patients waiting for him. Then came his message. He was far too busy taking care of epidemic vicitms to come out for mine. I should have to get the patients in by carrier.

How I wished then for a station wagon with removable seats such as is used in leper settlements! I sent word up to the hill. Was the Ford running today? It seemed that the engine had just been repaired, so it might run as far as Maradi without trouble.

Word came back. One of the tires was down.

A tire? That was a small matter. Usually whenever it was necessary to take out the 1932 Ford, that had been patched by makeshift parts ever since the war had made it impossible to bring in repairs, it took one or two days of a missionary's precious time to get it into chugging order. A tire? That would not be bad.

However, due to apparently deliberate sabotage, the tube was practically in ribbons. Necessity breeds ingenuity, and Ray de la Haye remembered the old trailer used for hauling bricks and wood. Because it had been impossible to get even tubes to fit its tires, old truck tubes had been stuffed into the tires somehow and inflated. We referred to the misfits as "the convoluted tubules," an abuse of the diminutive form, for the truck tubes made the tires look as though they had been made for a bicycle.

While the men worked at their tires, I worked with my patients. Hassan screamed and clawed deliriously at whatever was within reach. His brother was barely conscious, and as I worked with Hassan, he sat up and glowered at me with glazed eyes that seemed out of place in a living, breathing body. Three of the patients were delirious, and I shuddered as they glared vapidly at me.

By the time the convoluted tubules had been tucked into the right tires and inflated, Hassan and his brother had begun to respond to their treatment. The miracle drugs—too late to save our beloved Dr. Jotcham, buried in Katsina—were showing their marvelous power.

Sulfa drugs worked wonders for many of my patients. Poor living conditions and malnutrition made these people a special prey to every kind of violent infection. I knew that sulfa would prevent blindness in trachoma patients, but I had so little sulfa that I held it, grudgingly, for those patients to whom it made the difference between life and death.

For me to live is Christ was the word God had given me to live by, but I had hardly begun to fathom the practical aspects of my identity with the benevolent Christ I served—who healed everyone who came to Him for help. I saw only my dwindling stock of drugs and my mounting statistics.

I did everything I could to keep my expenses down to a minimum. I learned to use native oils, like peanut and palm oils, and shea butter, as bases for ointments I used. The French doctor gave me a prescription for bismuth-in-oil, used for the yaws injections. We made it in liter quantities.

Our people wanted something to "rub where it hurts," so I made gallons of liniment. When all drugs with counter-irritant qualities had been used up, I made a concoction with the ultra-hot local peppers as an ingredient.

Many of my patients were suffering from malnutrition and anemia. One of our own doctors had suggested that I could make my own ventriculin to treat anemia. I decided that the time had come for my venturing into this brand of drug manufacture on the day that I inverted a patient's lower eyelid and found it white. My Tallquist hemoglobin scale showed me that the man's blood was only faintly pink—far below the 30 per cent color plate, the lowest on the scale.

I told Mamman to eat liver in large amounts. He looked at me like a patient in a charity ward who is told he must have surgery that can only be done by a bevy of the most expensive surgeons in the world. Meat is a rare luxury on the menu of many bush people. Next market day, I bought my first calf's stomach, the source of ventriculin.

According to our good doctor's instructions, I shredded the proper tissues of this organ and put it out in the sun to dry. Unfortunately, it was the humid season, and after a day or two, even my boys—accustomed as they were to the high odors of drying fish and other native delicacies—encouraged me to abandon my project. My colleagues later gleefully referred to my valiant attempt at economy in this category as "Martha's high stomach."

Unwilling to abandon my patient to his condition, I furnished him daily with a ration of liver that made other patients drool with envy. Their covetous glances hurt, because I knew that good food would help others of my patients. I salved my conscience with the knowledge that the food was important medicine for this patient. The patient relieved me of the embarrassing situation by stealing a few bottles one night and disappearing. He probably sold the bottles next day, and got a third of the amount of money I had been expending on one day's supply of liver.

I was much more comfortable with my bush people than with visiting administrators, although dignitaries from the bush also often gave me times of uneasiness. Patients who wore the flowing robes and high turbans of high position, either political or financial, were a detriment to my most important work, that of drawing my family together for our informal Gospel gatherings.

One such resident patient was a man who reported that he was from Sori, though I learned later that that was the town comparable to his "county seat." The phonograph, a source of perpetual wonder to all my patients, attracted Madugu to the gathering, as it drew all other people from the bush. Fine Gospel records in the local vernacular, many of which were almost pure Scripture on one side with fine Gospel songs on

the other, were of incalculable value in my work, not only
because they attracted the crowds but because the people
listen far more intently to messages from the magic black
box.

When the phonograph was turned off, Madugu turned his
back deliberately on us while we repeated our Scripture, or
as I spoke to the people about what it means to be a Christian.
I noted Madugu's negative attitude, and with real apprehension I also noted the other patients' obvious respect for this
man from Sori.

"O Lord," I prayed silently, "don't let this man antagonize
the people against these messages! He could influence them
not to gather at all in the afternoons!"

I do not recall that I ever prayed *for* Madugu—only *against*
him.

Madugu, though haughty, was grateful. He came to our
afternoon "family" gatherings from a sense of respect to me,
I presume. Always, however, he sat gazing ostentatiously out
at the bush, his heart closed against the message, his back to
me and to those who were participating in the service.

He turned with some amusement, however, when one of
the boys, perhaps ten or even twelve years old, won his Wordless Book by repeating all the verses without being prompted.
The boy was delighted at his accomplishment, and turned a
couple of very graceful handsprings to show how he felt.

I saw Madugu eyeing the lad with aroused interest, and
noted the beginning of a gleam that betrayed his thought, "If
that little squirt can do it, so can I!"

From that day, Madugu turned toward me, and together
with the others repeated the verses that told the story of the
Wordless Book, and some of the other prayerfully selected
Scripure passages that I was teaching my family.

Madugu was there for a two-week period only, and much
time had been lost before he deigned to show interest; but on

his last day he did say his verses, and received his little Wordless Book.

As usual, when I gave away one of these books, I asked, "Do you believe the message of this book?"

"Yes, I do!" said Madugu, to my surprise—and incredulity.

Dadin magana, I thought. *Sweet words* to make me feel good. All Africans are adept at flattery and insincere agreement with someone they respect. Yet, though I did not believe a word Madugu said, for the sake of others who also professed to believe the message of the Wordless Book—and for those who had not yet made a profession—I went on.

"Do you believe the Scripture that says that Christ is the only way?"

Madugu looked me squarely in the eye and said that he believed this Scripture.

"Has any missionary ever come to your town, Sori?" I asked him then.

"No."

"Then if this is the only way, and your people will be lost if no one tells them, what are you going to do about it?"

"I'm going to tell them about Jesus."

Very well. Madugu was intelligent. His answers would help my patients who were truly believers. My one great burden was that my "family" would go home and gossip the Gospel in all the unreached places that we were contacting only through them. God had answered my prayers. Madugu had turned out to be a help instead of a hindrance. I praised Him.

I praised Him more, though, perhaps ten or more days later, when a tall, gangling stranger, who gave his name as Dogo—*Slim*—came to my desk at the dispensary.

"Do you remember Madugu—from Sori?"

I remembered Madugu.

"Well," said Dogo, "what he believes, I believe it too!"

Then Dogo proceeded to prove that Madugu had been teaching him, by reciting verses from the Wordless Book and others besides.

"We want a teacher. Our whole town wants to become Christian."

I wrote an eager note to Mr. Osborne, head of the station, explaining the situation to him. I told Dogo to take his request to the one person who might have a teacher to send him. Perhaps one of the evangelists could be spared—at least for a while. Here was an unsurpassed opportunity—unheard of in Moslem country. But there was no one to send. All harvest fields are white. To remove a worker from one field and place him in another is not the solution. The solution is *more laborers!*

Dogo went home. He came again later. His father, head of the town of Gidan Magaji, was repeating his plea for a teacher.

"We will build him a house," Dogo urged. "And a church."

All I could do was put them down on my prayer list and remind the Lord of fine young men competing for churches at home where the congregations are far too often unresponsive because they have been surfeited with opportunities to hear.

Not all of our work among the patients was in large gatherings, though that was the only way we could ever have reached all of them. We often snatched a few brief moments with individual patients.

Amina had heard the Gospel, with the others, before getting her medications in the morning and in our "family" gatherings. She was just one patient with a rather serious condition, but she was doing as well as could be expected, so I had paid only passing attention to her as an individual. Then, when the first rains came, bringing with them the strenuous days of the planting season, her husband appeared. He was going to take Amina home.

I protested that she was too sick to leave the dispensary, and too sick to be much help to him anyway. He had better leave her. He did not defy me openly, but next morning Amina was not there.

Only a few days later, it had become obvious that I had been right and that Amina could not work in the fields or pound grain. Her husband brought her back again with a ten-year-old boy, whom he left to take care of her. She seemed suddenly much worse, her first condition complicated with another more acute illness. Though she responded at first to an antibiotic, she took a sudden turn for the worse. We sent the little boy home to notify her family to get more help for her.

One of the other girls spoke to Amina about Christ, in those days after she was too weak to go to any more services, and she accepted Him as her Saviour. That afternoon when I brought her medicine there were several patients in the "ward." When I suggested a service, a boy brought me a stool. Because of Amina, I chose Christ's beautiful words recorded in John 14: "Let not your heart be troubled . . . in my Father's house are many mansions . . . I go to prepare a place . . . that where I am, there ye may be also."

I concluded simply, as to children, so that they could better understand. "Because Jesus said so, I know they are fixing up my house now—and Amina's, if the prayer she prayed this morning was from her heart."

Amina had been following the message, drinking in the assurance and hope of Jesus' promise to those who believe in Him. The eyes in the sunken hollows of her wasted face glowed with earnestness when she responded eagerly, her voice stronger than it had been all day.

"My prayer was sincere," she said.

Amina was weak so I decided to leave, though we had been there only a very few minutes. The little boy who had brought my stool looked thoroughly disappointed.

"Aren't you going to tell us any more?" he asked.

No missionary in Moslem country misses an opportunity

when presented with a willing audience. I withdrew some distance from Amina's bed and showed the boy my Wordless Book, telling him of the book in Heaven that registers the deeds symbolized by the black page, and that those transgressions are wiped clean from the pages of the books of judgment by Jesus' blood when anyone claims forgiveness by faith, as Amina had done.

"God has another book in Heaven," I said, "called the Lamb's Book of Life. The book has that name because God called His Son the Lamb of God which taketh away the sin of the world. When your sins are wiped off the black page, God writes your name in this book that shows you have been cleansed by the blood of Jesus."

"I want God to write me down," said the boy earnestly.

As I made plain the simple Gospel message, I traced the boy's name in the sand, of which the "hospital" floor consisted.

"By receiving Christ as your Saviour," I told the boy, "God gives you eternal life and makes you His son, and that is how He writes your name in His book."

Even though we had withdrawn from Amina's bedside, she must have been following our conversation carefully. Now she interrupted me, an anxious tone in her weak voice. With her ebbing strength, she raised up on her elbow. She seemed to be afraid that here was still something that she had not known and which she must do to be saved. It is hard to fathom or explain the illiterate's awe and reverence for any act of writing, so that even a scrawl in sand takes on momentous importance.

"Write mine too. It's Amina," she entreated. "My name is Amina." And again she repeated urgently, "Amina is the name."

I quickly allayed her fears, tracing her name too, on the floor with my finger. "God knows your name, Amina," I reassured her. "He knows all those who have received Christ. He won't make a mistake. You are His own."

A look of assurance and peace such as she had not before flooded her thin, drawn features. It was my last chance to witness to her. Before the next sunrise, she had slipped off to her new home.

Amina's husband had thought of her only in terms of her usefulness to him and had brought her back to me with an obvious air of finality, signifying "good riddance—let the white woman take her if she wants to." Amina would know, at last, what it is to be beloved. Amina, who had lived all her life in a darkness of ignorance that knows no real hope, had passed into the realm of light and glory. What a deliverance!

Amina, who had slept on harsh grass mats and cooked in earthen vessels over smoky fires, whose hands were rough, and who had trod hot, thorny paths with bare feet, whose clothes had been coarse from cotton threads that she had spun herself —Amina had slipped away to be served by angels in ivory palaces. How surprised and delighted she must have been when they put on her the soft regal robes of one accepted in the Beloved, and she was led along the golden street to the throne room! What an entrance!

I wish I could have seen it!

TWELVE

PRINCIPALITIES, POWERS, *AND GOD!*

Your adversary, the devil, as a roaring lion, walketh about, seeking whom he may devour.—I Peter 5:8
For ours is not a conflict with mere flesh and blood, but with the despotisms, the empires, the forces that control and govern this dark world—the spiritual hosts of evil arrayed against us in the heavenly warfare.—Ephesians 6:12, Weymouth

H ELLO!"
The students in the new Tsibiri Bible School looked up. An old man, his grizzly beard framing his face like shredded coconut on a chocolate pudding, seemed to be looking at the window, but he was not directing his Hausa greeting at the students.

"*Sanu!*" he repeated. "Good afternoon." Then he caught his breath with an audible gasp of surprise. "Well, what do you know about that! It's *me!*"

And so it was.

Glass windows are very rare in that part of Africa. Even government buildings substituted wide verandas for windows as protection from storm. But in a school, where it would be necessary to close windows during storms, and tin windows would leave the class in the dark, glass windows become a necessary luxury. The old man, passing by, had seen reflected in the glass the face of an old man who looked pleasant

222

enough to know, so he had stepped up to make his acquaintance.

The friendly old man was invited to visit the class in Bible School. He was not used to sitting on a bench, as the students were doing, so he sat on the floor, with just the edge of his fuzzy beard at the height of the top of the long table about which the students sat.

Bible Schools are the backbone of an indigenous church, the only practical solution to the vast need of unevangelized lands. The Bible School of Tsibiri was built of prayer and tears as well as of sun-dried brick.

For some years, money had been on hand to build a Bible School. Every time application was made, the government had refused permission for such a school. The reasons varied. Sometimes they were seemingly logical objections—often the flimsy quality of the excuses was as apparent as it was disheartening. Yet at last all conditions had been met. The permit was won by patience and diplomacy and much prayer.

By that time, however, World War II was making importation of building materials such as cement and metals almost impossible; each item was obtained under such difficulty that the project might have been abandoned by men of lesser faith than Ray de la Haye. So long had he been searching and negotiating for these materials that people, even in America, were aware of our needs and were asking God to supply. As early as the previous July, door and window frames had been ready, but building could not go on for lack of materials for the foundation.

The Bible School foundation had at last been staked out in faith. After many inquiries—and at a price—cement had been obtained, but there was no ant-coursing in French territory and no permit could be obtained from British authorities to export an item also much needed in Nigeria.

Ant-coursing is necessary to a permanent building, for if termites—which quickly find their way through cement—have ready access to the walls, even the native mahogany window and roof framework would need to be replaced very soon.

Ray said, "God has promised that 'no good thing will he withhold from them that walk uprightly.' Ant-coursing is not only a good thing, it is a necessity. God will supply by the time we need it!"

But it was *impossible* to get ant-coursing. There simply was none in French Niger. And there was small hope, indeed, of British authorities relenting on a hard-and-fast rule that would rob their own country of much-needed metal supplies. Ray was leaving Tsibiri, however, to get builders from Nigeria.

The boys gathered to push the Ford down the hill, the routine way of getting it started. Sometimes it didn't. But Ray was taking that risk on this long trip to Kano, since the old Ford was the only mission car in Niger. By long experience anyone who drove that car sought as carefully for a suitable parking place as a pilot searching a safe spot for landing a plane. It had to be a good place for a take-off. Ray smiled gaily with no apparent care in the world as he waved good-by. The Ford slid down the hill, then coughed and sputtered, and roared into life far down the incline.

The boys, who had pushed the dilapidated open touring car to the brink of the hill with practiced efficiency, dusted their hands on their clothes, and turned back toward the compound. We returned to our houses to pray.

The plodding, faithful Model A brought Ray back in good time, snorting and gasping under a small cloud of its own steam. Ray had no cloud on his forehead though. In his car was the needed ant-coursing. Even glass. The glass in which the grizzly old man saw his reflection came from Kano. That power had made the official sign the necessary permit that has also assured us: *The heart of kings is in His hand.*

Ray had brought Nigerian masons and carpenters, but the African building supervisor had been needed elsewhere.

"What are you going to do without the builder?" someone wondered aloud.

"I'll do it," said Ray, who probably had never supervised any building in his life. Ray was a musician—a scholar. Now he would be a builder.

Ray had been unable to get pan for the roof, but he built the mahogany frames—in faith—ready for the pan when it would come. For only that one season the roof was covered with thatch (which was of very poor quality so near the desert). The next year a gift from California—an inheritance turned over to the Lord——provided a permanent roof.

Rev. Carl J. Tanis, deputation secretary from the States, visited Tsibiri just a few weeks before the Bible School opened on February 9, 1947. He warned us that we should be prepared for trouble, for Satan had attacked every station where such a school had been built. Mr. Tanis knew the reality of these attacks from experience as well as from observation, for one of our mission's most effective Bible Schools is in Kagoro where Mr. Tanis labored as a missionary.

"The Devil does not sit idly by and let a Bible School run a smooth course," he said. "You'll have discipline problems you never dreamed of; your health will be attacked. You must remember that there is nothing Satan hates and fears more than a training school for evangelists."

Dan Nana, the evangelist from Hisatau, who was even then being used of the Lord in a special way, had moved into the narrow stall-like quarters with his family. Halima, his wife, declared enthusiastically to the other women, "Let's call our compound *Ba Tsegumi* (No Quarreling) ."

I had lived in Tsibiri all these months without discovering that the members of our local church came from two feuding families of the Gobir tribe. Those two families were represented in the Bible School too. And the feud blazed forth as these people were forced to live together in rather crowded quarters. A thoughtless word or gesture, misunderstood or misconstrued, was kindling on the hidden embers of prejudice. Smoldering antagonisms flared into uncontrolled, blazing anger, with biting words and raised voices such as one does not often hear in the villages, but which always attract a crowd. So Satan tried to destroy the testimony of *Ba Tsegumi* in its first weeks, and attacked repeatedly where he had found his tactics so successful.

Satan does not limit himself to open strategy. Ray de la Haye had been supervising the building of the Bible School structure during those weeks he had intended to use in planning and preparing his courses. No textbook but the Bible was available in the Hausa language. The students had only rather elementary educational preparation and would not be able to take notes from lectures. They would need a great many helps and outlines, all of which must be translated into Hausa. Ray and his wife, Sophie, were working at night to keep up with the class work.

Ray's break in health was inevitable. He came down with a high fever about a month after school had begun. Latent malaria often flares into an acute attack when people have become too tired, and it is our first thought in the tropics when a fever occurs without other prominent symptoms. When the fever did not respond to antimalarials, the French doctor was called to Tsibiri. He ordered more antimalarials.

After ten days of high fever, Ray was "rushed" (slowly in the old Ford) to Kano by Ralph Ganoe, a new missionary who, with his wife, Marjorie, had joined Tsibiri staff. Sophie remained to carry on classes in the Bible School. Rev. Newton Kapp, our district superintendent, came out from Maradi every day—by bicycle—to help carry on the work Satan had tried vainly to disrupt.

Ralph came back and reported that Ray had been so exhausted and weakened by his ride in the rickety Ford jogging over washboard roads, that all—even the government doctor who had been called in—had despaired of his life that first night in Katsina, where they had halted of necessity. The tentative diagnosis was typhoid. The prognosis was not good. They had wired Kano for a more comfortable car for the remaining 104 miles. Sophie, smiling valiantly, continued her classes in Bible School.

By April, Ray was able to leave the hospital, but it took a long rest in Miango, where it was cooler, before he could return to Tsibiri. Sophie joined him on the plateau, at Mr. Kapp's insistence. Our Piper Cub plane (God bless the church group that presented it to the Sudan Interior Mission!) took them to Jos on one of its first time- and life-saving missions. It was the end of May before Ray and Sophie de la Haye returned to the station.

And it was Sophie, of course, who gave us the pitch of our theme song, which we sang with the lusty vehemence of hope and a slight lilt of conspiracy in our voices.

> Got any rivers you think are uncrossable?
> Got any mountains you can't tunnel through?
> God specializes in things thought impossible
> And He can do what no other one can do!

When government officials had laid out the new town of Tsibiri and urged people to stake claims for building sites, Mr. Osborne, head of our station, had picked out a site for a church in town. Then, with some excitement, we had begun to pray for what was almost unreasonable to expect!

We needed a church, for the one we were using was so much too small that during the cold season we had services outside, within a *zana* enclosure erected solely to keep passing throngs from distracting too much of the congregation's attention. We all sat on grass mats directly on the sand. The sun, against which we had no protection, made us perspire and squint. We needed a church.

We knew that we could build a new church on our premises, but we were hoping for permission to build that church in Tsibiri—a church that would draw townspeople. All of us were well aware of the fact that in the Moslem North no permit for a Christian church within city limits had ever yet been granted. Still, Tsibiri was not nearly so fanatically Moslem as Kano or Katsina, south of us, Zinder to the east, nor—as I was to discover to my great sorrow—Madaoua to the west. The very fact that the town would take on a pattern different from the usual native village gave us cause to hope.

The French administrator was very proud of the new town of Tsibiri, his own masterpiece in design. With some fanfare, he came to celebrate the completion of the town, accompanied by other officials from Maradi, including the surveyors who had laid out the markers for the streets that radiated from the chief's compound like the *Etoile* of Paris. The chief and his cortege, in holiday garb, mounted on sleek horses, accompanied the French official on his tour of inspection.

For such an occasion, it would have been considered an affront had the mission had no representative to demonstrate our interest. Mr. Osborne and Mr. de la Haye, the men then on the station, had gone to pay their respects. During a conversation Mr. Osborne casually brought up the subject of the church.

The administrator turned to our Tsibiri chief and asked, through an interpreter, whether he wanted the church. The chief shrugged. He was plainly about to say that it did not matter to him, when the *malams* took him aside. When he came back from this impromptu conference, the chief said he did not want a mission church in his town. The commandant took the chief's decision as final. Satan had scored a definite victory, but he had also played into the hands of a God who could turn such a defeat into a challenge for far greater exploit.

Musa was an older Christian of a royal lineage, and shrewd in native diplomatic matters as his patriarchal namesake, Moses. He came to Mr. Osborne.

"I have staked out a very large compound. I shall build a *zaure* of some size. No man can tell me what I can or cannot do on my own property. I will use my entrance *zaure* for meetings in the town."

We were warned to keep Musa's proposition to ourselves. There must be no air of conspiracy about what Musa meant to do on his premises. In fact, we missionaries did not believe Musa had confided in many of the other Christians. Imagine then, Ray's surprise, when, in conversation with the chief's head scribe, he discovered that this man knew of Musa's plans, and it was down in writing in the chief's files that not a *zaure* but a *massalaci* (place of worship) was to be built. No protest had been made. The church was being taken entirely for granted. All conceded that Musa was acting entirely within his rights.

By Satan's strategy, it would be illegal for the mission to be involved in any way. God, Master Strategist, knew that nothing could be better for an indigenous work than that these believers cease to lean on the missionaries for money, plans, and initiative.

Tsibiri Christians began making bricks, using the rectangular forms borrowed from the mission rather than making the ordinary balls of mud that take much more hand plastering and never make a straight wall. They were going to do this

Building the Christian Church in Moslem City.
God stayed the rains!

right. They proposed to build a church seating three times the number of the average attendance.

The commandant came occasionally to view this new town and chanced to see a pile of these rectangular sun-dried bricks, unusual in native building projects. He demanded an explanation.

"They are building a church," someone said, by his ambiguity implying that the Europeans were defying an official statement. The commandant's wrath was not surprising. Even when someone explained that it was Musa's project, the damage had been done. The commandant's ire was already up. The commandant summoned Musa and ordered him to report at his office the next morning. That night we had a special prayer meeting.

We Europeans had done nothing toward the building of the church besides loaning the brick forms. It was a native project altogether, and one for which they had every right according to native custom and practice, but would the Frenchman see it in that light? Not all decisions are made according to the custom of the African. Would the mission be implicated in a charge of contempt of authority? What would it mean to Musa personally?

Royalty is not taken lightly by Africans, especially by those on whom the honor rests. Musa was by no means an exception to this tradition, and he had the added assurance of respect and veneration because he had a graying beard. He appeared before the commandant promptly next morning, not as a cowering subject, but as a man whose rights are being threatened. He spoke with the assurance that showed his belief that the man with whom he had to do would concede his rights.

Because it had become a community affair, with other Christians working, Musa could not say, as he had proposed to Mr. Osborne, that he was erecting a building over which he had complete and sole authority.

"The townspeople are right," said Musa, who speaks French, when the commandant made his charge. "We are building a house of worship."

"But," answered the white man curtly, "the people don't want it. And you have disobeyed my order."

"The people don't want the church?" retorted Musa. "For 17 years the Christians have been saving their offerings for a church. They are people of Tsibiri. Does that not prove that these are people who want a church?"

Musa went on to explain quietly, in commendable French, without fear or irritation, that the building was not a mission project but one he himself had instigated.

"The Mohammedans have their mosque," urged Musa. "We will not interfere with that. Why cannot we have our church? Why cannot I allow a church to be built on my own compound?"

Musa came back radiant. His first words to the Christians were, "The Lord has given us the victory!" Instead of ordering him to desist from his building, the commandant had given Musa a permit to buy wood for door and window frames.

Satan is not easily put to rout. He had lost in the diplomatic war. Now he began sniping. The bricks must be left to dry near the water holes where they were made. Every morning the Christians would come down to work to find many of their bricks had been broken. Finally, they took turns sleeping near the mosquito-infested brick field to guard their work.

Musa and the other leaders had planned a large building, and work was being donated. Progress began to lag. During those months of the dry season when building is possible, we were dismayed at the inaction at the church compound. When the rainy season was so near that all would be lost if they did not get a roof on the church, they returned to their project with renewed zest.

Dan Nana was sent out to an area where larger trees grew, and contracted with a local man for the number of logs they would need for the roof. The logs were to be ready by a certain date and brought to the road, where our trusty old Ford and trailer would pick them up.

Now that it was high time to get busy, there was a great deal of activity about the church. One of the elders had read of the large amount of money collected for a new mosque in another town. He gave the Christians a pep talk on giving money and labor. In a short while—with a guard to keep watch over bricks, it must be remembered—the walls of the church were up to roof level. The rickety Ford wheezed to the spot where Dan Nana expected the logs to be waiting for him. To everyone's consternation, not only were the logs not there but the man had not felled one tree.

Dan Nana looked at Ralph Ganoe in stupefaction (Ray was in the hospital at this time), then said, "There is only one explanation. The *malams* have threatened him. We offered him a good price."

Arrangements were made in another community for logs, but it was time *now* for that roof. South of us, people reported rains—heavy planting rains.

Musa reported another development. "People are bringing offerings to the *malams* of sheep and goats, to make medicine that the rains shall destroy our church. They are also praying that Malam de la Haye shall not recover, and that the Osbornes shall never return to the field!" (The Osbornes had recently been sent home because of Mr. Osborne's heart condition.) Far more powerful than the prayers of the Moslem *malams* was the rumor that, if a church was built, about one-third of the town threatened to move out of Tsibiri. The instigators of this movement anticipated, with malevolent guile, that the authorities would question them as to their motives for leaving Tsibiri. With one accord, ran the rumor, they would contend that they were opposed to the church in town and would not live near it.

Such united scheming foreboded the end of the church, no matter who was responsible for building it. Much more serious, such a demonstration of antagonism toward Christianity might also mean the closing of many doors of the mission's ministry in the entire French territory. The powers of darkness were set against that church and the Christ whose worship it would proclaim. And it seemed that the evil powers would win.

A planting rain fell in Maradi, eight miles away. The logs for the church roof were not ready; the inevitable rain must soon melt the unprotected walls. All the work would have been in vain. All the hoarded money had been spent. What result would the ensuing discouragement have on those believers whose faith was not robust at best?

A planting rain fell to the west of us. Grain was already green in the fields near Maradi. The Mohammedans prayed, and they brought more gifts for better prayers; but they did not pray alone. The Christians met for prayer that the Lord would stay the rains until His house was safe. One by one the logs were brought and work on the roof was done as quickly as the logs were available. But would they be in time? Heavy rains were almost generally reported all about us. Would God stay the rains for people who had probably been a bit shiftless? Would He make others suffer because of their procrastination during the dry season?

These questions were becoming a town-wide worry. It was generally conceded that God was obviously answering the Christians' prayers by withholding rain, but even the Christians were growing concerned about their crops. It was June. If the rains were held up too long, the short growing season might well be too short, and then no one would have a crop—Mohammedan or Christian. That meant hunger, for bush people seldom have a reserve of either grain or wealth for hard times.

Fields all about us everywhere were growing lushly. Only in Tsibiri had there been no planting rain, only a very few light sprinkles, the edges of rains that were bringing abundance to others. Villagers watched enviously as clouds bearing rain divided, encircled the community, leaving Tsibiri parched under the blazing sun. Another rain came toward the town and stopped just short of Tsibiri. Not one soul in Tsibiri called this a freak of the seasons or a chance dry spell.

When the last of the logs arrived, Moslems came to help the Christians finish their church. No doubt remained in their minds. The Christians had prayed. God had answered. The only way to get rain was to get that church finished.

Another of the Moslem prayers had failed. Ray de la Haye was there on the day that the last mud was put on the roof, and the builders announced that the church was complete. A shout went up over the town and a crowd gathered. Ray climbed a ladder and stood on the roof, above the milling spectators. He raised his arm to Heaven.

"We thank Thee, Lord, for answering our prayers and staying the rain so that we could have a house in which to worship Thee. Now remember Thy servants, who have labored so faithfully. They need to plant their grain. Open up the heavens for them!"

That night it rained. It was not a hard, driving storm to tear down new mud plaster, as could be expected during that season, but a soft, soaking, planting rain.

"We cannot doubt the hand of God in this," said my new boy, Audu Gumar, who had not as yet professed faith in Christ.

The next morning few patients were at the dispensary, for everyone able to work was out in the fields. One woman, who because of a bad ulcer could not help with the field work, voiced a common sentiment in a voice hushed by awe.

"*Ikon Allah!*" she exclaimed, as she discussed the grape-vine headlines of the day. Others echoed her sentiments, "The power of God! Christians' prayers *are* answered!"

Again Satan had overstepped himself. His opposition had made the Tsibiri church and God's answers to Christians' prayers the main topic of conversation for miles around. Years later, people from distant villages still mentioned this miracle with reverent solemnity.

Then the rains came, and with a vengeance—and so did their inevitable results for the Tsibiri buildings. On one occasion, the damage of a rain was a catastrophe mixed with blessing. A deputation secretary who had never worked on the field came to visit us. He had once made the remark in my hearing that he was often embarrassed to show pictures of missionaries homes in Africa because they looked so pros-perous.

He referred, doubtless, to the buildings in the Kano area, most of them as new as the recently established work. Dr. A. D. Helser, superintendent of that district, insisted that all buildings in his area be kept whitewashed and in good repair. British government policy in that same area required resi-dences to be built within a specified living standard.[1]

That deputation secretary made the rounds next morning, saw the sagging walls of the building where sleeping orphan children might have been pinned under a collapsing roof— a building that would have to be almost rebuilt before it

[1]The British government will not issue a permit to build any dwelling in the European section of Kano, whose plan does not meet rigid specifications, not primarily of appearance but for maintenance of health in the tropics. On the other hand, the French government is most interested in maintaining the "historic" flat-roofed appearance of cities near the desert, and overhangs which protect the walls from beating rains and baking sun are forbidden. Metal roofs must be concealed behind a coping. My own aluminum-pan roof was the first metal roof in the area, permitted because it was in the bush. It became a landmark for all air traffic in that region! This roofing pan had been supplied, months before, by one Sunday school class in Jackson, Michigan, but it had not yet arrived for this second rainy season.

would hold a new roof. The building in which Rita Salls
and Alberta Simms lived had a great crack in the east wall,
and one window had nearly been washed from the softened
wall. The roof leaked, as did mine, on my new house. If
that one storm did not convince that man that good houses
are far more economical—even if they look too prosperous
on pictures—then nothing ever will!

Good houses with ample overhang of roof to protect walls
are by far the least expensive when figured only in dollars
and cents. Missionaries may not deserve an attractive house,
but there is a subtle lift to morale with a probable increase
of energy and efficiency, when one changes from an ill-kempt,
leaky building always on the point of collapse to one whose
cement floors are carefully smooth, whose ceiling is clean,
with even the convenience of a glass window that can be
closed against the frequent driving storms without closing
out all daylight. Besides, an overhang makes a great contribution to health and vigor—thus to the work—by shielding
the walls from the blazing tropical sun. Solid walls are good
conductors of heat. A mud-walled house can become a veritable oven, hot long after the air outside is cool.

And there were all those hours—days that added up to
weeks—of perpetual patching walls and roofs by the men who
were needed in the Bible School, who should have been on
trek among the unreached villages, who could have been
ministering the Word among the Buzus whose nomad camps
encircled our compound during the "house-patching" season.
Girls had to go. Rita and Alberta went, because there was no
man free to go contact these Buzus for Christ. There was no
man to go to Gidan Sori, a Moslem town pleading to be taught
the way of Christ! Men were patching buildings!

Economy does not rest merely in the original price. Nor
can it be measured in dollars and cents when commodities
as rare as missionaries—male missionaries—and perishing,
undying souls hang in the balance.

Hang crepe on those buildings in Tsibiri, on those ugly-enough, tar-swabbed, eroded walls held up by heavy buttresses. Lament the Christ-consecrated life that was wasted plastering mud to them; let your tears rain on the grave that lies only a few yards off the compound. Hang crepe, weep, and remember the cost of poor buildings!

But we have not come that far. This was 1947—a year before the grave was made.

How many missionary-hours were spent tinkering on that decrepit old car is recorded only in Heaven's records. Before every important trip—and the faithful old Ford must make all of them, for there was no other car—two days were often spent in preparation. The car was followed by prayer that God would keep it together as far as its destination, sometimes several hundreds of miles distant, *with no garage on the way.*

And He did! Those "convoluted tubules"—a tube from a huge peanut-loading truck crammed into Model-A Ford tires —carried the clattering, wheezing old wreck for about 3,000 very important miles in trips made in the interest of the Lord's work. There was general jubilation on the day Ray returned from Kano with four new tubes that had been ordered nearly a year before.

One of these trips was made by Mr. Newton Kapp, who became district superintendent when the Osbornes left the field for furlough. The Sudan Interior Mission motto, found for many years at the bottom of every sheet of official mission stationery, is "to preach the Gospel not where Christ was already named" (Rom. 15:20). It is not difficult, on the fringe of the Sahara, to find places where Christ has never been named. Mr. Kapp went to interview proper authorities in Niamey to see why permission had been refused or delayed on several bases where the Sudan Interior Mission hoped to build stations.

The vast expanse north of us was still practically unreached.

Over 600 miles to the west of us one could travel, and find no missionary. Zinder, nearly that far to the east, had one missionary couple. As a result of that trip, Nikke and Kande in Dahomey, were opened to the Gospel. On the way back, Ray and Mr. Kapp were attracted to a valley along which there were villages in every direction—about 30 of them. They stopped the car and inquired the name of the town. It was Galmi. So we began to pray for Galmi.

Another of the matters that had to be taken up with higher authorities, though at another time when the governor visited Maradi, was permission for our mission to build near the new town of Maradi, also moved during the flood. The water had damaged our Maradi mission property and it had been condemned by the government. Mr. Kapp asked permission to build a mission house and church near the native part of Maradi rather than in the European section which was too far from the people we wanted to reach.

The governor was on the verge of giving his consent when the commandant objected. Once more it appeared that the cause of the Gospel had been thwarted, and that the mission would lose even a foothold already established, for it seemed that the governor was disposed to drop the matter of our location entirely. This has been the pattern of missionary delays so many times—and in other than French territory, of course.

Later, however, Mr. Kapp drew the conversation back to the subject. He stated that all the mission wished to build was a house and a place of worship. Maradi, because of its central situation at a source of supplies, was to become headquarters instead of Tsibiri, which is a bush station.

"Well, Musa in Tsibiri is building a church in town," the commandant said, objecting for the second time to Mr. Kapp's plan. "Why don't you do the same here, and that will settle your problem of living in the native section of town, which is not advisable from a health standpoint."

This suggestion was so far beyond anything Mr. Kapp had even dared dream, far less ask, that we had a special praise service for the marvelous way that God had again supplied more than we had asked or imagined possible. A church in a large Mohammedan center granted without a request for it!

Mission work is always intense and so is the pressure, for in frontier areas none can forget that thousands of souls are within reach, and that they must hear the Gospel if they are to be saved.

I shall never forget that last rainy season in Tsibiri. Even before the rains came, Ralph Ganoe looked down at me from a ladder set against the main house. He was smiling, his face eager, but he looked haggard and tired.

"What are you doing up there on that ladder with your hands full of mud?" I greeted him reproachfully.

"I'm going to do it myself this time," said Ralph. "I'm going to do a good job of it before the rains come." His face lighted up. "Then I can go trekking while the Buzus are here."

I nodded. I knew just how he felt. I did not even warn him that he was working too hard for a man in the tropics. I knew the goal of his long hours of labor—freedom to give out the eternal Word of salvation. Yes, maybe he could get ahead of the weather!

Ralph dug down deeply and filled in all craters and cracks in the walls. He had a smooth surface of plaster over the buildings, and a heavy coating of tar, when word came that the Osbornes were back in Africa. And, since this was Africa, right on the heels of the telegram announcing their arrival, the Osborne family drove onto Tsibiri compound with a sweet blast from the horn of a new Ford, successor to the antiquated Old Faithful that well deserved retirement notice.

The Osbornes' arrival meant a complete fruit-basket-upset for everyone on the compound but me. Rita and Alberta moved out of their rooms into a smaller one to make room for the Osborne family, which had grown since they had left the station. Twins had been born to them a few days after they reached the United States. Meanwhile, the De la Hayes were moving out of the Osborne house into the house then occupied by Ralph and Margie Ganoe.

"And," said Ralph, his eyes sparkling with elation, "we will be going out to Jiritawa!"

I knew what he meant. At last, he would be freed from the repair of the many Tsibiri buildings, to work in the town whose name means *Those Who Wait*. He had been longing for an opportunity to do real evangelistic and pastoral work. His dream was being fulfilled!

I remembered, while Margie and Ralph packed in necessary but ecstatic haste, what Jiritawa had looked like when I saw it three years before. Nothing had been done about the building since then, for we had expected the government to condemn it too. Ralph would have a good deal of repairing to do there, but it would be one or two buildings instead of a whole compound. Soon Ralph and Margie were gone, and our only contact was by messengers who came and went on market days. The old Ford had still served to move some of their loads to their new home.

One day, soon after their arrival, Mr. Osborne got into his car to drive to Maradi. As usual, the boys of the station had gathered and were waiting for Mr. Osborne's word to start pushing. As he settled into position behind the wheel, they moved to their own positions for a good shove, but with a soft whirr of the starter the new car sped from their grasp! The boys' hands fell slackly to their sides. None of us will ever forget the look of amazed frustration and disappointment on the faces of the boys, who had been looking forward to giving this bright, shiny automobile its starting impetus down the hill!

The Osborne twins, Jean and Ralph, were beautiful babies. Little Jean was as chubby as Ralph, but she seemed languid.

She had developed what some would have called "summer complaint." She had not been able to adjust herself to the climate which was then at its humid worst. Marie was a nurse, so we were sure that the baby would be all right soon.

Marie consulted me about her though, for the baby's pallor and listlessness were out of proportion to her symptoms. I soon became alarmed, for the child was wasting away incredibly fast. Soon she was so weak that Marie was handling her on a pillow. One week after the Osbornes returned to Tsibiri from furlough, little Jeannie had to be rushed away from the desert heat in an attempt to save her life.

They stopped in Kano for a few days, and it seemed that they would not even be able to reach the cooler plateau with Jeannie, but she rallied. This word came to us from the De la Hayes, for a few days after Jeannie had been taken to Kano, the De la Hayes, with Rita Salls and Alberta Simms, had left for their vacations on the plateau. By leaving at this time, they would evade the greatest heat, and, since all of them were teachers, they must all take vacations during the time school was out.

Mr. Osborne came back with little David; Marie and the twins had been taken, by plane, to the plateau. Reassuring word of Jeannie came from Jos a few weeks later, and Mr. Osborne decided that one of the first things he must do would be to make a tour of all the stations, some of which had been erected in his absence. Mr. Kapp and Ralph Ganoe were to accompany him. The project bore a far simpler aspect than if the old Ford would have had to make the trip.

Ralph must have worked feverishly in those few days, to make that run-down station livable, and to get it rainproof for Margie and for all their earthly possessions. Margie returned to Tsibiri to keep me company. For about two weeks we were left alone on the largest station in Niger. My own work continued to grow, and between us and the other work on the compound we were trying to get the Osbornes' house cleaned and whitewashed inside. Marie would have her hands full with her sick child when she returned.

About the middle of May, we had word that the De la Hayes and the girls were on their way home and were bringing with them some other French country workers. I told Haruna, the boy who did all my housework, that because all the other households had been broken up, for a few days we would be responsible for meals for all of them, as well as to prepare beds and baths for their first night.

Perhaps I should have broken the news of the household emergency a bit more gently, or offered him his choice of helper from anyone he could recruit in town. Haruna went home that evening and did not show up the next day for work.

Losing Haruna's help just at this time was a severe shock to me. I knew Haruna's cheerfulness and efficiency had contributed much to my own service by freeing me from any concern about the work in my house. Training a new boy takes much time and patience.

I did not have much time to grieve or worry about the loss of a houseboy. Two nights before our guests were to arrive, people called me to Gumar, a small village beyond Tsibiri, to see a patient. I found a girl who had been in labor over three days. Her condition was critical. I told her family that she must be brought to the hospital-unit at once. I hurried home to get everything ready for her.

The family had promised to bring the girl that afternoon, but I waited in vain. After supper, knowing that I would not sleep with that girl on my mind, I went back out to Gumar, trudging through deep sand all the way. I remained with her until after midnight, but I could do nothing for her out there.

They brought the girl next morning, during the hour I should be taking care of my clinic. With more than two hundred patients waiting for treatment, the young woman still had to come first. Neither Rita nor Alberta was there to take over the clinic, as they usually did in case of emergency.

I needed Margie, so I told Arzika to follow the previous day's orders for all medical patients who were doing well on their treatment, to do all ulcers and simple eye infections, and to hold for me all new patients or those who needed my attention. Margie, who had never done any medical work, and who had a tendency to faint, was to help with the delivery that I myself feared.

I had read far into the night in my book on obstetrics, because I knew that I would have on my hands a problem such as I had never faced before. It was actually worse than I had anticipated. I could not deliver even with forceps. The infant had obviously been dead for some time, and the girl's life was in danger from infection. Her life hung by a thread anyway, since she was in a state of extreme exhaustion. Contractions had ceased entirely.

After prayer, and consultation with Margie and with the young woman's father and her husband, I did a craniotomy, something I had never even witnessed. Even then, the beautiful big boy was hard to deliver. At last, the girl was quietly at rest. I was so utterly exhausted that my knees and hands shook uncontrollably, and I tottered on my feet.

"Can't you go home and lie down now?" asked Margie, still pale from the ordeal.

"I will, just as soon as I see a few patients that Arzika has not been able to take care of."

Arzika reported that he had taken care of a very big crowd, and he had over 50 new patients who still waited for my attention. It was nearly noon. New cases were always the ones who took most of my time each morning. I have forgotten what time it was when I finally pulled myself up the hill, too tired to eat the cold dinner.

My day was not done, by any means. I still had a very sick little mother down in the hospital unit. But even before I was prepared to visit her, Dan Nana, our young evangelist, came to tell me that Halima, his wife, was ill. For years, Dan

Nana and Halima had been praying for a child, and apparently their prayer was being heard. That afternoon, however, Halima developed symptoms that alarmed both of us.

I tried to forget the guests and the whole Tsibiri staff that we would have to feed that night, and concentrated on Halima's problem. That did not keep the crowd from coming, however, nor did it get the proper preparations too well in hand. It was a relief, though, to turn the extra station responsibilities over to the other Tsibiri missionaries.

No one was concerned the next day about whether my hospitality was of inferior quality or not. They were far too perturbed over a wire from Jos urging that Mr. Osborne join Marie at once, bringing their passport. Marie must be flown home immediately. Little Jeannie, who had apparently been getting along fairly well on the plateau, had taken a sudden turn for the worse.

How could we contact Mr. Osborne? He was somewhere on an involved tour, and telegrams in Africa have a snail-rate tendency to miss people who are moving about. We all felt sorry for Marie, just a few weeks in the country, and now to go back again, quite alone down in Jos to make all the decisions regarding her two other children.

Mr. Osborne was located, after some delay, and he rushed away to Nigeria. Ralph Ganoe had been ill on the trip, so ill that a few times their schedule had been delayed because he had been too weak to proceed. He and Marge were in Jiritawa, but we heard that he was better now since the trip was over.

Not many days later, however, I was called from my dispensary work altogether to take care of Ralph Ganoe.

"He has malaria," read the message. He would be moved to a hospital in another town so that he could be under the care of a doctor, so I got there as quickly as possible.

Ralph was suffering from the severe chills and weakening sweats of malaria, but no nurse who has given bedside care to a pneumonia patient can fail to recognize the disease when all the symptoms are present. I still could not speak French, but I asked Mr. Kapp to contact the doctor again, calling these symptoms carefully to his attention. Finally he also mentioned that I thought Ralph had pneumonia.

It is indiscreet ever to let a doctor suspect that a nurse does any thinking. A nurse obeys orders; she is not supposed to think. The fact that the doctor had been imbibing too heavily from a bottle did not help matters. The doctor told Mr. Kapp impatiently that Ralph had malaria. He could show him the slides, if Mr. Kapp was in doubt.

I had no antibiotics at my dispensary at the time, but I thought longingly of my bottles of sulfa drugs in Tsibiri, with a severe temptation to slip some to Ralph without charting them. I shook the temptation off, for it was not only unethical but dishonest. I used every spare moment—though Ralph was sick enough to require almost every minute of my attention—to keep up a detailed chart, hoping against hope that it would be read.

Ralph gasped for breath all that night, with only short snatches of troubled sleep. His pulse was becoming alarmingly high. We cut his shirts down the back to save his strength, for his constant malarial sweats made it necessary to change his bed frequently. By midmorning next day I was alarmed to note that Ralph was changing his position. A pneumonia patient lies on his affected side. Ralph began to lie on his back, and his grunting respirations were more labored and shallower than they had been during the night. Mr. Osborne returned from Jos that evening, and came to see Ralph. I confided my fears to him. Mr. Osborne drove back to Nigeria that night to send a wire from Katsina.

By morning, the doctor, sober for once, realized that Ralph had more than malaria. He gave sharp orders to his native assistant, who returned in due time with an outfit such as I had never before seen. He proceeded, with some cotton wads soaked in denatured alcohol and set ablaze inside these specially prepared glasses, to cup Ralph's entire chest. Ralph had to sit up while he did the back.

Dr. Hursh and Dr. Dreisbach, of Kano, arrived about two o'clock that afternoon. Plasma, penicillin—everything was done that could be done. But it was too late. Ralph died twenty minutes after our doctors arrived.

Margie had been taken to Tsibiri, and that was where Ralph would be buried. We hoped that Margie could not hear the carpenters sawing and hammering, and to spare her we had sent them to work down in the dispensary, where they labored through the night.

Africa is violent in the suddenness with which it often wrests life from those who are ill, but almost more brutal to the heart of the bereaved is the haste with which the body must be disposed. Not many hours must pass between death and burial. A funeral in Africa is robbed of the quiet dignity, the days of thoughtful remembrance and the emotional preparation for the time of burial. Except for Margie, all of us were busy with some part of the sad task of laying Ralph's body away. The wooden coffin must be stained and polished and lined. In May there are few flowers, but there were Bougainvillaea and one of the trees on the compound bore great clusters of rich yellow flowers. I had a few periwinkles. Have these simple white starlike flowers ever, before or since, been fashioned into a wreath?

On the morning of the funeral, I passed by the wall that Ralph had patched a few short weeks before.[2]

---

[2]One of the roofs later given to Tsibiri station was given by a family as a memorial for their son killed in World War II. They would gladly have given their son for the costly service of being a missionary, and he had planned so to live his life. Denied the joy of this sacrifice, they gave his insurance for the work in which he had hoped to participate.

People who would give their sons are the kind who furnish roofs, not measured grudgingly to the last skimpy square inch, but with enough overhang to free the Ralphs and the Rays and the other men for the work in the villages—in the Gidan Soris, the Jiritawas—so that there need not be so many who still wait and plead to be told about the way of Jesus Christ.

"I'll do it myself this time," Ralph had said, working himself to a state of fatigue that had broken down his resistance. "I'll do a good job, so that I can go out trekking!"

Ralph had never had that chance to go trekking, though God knows—and I am glad of that—how much Ralph's desire to do so was responsible for his death. I looked at that wall on the day of Ralph's funeral. The first lashing storms had undone much of Ralph's hard work. The walls needed mending again. I stumbled down the hill, blinded by tears. I was glad that Ralph could not see that he had spent the very hope of his life on a hopeless task.

The tropics had taken their cruel toll. Marie was on her way home with a little girl who was never to recover, but was to remain helpless for many years, a bed-ridden charge. Margie was a widow with one child, and she carried another living reminder of her widowhood, for another child was born eight months later.

Satan would have desired to use Ray's long illness to stop the Bible School, Marie's absence to take the whole family home, Ralph's death to discourage Marie. But because these missionaries knew the faithfulness and the love of God the Bible School went on, though Mr. Kapp had to carry a double load to do it; Mr. Osborne remained out on the field, though he had to care for little four-year-old David; Margie though a widow with two small children, remained in Africa, and came back for her next term asking that she be placed in Jiritawa, because she and Ralph had planned so much for these "waiting ones." That request, for very good reasons, was refused. The people of Jiritawa are waiting still.

The powers of darkness were not finished with their onslaughts. The De la Hayes had enough faith, and joy, and hope to help others, who might possibly have been weaker, through their sorrows. Satan made them his special target for that reason, or perhaps because they both worked in the Bible School. Four years after their little David was struck by meningitis, leaving his speech center paralyzed; little Teddy, the De la Haye's first-born, developed a malignancy which quickly robbed him of his life.

When Sophie wrote, telling me of their bereavement, she spoke little of her own grief, but of their joy that Teddy, by his simple testimony of faith in Christ, had led doctors and nurses to Christ in the hospital where he had spent his last days. I cherish her note still, and its keynote is on the front of the beautiful note stationery—"Rejoicing in hope . . ."

Satan would destroy, but with Christ the messengers of the cross are invincible. They sometimes pay an awful price for the privilege of battling Satan on his own territory, for that evil one does not yield ground easily.

When you hear a missionary appeal for funds to carry on his work, or to enter a place of "waiting ones," or even for roofs or for a home to live in, you may be tempted to growl, "Money! Money! That's all missionaries know. They don't realize how much this missionary work costs me."

Don't say it. Don't think it! Ask that missionary what his missionary work has cost *him*. I know one couple who can say, "It cost us two tiny graves in one term, and a little child, our last one, that must be cared for in hospitals, and who must have surgery again and again. This is what missionary service has cost *us*."

Ask Margie. "Has missionary service cost too much?"

You need not though, for Margie did not go out alone the second time without counting the cost.

THIRTEEN

"BEING MADE CONFORMABLE . . ."

> We know the Holy Spirit can touch with celestial
> fire the surrendered thing, and slay it in a moment,
> after it is really yielded up to the sentence of death.
> That is our business, and it is God's business to exe-
> cute the sentence, and to keep it constantly opera-
> tive.
> Death is the work of the Holy Spirit; and when
> you really yield yourself to the death, it is delightful
> to find how sweetly He can slay you.—A. B. SIMPSON

I BEGAN DRAGGING MY FEET so slowly that I was given a vacation from the dispensary. Rita Salls and Alberta Simms
took over. The girls were making the rounds one day, when
one of the inpatients, who was pounding grain, called to them.

"Why doesn't Maijinya come to see us?" she wanted to
know.

Rita told her I was tired, but would come down in a few
days. The woman stopped her work and rested on her heavy
wooden pestle to stare at Rita in sheer perplexity.

"How can anyone get tired," she asked, "just pushing that
little stick around?"

She was comparing her work—and pounding grain requires
tremendous strength and effort—with my own task of sitting
at a desk and writing records and orders, comparing the
weight of her pestle with my pencil! The responsibility I
carried every day was a bit heavier than a pencil, but it was
invisible. I was glad to share that responsibility with the girls
for the rest of the term.

249

My fatigue persisted. That last hot reason of my second term had been especially hectic, with an ever increasing list of patients. As people's confidence had risen, my responsibilities too had grown. They began bringing me patients they would previously have left at home to die. Four months before my furlough was due, I was sent home to get a good rest.

Even after I had been home nearly a year, I wrote headquarters that I was not regaining my strength. I offered to resign. Instead, my furlough was lengthened.

"You will be going to France, remember," wrote Mr. J. O. Percy, from the New York office. "You won't be back in the tropics for nearly another year."

Meanwhile, Mother had been keeping her refrigerator loaded with all the luxuries missionaries crave, and I had gained weight. When Mr. Percy saw me at a conference he exclaimed, "You look wonderful!"

A few weeks later I was on my way to France.

While I packed for this third term, I looked to the Lord for a portion of His Word that should be especially mine. He gave me one. As I had hesitated about accepting, for my travel during the war, His Word that "for me to live is Christ, and to die is gain," so now I trembled at the Word God began to lay on my heart.

> "That I may know him, and the power of his resurrection, and the fellowship of his sufferings, being made conformable unto his death" (Phil. 3:10).

My Lord had shown me, by His abounding grace and provision, the glory of His identity with me—*for me to live is Christ*—whenever I had needed anything from Him. I had learned to know Him in a way that was far above what I had previously dreamed possible this side of Heaven. Now I knew that I was just beginning to know Him; His gracious fellowship was growing every day more desirable to me, now that I had tasted—just tasted—what true communion might mean.

"That I might know him" was the sincere prayer of my heart, and I needed to know in my own life and for greater effectiveness in my missionary testimony "the power of his resurrection." These things I wanted.

But was I willing to pay the price? Resurrection follows death, and death comes by suffering. Could I accept them? I was afraid. I trembled literally when at last I committed myself to this challenge on my knees. Had I known to what I was binding myself, I might not have had either the faith or the courage to do so. But I did, and because I have only brushed the surface of its meaning lived out in daily life, it has become my life verse.

I arrived in France during the first days of January, in 1950. Paris, saturated with a tumultous history, caught my fancy. I have always enjoyed language study, and I enjoyed the study of French; but after the first few months I had to cut down on the number of classes I was taking. Dr. Burt Long, also there to study French—and a brilliant student—wrote to someone at headquarters that he thought I was in no condition to face a term in the tropics. I received letters from three of the top men in our mission organization, from three different addresses.

I had met Rev. G. W. Playfair, general director of the Sudan Interior Mission, and his gracious, motherly wife a few times briefly. Each time he had impressed me with his humility and fatherly interest in our concerns and problems, though they were trifles compared to the responsibilities and burdens he bore. Now, he wrote from a hospital bed in London: "We send people home—not to the field—when they are tired."

The other men who wrote me were of the same opinion. Their solution of holding me in France until I felt fit did not appeal to me. I had been at home resting without any sud-

den rebound of vitality. Paris in winter—living in an un-
heated room—is no health resort. I had not come away from
the States pretending to feel truly fit. In New York, I had
been told that I should give as much service as I could. On
that condition I proposed to proceed to the field at the end
of the ten-month period we all were expected to spend in
France.

"If you'll only warn the people with whom I am to work
that I may not be able to give full service," I wrote to Mr.
Percy, in a letter dated September 25. "If there is anything
in this world that I hate it is to be considered lazy. I also
hate to have special privileges like long furloughs . . ."

Although I had brought equipment for the large medical
work in Tsibiri, I had been warned, by this time, that I would
not be sent back to that station. I had loved that work and
I was disappointed, but I knew that it would be better left
in the hands of Joan Jackson, the capable nurse who was then
in charge there. I became eager to see the new station to
which Dr. Burt Long and his family were preceding me. That
hospital was in Galmi, the town in that well-populated valley
for which we had been praying for some years.

November 8, I got my first look at Galmi station. The great
stone hospital sprawled out like a great *T* on a stony hill. I
learned that all of us, except Dr. Long's family, would be
living in one wing of the hospital until builders arrived to
erect the other houses.

The doctor's house was some distance down the desert
road. The foundation for a chapel made another break in
the bleakness of the hill.

Stone buildings! The hill on which we lived was of a soft
stone that could be cut into shape. What a building material
in contrast to the sand of Tsibiri! There it would have been
hard to find a stone the size of a pea. Here, on the contrary,
it was almost impossible to find soil to plant a few beds of
flowers.

And so, in a new and different setting, I began my third term in Africa. The next days were to be like the memory of a horrible nightmare.

Two ranges of hills funneled a violent wind down upon Galmi at all seasons. In the doctor's new house, so recently erected, the kitchen door had already been moved from the windward side to a more sheltered spot, because soot and ashes were swept through the entire house to the farthest bedroom by the unremitting force of wind. It blew in Galmi when in Madaoua on a level plain about 30 miles away; it was comparatively quiet.

The harmattan season always brings harsh, hot winds anywhere in the Sudan. These winds veiled the landscape with a shroud of red powdered sand from the desert. Even in Niamey, my face and hands had become chapped and dry. Now the membranes of my nose became so dry that they bled. This was no surprise. It happens to all of us during this season.

The harmattan had been bringing me hay fever too. During my last year in Tsibiri, I had suffered with it a great deal. I had brought with me a new prescription for hay fever that was supposed to relieve the congestion without making me drowsy. I was sensitive to the drug, however, and I had to stop using it because it overstimulated me so much that I was getting almost no sleep at all.

My nose and throat became so sore that eating or drinking, and even breathing, was painful. I lay awake at night now, because congestion had closed my nose entirely, taking sips of water to moisten my cracked lips and parched mouth and throat. I kept wondering why I did not become acclimated. I seemed to be burning hot even at night, and aching right down to the bone.

The alkaline water, in which soap formed curds instead of suds, had to be brought on the heads of a carrier from a well about a mile from our compound. A well had been dug on our rocky hill, but it had never yielded more than a few calabashes of muddy water. Some days water was so scarce that we could have no baths. That, in Africa, is tragic!

I had to unpack and get settled for work. Due to some oversight, my furniture had not been sent from Tsibiri. Drearily I unpacked boxes, spread the contents about on the floor, then put shelves into the packing boxes to make them usable for furniture.

Even the hospital seemed to mock at my expectations, for it stood, with the exception of one room, barren of furniture and equipment. The long-awaited carpenters were being held on another station indefinitely. The French government pharmacist who visited the station about that time added his own bleak note of warning.

"You can expect meningitis in two or three weeks. Some cases have already been reported to the east. Since the disease is showing itself early in the dry season and lasts until the rains begin, we can expect a severe epidemic."

How could we admit and care for victims of that horrible disease with no setup to care for hospital patients—and with white people living in the same building?

Reeling with headache and disappointment, I dodged a stone in my path, as I crossed the compound, only to be tripped by a stick. I had broken two bones while in Paris and I had every reason to believe that night that I had managed to break another of my bones which, the Paris doctor had told me, were decalcified.

I was a bit grim that night when I prepared to kneel for my quiet time. I was ready to do some first-class murmuring to the Lord: "Why hast Thou brought . . ."

A quotation from Hudson Taylor, read only the previous week, flashed into my mind. "Recognize no second causes," wrote this man of faith. "These things are from the Lord!"

"Well, *this is it*," I told myself. "Being made comformable unto death is a bit painful, but it's what I asked for. May God help me not to whine!" Still, I wondered if I hadn't had almost as much as I could take.

Next day, however, was worse. My throat became so unbearably sore that Dr. Long prescribed sulfa. Taking time off to be sick, I also took my temperature. The thermometer ran up to around 103 degrees. What I had been blaming on the climate had just been fever all along and that, as well as my aches, was alleviated very quickly with a little medication.

Strange that the physical pain of those first days should remain so clear in my mind. It was to be the prelude, merely, to a suffering far more intense and unforgettable.

At the 1948 Keswick conference, Rev. Theodore M. Bamber spoke on my life text, Philippians 3:10. "The great business of the Christian is not living but dying; not how to live a victorious life, but how to negotiate a humiliating death. . . . The Lord will accept you for death as surely as He accepted Jesus. If you mean death, God means it. It was not enough that Jesus should set His face steadfastly toward Jerusalem, and keep on getting nearer the Cross, hoping and trusting that somehow or other it would not be essential. There was no lamb in the thicket for Him, and there will be no lamb in the thicket for you or for me.

"If you mean death as God means death, then every circumstance in life will begin to operate, through the chief priests and scribes and the multitude, to bring you to where God wants you, and you want to go. God will accept you. . . . Circumstances and enemies and friends . . . bring you where God wants to bring you."

Had I had a choice, I should have fled from this death, renouncing my willingness; but God knew that deep in my heart I still desired His best for me, though I cringed as Jesus never did. I, too, stumbled under the cross, but I did not fall with a thought of compassion for another who also suffered. I was too engrossed with the pain being inflicted on my own ego.

So occupied was I in my pain that I rebelled at the cross, and God's face became obscure behind a cloud of bitterness against a succession of minor crises that restricted the scope and effectiveness of my ministry. I fought the tightening meshes of circumstance as one lashes in blind and frenzied desperation at the strangling tenacles of an octopus.

Having lost conscious contact with the source of power, it did not take great depth of insight to fathom that, as a nurse and as a missionary, I was hardly worth the continuation of an allowance in Africa. My mortification was greater because others were involved and inconvenienced by my shortcomings. The final and ultimate humiliation came with the realization that I was generally considered a shirker.

How gladly would I have twisted myself out from under this opprobrium! I would cheerfully have worked day and night to disprove the stigma of my own small Golgotha, but that was not the divine plan. My ego needed to die, not to be revived. For death, I needed defamation—not vindication.

By working furiously to demonstrate my industry, I managed to scald my leg rather seriously. This time I became completely worthless to the work, and the burn healed far too slowly. Instead of regaining a reputation for being industrious and helpful, I was a care and a hindrance to others' work.

When Dr. and Mrs. Long left the station for a few months at language school, I determined to begin assuming my duties, no matter what pain I should suffer. After only one afternoon at the hospital, however, my foot became so badly swollen that a latent and unsuspected infection became suddenly virulent, and climbed my leg in angry red splotches along the course of a vein. I ran such a high fever that I could hardly raise my head. I began to wish ardently for physical release. Death would be such an easy solution to all my problems. But it was not physical death that God was preparing for me.

Had I submitted to His death more meekly and graciously,

it surely would have required fewer disappointing circumstances. God brought just as many as I needed.

Bright dreams, high aspirations, even a commendable ambition, lie buried in that wind-blown, rocky valley—buried under an avalanche of circumstances. Even in my last days in Galmi—for I requested a transfer—while I was packing to leave the station, I was bitterly disappointed in Haruna, who had served me faithfully during the previous term and had become like a beloved son. He began, at this time, a series of grave thefts that continued after I had to dismiss him. Finally, he was imprisoned, torn from his cherished family—his wife given to another!

"If you mean death as God means death," was the gist of Theodore Bamber's message, "God will accept you for death. Circumstances and enemies and friends will bring you where God wants to bring you."

Circumstances. Friends. I was still to meet my *enemies.* And I had not long to wait.

"But God is faithful, who will not suffer you to be tempted [tested] above that ye are able." I was to have some bright days of fellowship before I faced my foes.

I was elated when I was asked to relieve Joan Jackson for her month of vacation on the plateau in the middle of October, not quite a year after I had come back to Africa. Tsibiri had always been the station of my heart's fondest fulfillment. I was eager to be back among the friends of this largest Niger station too.

Elaine Berdan[1], another nurse, far better qualified for hospital duty and a qualified laboratory technician, had arrived from France to take my place at Galmi. I would be sent to begin a new dispensary in Guesheme, a station that was to be built soon—a new frontier nearly 200 miles southeast of Galmi. I was delighted with that prospect too. This would make the third dispensary permitted us in Niger!

---

[1]Now Mrs. Charles Carpenter

The work in Tsibiri had continued to grow by leaps and bounds—the bounds in statistics usually coming during the dry season when the nomads moved down from the north. This, being October, was high-tide in the flood of patients. On some days there were as many as 500. Two missionaries and three local helpers were needed to take care of the throngs. Many of the patients knew me, and I was glad to meet them again. It was like a reunion with friends, and I reveled in it.

When Joan Jackson returned from Miango, it was time for me to go on vacation, and since Tsibiri was halfway down to the plateau from the new station, Guesheme, it was only practical to take it at that time. Besides a vacation in Nigeria, I managed to work in the fine Kano Leprosarium for a few weeks while I waited to get some passport difficulties ironed out. I also had a few happy days back in the Kano Eye Hospital.

When I returned to Niger, I moved my things from the lovely stone duplex in Galmi, the best building in which I had lived on the field, to a round, thatched hut, the lowliest and smallest home I had had in all my years as a missionary, but I did it light-heartedly. I had learned that happiness does not consist in things.

This hut was in Madaoua. Guesheme, the new station, could not be built because funds had not yet come in for the building. My stay in Madaoua would be temporary, but would permit Jim Lucas, head of the station, freedom to do a great deal of trekking while I was there. Madaoua, I was told, was such a hard town that Jim felt his time wasted there. So bitter was the antagonism that he had begun to spend much of his time in smaller villages that were more friendly and probably more receptive.

About a week after I had settled into my hut in Madaoua, I was back in Galmi as a guest of Elaine Berdan's at the annual missionary conference of our Niger field. While talk-

ing to the group that had been crowded into the nurses'
duplex for the night, I described a method of using bandages
(starched and lettered) instead of flashcards to teach illiterates to read. I had stumbled on this method in Galmi where
I had mixed nursing with school work. Mrs. John Ockers
sat up with interest.

"Why don't you come with us on our trek to Sai? That
chief is eager for education. He has asked us to teach his
young people."

The upshot of the matter was that I spent another fort-
night in the Tsibiri area on a trek memorable for the fact
that eight wives of that one chief accepted the Lord as their
personal Saviour.

I had barely unpacked back in Madaoua when I was called
to Tahoua. Don Darling, our mission builder for Niger, was
in that barren vastness with his family, building the first
station in strictly Tuareg country, a station for which many
had prayed for years.

I was sent to take care of Linda Darling, who had come
down with a mysterious fever there in Tahoua. When I left,
a few days later, there was a small grave in Tahaoua. Again
the desert—and the evil powers that had reigned unchal-
lenged for so long—had exacted a heavy price from those who
dared push forward the Gospel frontiers.

With the exception of Tahoua, Madaoua was the Sudan
Interior Mission's northernmost station. The population of
Madaoua is divided between three tribes, the town Fulanis
(the ruling class of these nomadic herdsmen), the Buzus,
nomadic tribe of the desert, and Hausas. Women are not
locked in in the same strict sense as were the women of Jega,
for most of the compound walls here were of grass.

Though the women are not locked in with tangible walls,
a great and invisible barrier surrounds the minds and hearts
of the people, a wall, I found, that was heavily buttressed
with fear. Alice Lucas took me to several Buzu compounds,

where the people were friendly, she said. We also made a visit of respect to the large mud-walled compound of the chief of the Fulanis, where we were received quite graciously by the head wife. This *uwargida* did not object when Alice suggested that the "stranger" wished to read to them from God's Book.

I chose to read one of David's psalms, as he is one of the Old Testament characters whom Moslems regard as one of their major prophets. After a few minutes two of the women started to interrupt and chatter with the obvious intention of disconcerting me. I reminded them that I was reading from the Word of God.

"I don't hear the name of Mohammed in your reading," said the *uwargida*.

"I am reading only as God gave us the Book."

"You have your way; we have ours. We do not want to hear any more."

Had she been one of the *malams,* I could have reminded her that in the Koran Mohammed instructs people to give reverence to the psalms, and they would have allowed me to go on probably. Here was the hardness of Islam, the fanaticism that closes the heart and mind against the truth, coupled with ignorance that does not even desire to know.

The first day I went into the town alone, I asked God to guide me. I found a woman sitting practically in her compound doorway—for here in Madaoua only the compounds of chiefs or of the very rich have an outer court, and many have no *zaure* entrance hut.

"We are glad you have come to call," she said politely, "but we haven't time."

"Oh, I have no intention of making you entertain me," I said. "Just go on with your work. I'd like to get acquainted."

"You'd better go on," she replied uneasily, "we're busy." Then as an afterthought, "Here! I'll take you to the place where they haven't so much work."

"I'm not doing so well," I whispered to my Lord. "I am being shown out of this woman's vicinity." Nor did things look much better when the woman ushered me into a compound where I found only two men under a large *rumfa*. A woman does not ordinarily visit with men unless other women are present.

"Here," she said to her neighbors, "is a guest." Then to me she said, motioning toward the men in characteristic Hausa fashion by pointing with her heavy lips, *"Malamai na!* (They're both *malams!*) "

A woman brought a mat from inside the compound. It so happened that my Hausa name, given me by Alice Lucas' cook, was Hawa[2]. And Hawa was the name of the *uwargida's* daughter, who was married and had moved to some place in Nigeria. That gave us two things in common—a name, and some knowledge of *Kasar Ingilishi* (English country). The restraint was broken and we had a nice visit.

It was a *malam* who approached the subject of religion. We began by discussing the psalms of David. Knowing the dread uncertainty of the Moslem religion, I spoke of David's assurance of his eternal home, and from there I was able to lead the discussion to the certainties of the Gospel. It turned out to be a fine service, and several women from other compounds came in to see me. I was amused to note that the woman, who did not have time at her home, did have time to come here to listen, though she had to leave her work altogether.

My experience illustrated how fearful the people are of the displeasure and censure of the *malams*. However, the woman and her friends must have been some of the town's best gossips, for from that time I was welcomed into almost any home where I salaamed. In Hausa country we do not knock at doors; we do something much finer, for we stand outside and call, "Peace be upon you!"

[2]Eve. *Maijinya*—nurse—was not appropriate here, since I had no permit to do medical work in Madaoua.

"And upon you, peace," came the response, almost invariably, in those first weeks. The women were sincerely glad to see me and embarrassed me with gifts. I had learned long before that to refuse a gift is the worst rudeness. Daily I came home with something, or even was followed by a boy who carried things to my home for me.

Naturally I was given another opening to the homes when I gave them gifts, but there were so many friendly people, it seemed that I did not need to rejoice about a new opening as we had in Jega.

Those happy days were in March. One month later all was changed.

The *malams* of the Sudan have been well described in Matthew 23, right down to details like wide borders on flowing robes, phylacteries, and public almsgiving. For their prayer rituals, they usually came outside their compounds "to be seen of men." More deadly is another resemblance, for they too "shut up the kingdom of heaven against men" for they neither go in themselves, nor allow others to enter who would desire to go in.

Malam Sule, one of the most powerful *malams* of the Sudan, lived in Madaoua, and everywhere I went I saw groups of *malams*, disciples of the renowned older man, sitting together laboring over the Arabic characters of the Koran, or copying, by hand, entire commentaries, or the Koran itself. People left Kano, the great citadel of Islam, to get instruction from this man. Naturally he wielded a still greater awe among the illiterate followers of Mohammed's doctrines.

One day, when I returned to a home where I had been received repeatedly as a friend, I did not receive an answer to my salutation of "Peace!" I called again, for I was sure I had seen someone move inside the huts. I was perplexed because I received no answer, but thought that perhaps the women who knew me were not at home. I went to another compound.

Here the women were outside their huts, pounding grain. They did not answer when I called to them. But I was certain of a welcome here. I had been in this home often. Now these women were very patently embarrassed, and seemed to be wondering how they should get rid of me. They answered my greetings in subdued monosyllables. They did not put down a mat. In Africa, etiquette dictates that a guest must be seated even before she does very much greeting. They left me standing. Wondering whether they would remember their manners, and ask me to sit down, I remained there quietly for a moment. They turned their backs to me, waiting for me to leave.

Nonplused and confused, I went to another compound where I had often been laden with gifts by the women, who had always delighted every time I came to see them. Here, too, I found the same attitude of unfriendliness. Already alert I watched for some clue to their actions.

As I entered the compound, I observed the women dart quick, fearful glances toward the compound entrance, as though to assure themselves that no one had seen me enter. They looked at each other as though wishing the other would have courage enough to take the initiative. Here, too, I was left standing. I could see no real unfriendliness in the embarrassed women's faces, only fear—stark, wild terror.

As I trudged through the deep, hot sand, back to the mission compound, after a fruitless, frustrating morning, I tried to imagine what terrible threat had been able to make every one of these women cringe as though she feared some evil and supernatural retribution.

My disappointment deepened day by day, for the dire threat issued by the *malams* had preceded me into every home. Wherever I went it was the same. No answer to my salaam. No mat. No welcome. Fear!

"Even if I would talk to these women about the Gospel," I told Alice, who had not been able to go into the town for

some days because of illness, "they are far too frightened to
pay any attention to me. If my presence brings them persecution or even the greater fear of a *malam's* curse, then I am
cruel to torture them with my visits. And they may begin to
resent me and the cause I represent, if I continue to visit
them."

In Jega, my alternative to getting into compounds had
been to make friends of the children, who in time invited
me into their own homes. So I took used greeting cards
with me, and handed them to children I met. I developed a
fine long train of youngsters, and, because it is not illegal in
French territory, I gathered them under a tree for a story.

Not many days after I began this method of finding an
audience, I had to go all the way to the east part of town
before I gained a good following near the French school. I
thought little of it. Children of African villages all collect at
any part of town where there happens to be some attraction
or novelty. Some other interest had drawn my little friends
elsewhere.

After a nice visit, three of the boys from the school came
back with me, carrying my books, and chatting of this and
that.

"*We're* not afraid to be seen with you," one of my escorts
offered, as we were crossing the wide market place, which
was unshielded, of course, from hostile eyes that might be
peering at us.

"We're from the school. And our fathers don't live here,"
supplied another.

"But Sule got a terrible beating."

"From his father, because he carried your books the other
day."

A "terrible beating" is no laughing matter in Africa. I
shuddered. My presence *anywhere* was actually causing bod-
ily harm to people who were seen with me!

Alice and I talked about the situation. We agreed that

this was the kind of town against which Jesus instructed His disciples to shake the very dust from their feet. After years of labor, the Lucases could not point with confidence to any one person in Madaoua and say that he was a Christian.

I went to my small thatched hut, remembering to set out the bucket of water that would, in that scorching May weather, become uncomfortably warm for a bath if left more than an hour. I was suddenly aware of the rigors of missionary life so near the Sahara. Was it all worth the effort and discomfort and frustration involved?

"What now?" I asked God, somewhat bitterly. "I am just wasting time here!" Then, without waiting for Him to show me the next step, I said impatiently, "Why?"

I remembered that wonderful term in Tsibiri, the thousands of souls I had contacted for Christ there. I reminded God that I had tried faithfully to meet every challenge He had presented. Why had He allowed me to come here where all opportunity was now cut away. *Why?*

I remembered the trek to Sai more recently, during *this* term, and recalled the eight women who had accepted Christ in one evening. Why was I kept here where women were afraid even to listen to me. *Why?*

My bitterness grew as I remembered that people were waiting right now in Guesheme, with hearts already prepared by the faithful witness of one lone Christian. We had hoped to enter Guesheme before the rains. Now the rains were near, and it would be several months before we could think of building. Money that had come in would not do more than build a few boys' houses. I had offered to go out to start the work, living in the boys' quarters until money came in, but I was not allowed to go to such an isolated district alone.

Islam encircled that pagan area. I thought of the fanatic missionary activity carried on by the agents of Islam. Pagans come to Christ by thousands in comparison to the single Moslem who accepts Him. I was getting a sample of how

difficult it is to work among people once they have been won
to Mohammedanism.

"Why?" I moaned again, fretfully. "Why am I marking
time here in Madaoua?"

I wonder if Moses ever became as impatient in his forty
wilderness years as I did in these days—were there forty of
them? And, as God answered Joshua's *wherefore* with one of
His own, so He answered me now, "Wherefore liest thou thus
upon thy face?"[3]

God's *wherefore* tore right through the show of all my important reasons for wanting to leave this fruitless place.

"You merely want to vindicate yourself as an effective missionary—isn't that it? You want numbers."

I held my peace, for I could not argue with the shocking
truth, and it took me some time to recognize it for what it
was. My primary motive had lain, all the time, exposed and
naked before God's eyes. My service of that term lay, decay-
ing and useless—wood, hay, stubble—on the altar of pride;
and pride is a world away from the death and the resurrection
power of Christ.

God in His gentleness and longsuffering still offered me
beauty for ashes, the garment of praise for the spirit of
heaviness. I continue to be amazed that He did not turn
from me.

"Perhaps I have placed you here in Madaoua for one soul,"
He said then. "Will you stay for that one soul?"

I bowed in affirmation, mute with shame at what God had
had to point out to me in my own heart and life.

"And if you yourself, and no one here, will ever know if
you have won that soul, will you stay?"

"Yes," I said.

So I became willing to invest the six months that would
have to elapse now—for with the rainy season soon to begin,
that time must certainly pass before Guesheme station could

---

[3]Joshua 7:10

be entered—going about to find that one soul for Christ. By
God's own Word, I knew that a soul is well worth a six-
months' investment of time.

But God was not quite through with me. He led my attention to an article in an out-dated, yellowed copy of the *Good
News Broadcaster*.

"Much discouragement on the mission field," I read in
this article, "is due to exactly this idea of 'investing talents
and time where one would see more spiritual dividends.'"
The author, whose name I have forgotten, stated that the
Word challenges us to present our bodies a living *sacrifice*.
A sacrifice has no returns—no dividends.

Being made conformable unto His death. This then was
the experience for which I had bargained when I desired to
know Christ. As I accepted this facet of His death, I began
to know in a way I had never before experienced it His
peace, and ultimately, His joy, exactly as He has promised
them.

One of God's little feathered creatures had chosen the tree
over my hut for its nesting place. My heart, at last, was
attuned to listen with eager confirmation to the rhapsody of
unadulterated joy that it poured forth, swelling to such an
ecstacy of pure delight that the bird seemed in danger of
bursting its tiny throat. Now I could thank God for giving
me this house with thatched roof, for, though it let through
much of the dreadful heat, it offered no barrier to the bird's
cheerful song either.

My attitude was changed—my circumstances were not. I
went back into the town, but every compound, it seemed, had
been contacted by *malams*. Fear had turned to hatred in
some of the set faces that had once lighted with welcome
when I appeared at their door.

I trudged from one place to another. Some people ignored
me altogether. None offered me a mat to sit down on. Had
I been selling—for a commission, no matter how great—elec-

tric fans or ice-boxes or even medicines to relieve their tem-
poral sufferings, I should have flung my portfolio or demonstration kit into my car and said, "Well, then, let them burn
up in the heat; let them rot in their disease. They don't want
anything else." But now I remembered that what I was
bringing them was more important than an alleviation of
physical suffering.

Truly as I walked those loose, sandy paths, I began to
know a little of the meaning of fellowship with Christ's suffering. He had come from heavenly palaces of incomprehensible glory to walk barefoot among men, yet He was de-
spised and rejected by these creatures whom He had formed,
and for whom He purposed to die! If I grieved merely because people refused to hear the *message* of Christ's atoning
death, think of what agony of heart must have been His who
came to offer His life.

During these days, He walked with me down each burning,
sandy path, and I, in spirit, walked with Him down the
Judean streets where He had been rejected and mocked. I
began to know Him a little, the King of glory who was also
"man of sorrows, and acquainted with grief." And I was
prompted to write of Madaouo: *Put off thy shoes from off thy
feet, for the place whereon thou standest is holy ground.*[4]

One day I left my fruitless wandering about the hot deserted paths, and turned into a compound I had never before
approached. I did not waver or hesitate when a servant met
me at the entrance and stared at me insolently. I asked for
the head of the house, Malam Sule.

The servant withdrew, and returned. "Come then. You
shall meet Malam Sule."

I was led into a large *zaure*. It was filled with disciples of
the great teacher. They bent ostentatiously over their hand-
written Arabic books and pamphlets. A large man rose, his

---

[4]Exodus 3:5

robes billowing. The atmosphere was electric with suspense. *What was I doing there?*

"I am Malam Sule."

"I want you to give me a teacher," I said, coming bluntly to the point. I felt, rather than heard, the gasp of surprise or elation that passed about the dimly lighted *zaure.* "I want to learn *Ajami.*"

Ajami is Hausa written with Arabic characters. There is no connection between learning *Ajami* and becoming a Mohammedan except what has been built up in the minds of the common people. None of them learn Arabic script but for the one purpose of becoming a teacher and propagator of Islam. I saw Malam Sule's eyes light with triumph.

We haggled a bit about the price I should pay my tutor. He gave me a young *malam*—for he had power to assign a task or forbid its acceptance—and stipulated my hours of learning. He did not furnish the textbook—I did that.

The young man whom Malam Sule assigned me was a fine, intelligent *malam,* who asked me to come to his home for my tutoring. His wife was a sweet young girl, and we immediately liked each other. We visited often, if Malam Isa was not at home when I came. We even discussed the matter about which my textbook dealt—and which her husband was helping me to read.

During those next days, I studied hard at my *Ajami,* learning to write sounds by means of curved lines, with vowels either left out entirely, or put in—my *malam* could teach me both ways. I learned the voweled way, because that was the way my *Ajami* Gospel of John was written.

Though I never did learn to read *Ajami* fluently, I could read Arabic numerals, of course. To Malam Isa, who knew how little I could read, I suppose I appeared to be searching at random, looking for interesting curvatures in the lines that are read from the right side of the page to the left. Actually, I selected those portions of John's Gospel that are rich in their message of salvation and grace. I stumbled often over the portions I could easily have rattled off from memory, and my tutor was forced to read them over and over for me. Malam Isa read well, and at last I perceived that he was reading ahead, while I struggled with the convolutions of Arabic. Then I let him read to me. He did read, eagerly and thoughtfully.

I began to write a bit, and was sincerely regretful that I had not learned my Hausa by writing it in *Ajami*, for intonation had been one of my greatest weaknesses. Intonation—stress or tone of syllable—and length of vowel are written right into *Ajami*. By writing a word according to my *malam's* insistence on accuracy, I was learning to pronounce my words more correctly. So I was learning more about the Hausa language, while my young teacher was learning about Christ.

One morning he came to me before our early breakfast. He had never come to my house for any of my lessons. By looking at his haggard face, I knew why he was there. He had not slept.

"I know this is the way," he said. "How can I start following Jesus Christ?"

"You are right, Malam Isa. Jesus Himself said—if you recall what I was trying to write yesterday—'I am the way, the truth, and the life: no man cometh unto the Father, but by me!' Jesus is the way; and He is the only way."

By the way he stated his next question, I knew he had come to me for a certain set of rites he should practice, as he had learned certain rituals to perform before he could be considered a Mohammedan in good standing. I explained that one does not become a Christian by obeying a set of religious precepts or practicing a Christian ritual.

"You notice that we do not pray to be seen of men. It is because our religion is of the heart. And it must be in truth. You know the plan of salvation, for we have discussed it.

'Believe on the Lord Jesus Christ, and thou shalt be saved.'
Remember that Jesus said, 'Ye must be born again.' "

"And how is one born of God?" asked this rich young
malam, who, like Nicodemus, had come to me under cover
of the morning dusk.

I reminded him of another verse he had seen in John:
"As many as received him, to them gave he power to become
the sons of God, even to them that believe on his name."

"Let me read you something else written by this same
disciple of Jesus," I said, turning to John's epistle. " 'Whoso-
ever shall confess that Jesus is the Son of God, God dwelleth
in him, and he in God.' This is the new birth—the spiritual
birth: the Spirit of God Himself dwelling in you. That
new life is eternal."

Malam Isa trembled. No Mohammedan accepts the deity
and sonship of Christ. He began to see clearly why the two
religions can never meet. I realized now that Malam Isa had
intended to continue to earn his livelihood by continuing to
practice as a Mohammedan *malam,* but enjoying the greater
assurance of Christianity by being a secret believer. Now he
knew that he could not be a true Christian and a Mohammedan at the same time. Great drops of sweat stood out on
his forehead as he realized that following Christ meant making a choice between the two. As a Mohammedan he could
not confess Jesus as Son of God; as a Christian he must. I
reminded him gently of the assurance of the Christian life,
of passing beyond judgment—from death unto eternal life.

"Eleven years," he said, every line in his face showing the
agony of his struggle—"eleven years I have been learning so
that I could become a *malam.* I came to Madaoua after I
had learned all I could learn in Kano."

He was bowed together in distress of soul, then he straight-
ened, his face hardening, "I can't lose all that time!"

Eleven years—and he was comparing them with the eons of
eternity. But his eyes were hard now, and so was his heart—

it seemed. My words appeared to fall on deaf ears. "Not far from the kingdom," seems a good thing to say of a man, but it is a tragic thing—and terrifying.

Malam Isa found an excuse for terminating his work with me, and I was never able to speak to him about the claims of Christ. I do not know whether he was as successful in dismissing the Holy Spirit. I have reminded the heavenly Father about this fine young man through the years that have passed.

Eleven years! Fear of losing face before friends. Empty rounds of empty pleasure. Fame. A secret sin. These are the trifles which when viewed nearsightedly loom larger than eternity.

FOURTEEN

A TREK, A SCHOOL, AND A CRUISE BY BATHTUB

Simon, son of Jonas, lovest thou me? . . .
Yea, Lord; thou knowest that I love thee. . . .
Feed my sheep.—John 21:16

I HEARD VOICES OUTSIDE my little thatched hut. I looked out, quickly through the two-by-two window, amazed and incredulous. Two women were coming to visit me!

I had ceased going to visit the women in their homes during the time I had been concentrating on my course in *Ajami*. It had become too apparent that my presence might endanger those whom I would so much have liked to help.

As I swung the door open, I saw that one of my guests was nearly blind.

"We have heard," said the younger of the women, "about the blind people whom you have sent to Kano Eye Hospital. Everyone is talking about the astonishing fact that the doctor can make them see again. I have brought my sister to you, also."

I examined the blind woman's eyes, regretting that I could not give a very hopeful verdict.

"The people whom I sent to Kano had cataracts. Your sister has glaucoma. However, I am willing to do everything I can for her, since there is also an operation for this condition. I'll be glad to write to Dr. Hursh and tell him about

273

your sister's eye. He may send me medicine, or he may ask
me to send her to him."

The sisters were delighted when I told them that I knew
the doctor, and that I had even worked with him for a few
months. They talked without the self-consciousness of bush
women who are meeting a white woman for the first time. I
was so glad to have contact with women of the town again
that I was overjoyed to entertain them as long as they would
stay.

Hausa etiquette demands that one escorts guests some distance on their way home after a visit. I wondered if these
women would want to be seen with me, but I did take them
to the edge of our compound.

"Why don't you come with us?" offered the blind woman's
companion, with seemingly no fear of the consequences of
her proposal. "We would like to have you visit our compound and will show you the way!"

My heart picked up a few beats, thumping out blood that
was fairly dancing with exclamation points. I was being *invited* into a home!

My guests continued to chat casually as we strolled through
the town as though they were oblivious to any stigma attached
to me. Yet these women were well informed about what was
going on in Madaoua; they pointed out various spots of interest to them, giving me the history of some of the families
I also knew. It appeared that they were both completely indifferent to the edict that frighened other women nearly beyond reason. As we passed the chief's high-walled compound,
they spoke of him by his first name.

"He is our brother, you know."

I did not know, but everyone else in town did. Gossip is
a wonderful and a terrible power. David, who knew whereof
he spoke, said, "Surely the wrath of man shall praise thee; the
remainder of wrath shalt thou restrain."

I had walked openly through the town's market place with

the chief's sisters. I was being accepted as a guest and pupil in the home of Malam Isa, under the order and sanction of the most powerful and influential *malam* in town. Surely the *malam* must have had a complete reversal of opinion. Was it not he who had dictated the decree that I must be ostracized and banned from all homes? The *malam's* fear of my harming their cause had been stilled. Had I not taken up their own form of *karatu?*

I visited with my new friends often, at their own insistence. Other women dropped in to chat. Soon my welcome in the homes was as open as it had ever been. The storm of threats had blown over.

Jim and Alice Lucas were due furlough at the end of June or early July, and plans had been made for another couple to replace them. At last it was decided that those workers were needed more in another part of the field, so the barren, fruitless station at Madaoua would be closed for some months. I would be sent to Tsibiri to help with the medical work.

Needless to say, I was overwhelmed at the prospect of returning once more to the work that had been my greatest joy. I had been keeping in touch with those of the staff whom I knew. The work had been growing continually. Joan Jackson, a new nurse, was doing a wonderful job there with the help of Evelyn Ockers. Both of them had been there in October, when I relieved Joan while she was in Miango. I had met the others on the station at the same time, and had renewed friendships during our mission conference at Galmi. How wonderful to work among these old friends!

While ruffling through some papers I was packing, a letter dropped out from others. It was one Alberta Sims had sent me which had been waiting for me in New York when I arrived there on furlough after six weeks on a freighter.

"Do you remember Madugu?" she asked.

Of course, I did. Madugu was the patient who had carried the Gospel to his family at Sori. His father had sent several requests for a teacher. I remembered Madugu.

I reread Alberta's letter. In it she recounted that, through Madugu's testimony and influence, his father, the *maigari*, had made a proclamation that the people of his village could dispense with the Moslem fast and go about their farm work, for he no longer saw any need for it.

I looked up from the old letter, praising God anew. To openly break the fast is the acid test of one who turns from Islam to faith in Christ. Persecution invariably follows such testimony of faith, for such it is, indeed. Moslems would not break that fast for genuine fear that they would be excluded from even a hope of Heaven. The fast of Ramadan is the chief of the "works" to which the devotees of Islam cling for whatever meager hope they have.

"Madugu has won at least ten people to the Lord in Sori," Alberta reported in her letter. She added, "They are begging for a teacher so that they can learn more about what it means to follow Christ. They are all illiterates, of course, and one can hardly understand how they can develop a Christian community unless they have help."

I knew that Madugu had been at the dispensary only about two weeks. He had learned ten or twelve Scripture verses. I did not know how much he had understood about Christianity beyond the bare essentials of what it means to be saved. Madugu's name had been on my prayer list ever since I had first learned of his witness, and I had had a burden for that entire village that was down on my list as Sori.

Even as I praised God for the old *maigari* and for Madugu's testimony, the letter began to tremble in my hands. I loved Tsibiri medical work. I wanted to enjoy the companionship of my friends. I had been very lonely during so many months of this term. Guesheme would be another isolated and lonely place.

No one at Tsibiri dispensary is going to be absent from the station. They have been carrying on very well without you.

I began to see clearly what my next step must be. I wrote Mr. Kapp, our district superintendent, for permission to trek to Sori. I would need to pack the necessary equipment to take with me.

I explained to Mr. Kapp why I should like to go and live in Sori during the time I was waiting to be transferred to Guseheme.

"If we cannot furnish a pastor, we can teach someone in the town to read the Bible. Then they can learn the answers to their problems, and get their guidance for a Christian community by searching God's own Word."

Mr. Kapp had never heard of Sori, but he gave his consent. After I arrived in Maradi and began inquiring whether anyone had ever contacted the people of Sori, I learned to my dismay that no one seemed even to know Madugu's story. Alberta Sims and Rita Salls were at home on furlough, and the entire Tsibiri staff had changed.

Though my sense of duty was as strong as ever, my enthusiasm for this trek ebbed somewhat when it became obvious that the people of Sori had given up asking the mission for help, and had lost contact with Tsibiri station. What did it mean? After four years how much life would I find? Would they still want a teacher? Perhaps their desire for help would now be bitter antagonism because of our apparent indifference.

I decided to send a messenger to Sori, asking if they would like to have me come and if they would have any sort of place for me to live if I came. While I was making arrangements to send this messenger, Dan Nana, the evangelist who had accompanied me on my trek into the desert, appeared at the door of Mr. Kapp's office.

"I know about them," he said. He explained that Sori is actually comparable to a "county seat," and that the name of Madugu's village was Gidan Magaji. "But if you want to go *there*," Dan Nana said, "you'll have to go at once. In two weeks the river will be so high you won't be able to cross it."

"In other words," said Mr. Kapp, "you will have to make it a ten-day trek. You won't want to risk being marooned for the duration of the rainy season."

"Madugu's older brother is now *maigari* there," Dan Nana added. "The old *maigari* died last year."

I was stunned by Dan Nana's casual statement. That *maigari* now dead was the man who had sent so often and so vainly for a teacher. He was the man who had offered to build a church and a home for a teacher. He was the one who had canceled the Moslem fast in his town. Now he was dead.

Had Madugu known enough of the Word to show him to saving faith?

Here is the tragedy of missions. Men—sincere, zealous, red-blooded young men—are *competing* for a place to serve Christ in their homeland, *but this old maigari had died, pleading for more knowledge of the way of Christ!* I could have wept. I might go now to teach them what I could in ten days, but for frontier work, for trekking, for establishing churches or training leadership for a Christian community, God has never intended to use women. It is man's work—a work that demands strong sinews in arm and soul.

While I made further preparations in my room in Maradi guest house, and waited for word from Madugu, John Ockers, who had been trekking around Tsibiri whenever he could be spared, came into Maradi. When I asked him, as I had asked the others, if he knew anything about these people in Gidan Magaji, I received an enthusiastic response.

"Madugu?" he said. "Yes. I stopped in that village last year on a routine trek—for about an hour or so. Madugu quoted all his verses to me in the first few minutes I was there. They still ask for an evangelist and are offering to build a church."

I had ten days. They wanted instruction in the faith. I wanted to teach someone to read. How much would I accomplish in ten days? I must make very definite plans so that no precious time should be lost. How could I do what must be done?

Ten days of concentrated doctrine—taught to people who have never learned to concentrate and could not take notes? Should I concentrate on teaching someone to read? My "bandage" system of reading instruction was rather fast (Dauduka, whom I had taught to read in Galmi was even then in the Tsibiri Bible School, and doing very well); still I could not hope to teach anyone to read the Bible very fluently in ten days.

Madugu sent his answer without delay. The people were preparing a house for me and eight carriers would be waiting for me by the bend in the road nearest Gidan Magaji on the morning I intended to go there. Madugu would furnish a horse for me to ride. The jeep, he explained, could no longer get across the river.

I went to Mr. Kapp with a pounding heart but with not too much hope that my decision would carry much weight. Our district superintendent was very careful of his missionaries. I had had quite a bit of difficulty in gaining permission to take a two weeks' trek alone up toward the desert, under far more favorable circumstances.

"I need more than ten days for what I have to do in Sori," I said. "I want your permission to remain there."

"And be marooned?"

"And be marooned." I laughed. "What of it? I'll just be on one side of a river. You'll be on the other!"

"But that means that you will be cut off from any help during the entire *malka* season. What if something goes wrong? You might get sick."

"I'm a nurse. I know how to take care of myself. I have learned to live in this country."

Having obtained Mr. Kapp's reluctant consent, I began to plan the equipment necessary for prolonged isolation in the bush. First of all, since my primary object in remaining throughout the rainy season was to get the Bible into their hands, I had to have books and other equipment necessary to teach elementary reading. To make general religious instruction more effective, I decided to take the fine supply of visual-aid materials that the Lord had supplied while I was at Madaoua. The phonograph, with the Christian Hausa records, would attract many to the services. I could not imagine being without my typewriter for two months, for a missionary is never without the responsibility of keeping in contact with the home constituency. I needed the specific prayer help at this time more than at any other.

Eight head loads. All I wanted and all I needed had to go into those eight head loads: working equipment, clothing, tins of food, pots and pans, cot and bedding, mosquito net, a lamp or lantern—these were just general essentials. Packing for a trek is not like packing for a camping trip in civilization where forgotten items can easily be replaced enroute. The planning must be detailed. There are no drug or dime stores in Sori. If I forgot a toothbrush or other small inconsequential items like matches, soap, kerosene, or salt, I might miss them a good deal. Forgetting a small thing like an antimalarial drug might be tragic. In making up my list, I decided to include my cat.

A cat on trek?

With eight 60-pound headloads as my limit of baggage, taking a cat on trek may sound like sheer, impractical eccentricity. On the contrary, my pet had top priority on my list of essentials after the trek I took with the Ockers to Sai, where hordes of rats and shrews literally overran my bed every night.

Abubakar, a young boy who had repeatedly asked me for work and who seemed interested in the Gospel, was one more addition to the trekking equipment I decided to take. During the farming season it might be very difficult to get local help, still it would be well to be freed of all household chores, no matter how simple I kept them. Naturally, he would be sitting in on the religious instruction I would be giving the people of Gidan Magaji, and might take a definite stand for Christ as a result. I did not have to count Abubakar's loads with my load weight, however, for he would be carrying his own bed roll. Trekking, for the African, is much simpler than white people make it!

At 8:30 on the morning of July 22, the Kapps took me as far as the jeep could go. Someone had assured me that the village of Gidan Magaji was only four or six miles beyond this bend in the road. I expected to be there by lunch time.

A few blasts of the horn brought some natives to the car from a small village not far from the road. These men took my loads from the jeep, telling us that Madugu was in the village. I waved a merry farewell to the Kapps as the jeep swung around and back toward Maradi.

When Madugu came, he seemed aghast at the loads I had so carefully trimmed down to eight-load weight. He had brought with him only two boys and one was just a very little shaver who could hardly be expected to carry much. Abubakar, too, was of slight build and had his own blanket roll to carry.

I was not enthusiastic over Madugu's suggestion that I leave part of my things in this native village. It was a frightful strain on my limited confidence in African honesty in general, and not a reflection on the character of these villagers in particular, for I had never seen them before.

I tried to hire local carriers, but ran into the same trouble Madugu obviously had had in fulfilling his promise to bring eight men. Of the three who had come from Gidan Magaji, Madugu was the only fully grown man. This was the farming season. Men were in the fields.

In Africa, a horse is a creature of pomp and royalty. Madugu looked shocked when I suggested that some of my things could be tied to the horse's saddle. Since it was only four to six miles from here to Gidan Magaji, I thought I could easily walk. I told them so.

"The river is hip-deep," said one of the men, taking Madugu's side.

"Well, we can unload the horse at the river, and I'll ride over. Then you can reload."

Madugu shook his head, but tried my plan when I insisted. The load was poorly balanced, and the saddle swung under the horse's belly. I was suspicious that Madugu had contrived the failure.

Reluctantly and with a good bit of uneasiness, I began to reassort my loads so that I would have food, light, and a bed for the first night. Here also we had some slight differences of opinion. We agreed on the bed bag as being important, but the phonograph, which I would have placed last on my list of important items for my first night in the bush, was quickly placed on the pile of things that must go. My cat must perforce be classified as essential simply because she could not be stored indefinitely in the screen box in which she was being transported. We were not a very impressive safari as we started off. I was the only one on a horse.

I quickly became reconciled to the fact that the horse I was riding was not being used as a pack animal. We waded through long stretches of swamp dotted with thorn trees. Wading would have been impossible unless I had kept on— and ruined—the shoes I needed for the coming two months.

The horse snorted when he was drawn into the river by Madugu, and slipped awkwardly in the sloping streambed. I could do nothing but draw my feet from the stirrups and hope the horse would find his way across without stumbling into a hole. Madugu and the boys struggled silently and un- complainingly against the clutching force of the stream whose sullen red current writhed menacingly over what had been a dry stream bed until a few weeks before. I could see that it was not easy for them to keep their footing and impossible for them to see the depth of the next step ahead, and they were balancing on their heads loads that weighed half as much as they did. Shilling, the boy who carried my bed bag, fell headlong just as he reached the far edge of the water. The bed bag fortunately fell toward the bank, not into the water.

I knew that the *malka* season of torrential rains would fill the watercourse with a vicious, raging flood in less than two weeks. From then on until the end of the rainy season, nothing but a helicopter would be able to reach me—and there were no helicopters in that part of Africa.

The finality of the crossing held for me neither qualms nor regrets. I had asked to be marooned. The wonder of it was that I had been given permission to spend all this time at a project that seemed primarily my own interest. I sent up a jubilant breath of thanksgiving and a prayer for guidance that I might use the time well.

Madugu, glancing over his shoulder, must have noticed that I was tired.

"You'll be glad when you get there, Maijinya," he called encouragingly. "The whole community is going to welcome you. We have told everybody. Even in Nigeria they know you are coming!"

"Nigeria!" I retorted. "But that is far south—British country."

"The whole world knows about you!" he replied enthusiastically.

I laughed, pondering the efficiency of the tom-tom news service and the smallness of an illiterate's world. During my projected stay I sincerely hoped to widen those horizons by teaching some of them the magic of the printed page.

One of the carriers, Kudu, whose name means *south*, said, "I'm a believer."

"So am I," said the small Shilling, whose conviction radiated right through the smudged perspiration on his face.

"You'll have a thousand," said Madugu.

"What is this to which I'm riding?" I asked myself. "Is it one of those miracles that missionaries in Moslem areas hardly dare dream about—and read about with envy?"

Tears of joy welled up in my eyes and overflowed my heart in humble praise, as I searched vainly for adjectives of the extravagant, supercolossal variety, but found none to express the wonder of what had happened because one person had shared the tiny spark of light he had received during two weeks at the Tsibiri dispensary.

So, despite fatigue and hunger, my ride was shortened by anticipation of rich days ahead, though I frankly admit I was very glad when not long after sundown we did reach our destination.

I was taken to a compound opening directly on a large open "square" in the center of the town. Dogo (Slim), the tall, gangling man who had come to the dispensary four years before to ask for a teacher, was my host. He grinned his sincere welcome, exposing a sadly incomplete set of teeth deeply stained with kola nut.

"If it were possible to build a *shigifa* during the rains, we would have done so," Dogo apologized. I am sure he spoke the truth, though there was no *shigifa* in the entire village. Had there been one, I suppose it would have been offered to me.

The newly thatched hut Dogo had prepared for me was actually outside his own compound but walled with *zana* mats, so that it offered a possibility for almost complete privacy. I could not have asked for better arrangements.

A crowd was gathering. "To hear the gramophone," Dogo explained.

"Please give me time to get some supper," I said. "Then I'll bring the phonograph out to the square."

I had left Abubakar and the two boys behind out of sight, but they were soon there, too, breathless with haste. *They had run with their loads for fear they would miss the phonograph!*

Actually, though I was nearly famished, my greatest preoccupation was to get something to assuage my thirst. I had left my kettles behind, but willing hands offered all the metal cooking equipment in the village—a tin pail and a tiny iron stewer. Fussy as a nurse becomes in the tropics, I did not even look to see how clean or dirty the utensils were. I just told my new, inexperienced boy, "Get some water boiled!"

"Water!" I could think of nothing else. Under the mistaken idea that my ride would be one of only four to six miles, I had taken only one small canteen of water and had drunk deeply before I realized that the water would have to be rationed carefully during lengthening hours of a torrid day. I was limited to the water in my own canteen because, no matter how great thirst may be, by bitter experience Europeans have found that one indiscreet drink may mean months of suffering—even death.

My thirst had grown through the day as my painfully hoarded supply of water dwindled to a few warm ounces that sloshed temptingly about in the nearly empty canteen. Though I had thoughtfully planned cautious sips to go with my hurried meal of tinned meat and bread, my thirst was greater than my self-restraint, and by the end of the meal I was calling eagerly to Abubakar to see if the water were boiling. I drank it, too, just as it was, for my tea and coffee were still in the loads left behind. Then, pouring two cups of water to cool in my absence, I went out to the town square for my first service.

I was glad that Gospel Recordings, as well as some individual missionaries, have made some fine records in the Hausa language. I was too tired to do much speaking that night, but I was not only confident that the phonograph, because it was such a great novelty in this bush community, would have an attentive hearing, but that the message was as good as any I could give them.

When I set up my cot later, I found that I had used up about half the floor space in my new home. The mud walls were six inches lower than shoulder height, which meant that I had to double over to get out of my door, but I was able to stand upright anywhere in the central part of the hut. I realized, looking at the size of my feet, that I would need to plan carefully if I were to store all my equipment in this hut— and still leave room to stand up. But I was thankful for the fine rainproof roof. The offer of a larger hut with a leaky room would have been quickly rejected.

Next day Dogo brought another thatched roof (guaranteed for shade only) and mounted it on poles to form my school and reception parlor. I made use of it at once, though my books had not yet arrived, to entertain all the dignitaries in the vicinity that called to pay me a visit of respect. Many people made a day's journey to see and hear the phonograph that spoke their own Hausa language. I was often amused at bewildered conjectures about the wizardry required to trap a man in the little black box.

These visitors knew why I had come to Gidan Magaji, and very few left before I had opened "God's Book" and talked to them of the Lord Jesus Christ. We had a service in the square every evening.

It was two days before my loads were brought by a fresh group of carriers. The others still had sore necks from balancing their heavy loads. It was good to have fresh clothes and cooking materials.

My largest packing box had been planned so that I could set it on end, and by sliding in a few plywood boards for shelves, it became a general cupboard, not only for dishes, but for books or any equipment that must be protected from white ants. I mounted my cupboard on four tins, part of my grocery supply. Other furniture consisted of a deck chair, folding camp table and chair, and a cook stove. The latter was made of the end of an oil drum mounted outside on three broken earthen pots furnished by the women of the village. Later, when food spoiled too quickly in my tight cupboard, the screen carrying-box for my cat was thoroughly scrubbed and used as my "ice-box."

At some distance from the compound, at the edge of a field of guinea corn, was my "bathroom," formed by a high *zana* mat set down in the form of a loose, humped *6*, or a *C* with one edge pushed in. This arrangement gave complete privacy, though there was no door.

While in Galmi, where I had been in charge of school work, I had stumbled on a method of using bandages to teach illiterates to read. On two strips of well-starched muslin bandage, I had printed the consonants in the order of their most frequent usage in the Hausa language. On the two other strips I printed the vowels in the same order.

Hausa, trade language for millions of people, is phonetically a simple language, with syllables formed generally from a single consonant followed by a single vowel. I could draw these bandages through a slitted cardboard to form countless combinations of two-syllable words.

Illiterates often have a fatalistic disbelief in their ability to master the mystery of the printed word, for a page appears like a forbidding array of thousands of unintelligible hieroglyphics. If they can be given a quick, encouraging start, half the battle is won.

By the end of the second hour of instruction, my students were keeping score, in the sand, of words they could read without assistance from me. To their amazement and pride, the count reached more than 100 words.

Although my class periods were limited to the afternoon hours, when my pupils came in from the field, tired, pouring with perspiration, within two weeks a couple of the young men had finished the well-planned British government primer designed for illiterate Hausa adults, and were reading—haltingly—almost anything I placed in their hands.

In one of my talks in the square, I mentioned that I had had Madugu's name on my prayer list for four years, or ever since I had known that he was winning his fellow townsmen to the Lord. Dogo came to me, one evening, with a group from the village. He addressed me, as all of them did, by my Hausa name.

"Maijinya, you ought to make a list of Christians now. Write *us* down in your book! You can put me down, and my wife, Hawa."

"Write me and my wife down too," exclaimed Jadi, one of my star pupils. Jadi had once aspired to be a *malam*. During my first days in Gidan Magaji, without any suggestion from me, and without my knowledge, Jadi burned his wooden slate, symbol in his mind of the Mohammedan religion. Even then I began dreaming that he would become a *malam* of the Christian faith—that he would attend Bible School—a dream that was soon to come true.

Others were standing over me as I wrote down their names.

"I'll get you some more," said Dogo. "I want them to come here and give their word themselves. We can't take lightly what is written down in a book."

Illiterates have an almost superstitious respect for a "paper." Dogo was so eager to get his list up to date that he used a bit of strategy that required me to be an innocent accomplice. He asked me to write a letter to a man called Dan Malam, asking him to come the same day if possible. I heard him murmur to the messenger, "He won't trifle with a paper!"

Nor did he. Dan Malam soon arrived from a distant town, a friendly faced old man with frizzly, frosty whiskers. No one had read the letter to him—for no one in his town could read —but he had taken it as a "summons," just as Dogo had predicted. He waited patiently until Dogo arrived.

"This is another one for your list," Dogo announced. "He had two wives, and gave up one after he talked to Dan Nana."

"This explanation brought light upon two things besides the evident sincerity of Dan Malam. I had wondered why Dogo had not brought Madugu to be written down on my list. *Madugu had four wives.*

I now saw that these people had more information about Christianity than I had anticipated. Dan Nana, stationed about a day's journey from here, had been here occasionally, as many as five or six days at a time.

"And when he came," supplied one of the boys, "we didn't sleep."

I had planned to approach the matter of polygamy very carefully, as it is not a matter essential to salvation, though it is one of the greatest and saddest problems of establishing a church in this land.

Any who ponder thoughtfully and kindly about this unfortunate family situation will understand the heartache and prayer burden that were mine. I saw Madugu's face grow sadder as each of our services unfolded more of the spiritual riches that are ours through Christ. It seemed that he felt himself excluded from these blessings. Yet this was the man who four years ago brought the message of salvation to his village and won others to faith in Christ.

I told Madugu that his having several wives could not keep him from eternal life, though it would exclude him from church fellowship.

"My loyalty is with the Way," he said. "See, I am going to send my daughter to your school!" But his face remained sad and he never came to be written down in my book, though I sincerely believe that the Lamb has a record of his name.

What his battles were he would not tell me, a foreign woman. I believe he had broached the subject of the new faith to his wives, for in his compound the women not only made me feel unwelcome but they were hostile. They hated the Christianity that threatened to break up their home. Two other polygamists in Gidan Magaji reacted almost as did Madugu, though his sadness was more obvious and pitiable.

I had ample evidence in those first days that those whose names were "in my book" sincerely desired to live as Christians should. Kudu, meat-starved as are all these people, brought me a small alligator. "Do Christians eat these?" he asked.

Jadi's problem was more serious, as I could tell by his evident agitation when he came to see me. Contrary to custom, he came right to the point. Only an overpowering emotion could make a Hausa plunge right into an unpleasant subject.

"I lied to you yesterday. My wife refuses to be in your book. Strike her off!" He hesitated, trembling visibly. "Can we be patient, and talk to her a while, to see if she can be persuaded?" he wanted to know. "Then—if she doesn't yield —I'll *change* wives!"

His relief that Christian principles would not advocate an exchange of wives was pathetic, for, said he, "I love her very much."

It is natural that there should be persecution. Amadu and his wife, from another town, were told that they would have to leave Badeta when they publicly made it known that they wanted to become Christians. They were making plans to move to Gidan Magaji. Two other inquirers from that town ceased to come to the services.

Dodo was a snake charmer, and he generously offered to round up a cobra and a few vipers and demonstrate his skill, if I were interested. "I know just where they hole up. It won't take long to find them."

I declined this form of entertainment so abruptly that a

crowd of curious bystanders had a good laugh. I remembered with vexation that I had failed to bring my snake-bite kit.

These were the pillars of the church in Gidan Magaji. I was irreverent enough to wonder, during one of our Sunday services, what would happen if I could lead that picturesque delegation into a fashionable church back home!

For such occasions, Madugu wore his turban and a flowing robe that denoted his position of honor in the community. Dogo's floppy, homespun gown, usually hanging from one bony shoulder, and growing, week by week, a trifle stiffer about the neck and darker in color generally, was about the average costume for older men. Jadi wore a new leather loin-cloth, very picturesque because of the various odd-shaped ends that dangled from it here and there for ornament. The children did not bother about clothes at all, and—on second thought—I decided that I should have to leave the women at home; they would scandalize their proper and respectable sisters in the faith.

I would have been proud to let my naked little urchins meet children from more fashionable Sunday schools, how-ever, to match them in a Scripture memory contest. Even little Illo, who was no bigger than a minute and could not pronounce his words very clearly, was repeating about thirty verses that I had taught the young Christians in such sequence that one verse naturally and logically led into another, for only so would they be able to prompt each other if a verse was forgotten—at least until Jadi and Dan Naito could find their way around in the Bible.

Perhaps, in another sense, my group of bush believers would compare favorably with a group of more properly clad members of a church at home. This mere handful of Chris-tians offered, once more, to build a meeting place, to be used as a school on weekdays and as a sanctuary on Sundays, a *shigifa* for the teacher (which means a better house than their own homes), and Dogo urged that I remain, and they would build me a dispensary!

And who were these generous souls who could afford such bounties? I got an unrehearsed glimpse of the "bank account" upon which they must draw to make good their offers.

Two weeks after I arrived in Gidan Magaji, Abubakar came to me and said that he was leaving. He was not dissatisfied, he said, with my treatment of him, or in the amount of work he had to do.

"I just can't stay here in this village," he confided, "because I can't live without *tuwo da miya*."

I recalled another trek on which I had been treated quite royally by the chief, but my boys complained afterward of the lack of proper food given them. I knew Abubakar had enough money to pay well for food, so I decided to find out why he was not able to get the mush and gravy that is the staple food—not a luxury—for Hausa people. I went to Dogo with my problem. I discovered that everyone in Gidan Magaji was living on *fura* during those hard days of the farming season—a gruel made of grain and buttermilk.

"You see," said Dogo, "we have nothing to make the gravy."

I remembered Kudu, then, and his question about eating the alligator. These people could not afford meat or fats to make the *miya* without which *tuwo* is quite unpalatable.

Never had I known for how much I ought to be grateful until I lived those weeks in Gidan Magaji. I was almost ashamed to eat meat, guinea fowl eggs, or to use goats' milk, or even the Fulani butter that had to be strained and boiled to make it safe to eat. Adults were more discreet, but children gazed with hungry eyes, quite without envy, at what missionaries call a "bush" diet.

I recall, only too well, throwing away the wrapper that had been about some cheese my mother had sent me from home. Children passed the tin-foil wrapper from one to another, just to get a "lick," so they could taste the delicacy that I had enjoyed. I had brought a tin of cookies to use instead of desserts. I think I ate three of them. I had much more pleasure watching the children eating the rest, impressed over and over again at their spontaneous generosity as they shared with each other.

My canvas cot, rusty folding chair, my meager supply of battered trekking kettles and unmatched dishes, my stove, made from the end of an oil drum—all these were, for the people of Gidan Magaji, unattainable luxuries.

These were the people who offered to build me a permanent house and dispensary, and a church. These were the people who brought eggs and chickens, even grain, as their "contribution" on Sundays. These were the people whose fear of hunger caused them to give up Sunday farming with reluctance—and these were the people who were now rejoicing, for said they, "The whole world says there are no farms with grain like ours!" So these people, whose "deep poverty abounded unto the riches of their liberality," began tasting the faithfulness of our wonderful Lord!

I deeply regretted that I was able to do very little work among the women. During the morning and early afternoon hours, the women were out on the farms with the men. I got up at 5:30 in the morning, but by that time the women had pounded grain for their families—a long, arduous task—cooked breakfast, and were out on the farms. The villagers called my rising hour "midmorning."

When the women came back from the fields, they had to go to the well for water and to pound grain for their evening *fura*. That was the time I had my reading class with the boys who dropped wearily down on my mat in my "reception parlor." In the evening, the people—men and women—gathered for a meeting in the square.

After that meeting, I sometimes took my visual-aid materials to the various homes, and by the light of my pressure lantern told some of the Bible stories that would appeal to the women, often by request repeating the previous Sunday's story, for many of the younger wives were not allowed to join the large mixed crowd that came for the Sunday services.

Most of all, the women loved to sing and so did the children, and they were proud of the wonderful way their children were memorizing the Word of God. Only in Madugu's compound, and in other compounds where there were more than one wife, was the welcome less than gracious, though the women were tired after their long, grueling days.

One of the women brought me the first tender ears of corn during those days when the guinea corn that closely encircled my own little hut had also grown rank and ten feet tall. The heat during those days became very oppressive because the humidity was held by the cornfields that permitted little breeze to reach my hut.

I had always liked corn and was glad for this variation to what was, for me, a very restricted diet. I had lost my appetite as the humidity increased and was bothered with a slight but stubborn nausea. On August 19, I sent a request to Maradi for more tinned foods, hoping that a better diet would relieve my symptoms. But I had waited too long for such things to be sent. Even before my messenger got back, I heard that a woman and her child had drowned trying to make the river crossing.

I missed Abubakar sadly during those days. As long as I was well, his going had not mattered too much. Now I began to feel very much alone, isolated from anyone on whom I could call to care for me if I should grow worse. But then, of course, I would not allow myself to grow worse. I had to spend more time on a better-planned diet. That was all.

During the first week or so, anyone from any village nearby had made a point of calling at Maradi or Tsibiri stations to see if they could bring a message or parcel for me. My communications with both stations had been far more frequent than I had anticipated. Evelyn Ockers, from Tsibiri, had even kept me supplied with bread.

My messenger returned several days after I sent him, without the tins I had requested but with a very welcome accumulation of three weeks' mail. Evelyn had sent a loaf of bread, but that, as well as the mail, had been well dunked in the river. My messenger said that he had placed them all in a calabash and swam over with them, but it had not been easy. He reported that the number of people dead at the river crossing had risen to six. I was now marooned.

I was still ill. In spite of rigid precautions against malaria and food contamination, both common complications of trekking life, I was suffering more and more from nausea that I was trying to attribute to some article of my diet. I eliminated one by one, those that aroused my suspicions, until finally the nausea thoroughly eliminated them all.

I started with the corn, for I seemed to feel worse after having eaten that. That should have given me a clue to the fact that my nausea was not caused by tainted food but by the butter that I had generously spread over the roasting ears. I further complicated my self-diagnosis by taking atabrine when I discovered that I was running a fever. Atabrine is a yellow dye and, if taken in therapeutic doses, usually makes the skin yellow. So I hid from myself one prominent symptom of infectious hepatitis—the jaundice, which never did show too well in my eyes. My hut, in the middle of tall corn, was too dark for me to note any change in my appearance. I was too ill by now to spend much time looking at my reflection in a mirror anyway.

Meanwhile I had kept up my classwork in the afternoons. Jadi was beginning to write little notes that were somewhat difficult to decipher because he forgot his vowels, for he had previously learned to write unvoweled Arabic. During the day I spent more and more time in bed, not only because of the nausea, but because I was growing weak.

"Hurry and get well," urged Kudu. "I have a fiancée in another village, and I want her to become a Christian before we are married. She wants you to come to tell her what she needs to know."

The children could not believe that I was ill. At first, when they clamored for me to come out to them I could not resist them, but would set up my deck chair in my "reception parlor," relieved to be outside the hut that had grown suffocatingly hot as the corn grew taller.

Later when I could not come out to them they clustered about my door, singing the choruses I had taught them and repeating in proper sequence the Scripture verses they had learned. They had found the best way of cheering their patient. I had not come in vain. My work would go on. I had taught at least one to read well, and had furnished him with a Testament. The Gospel was singing in the hearts of many.

As one day of nausea followed another and I grew worse instead of better, I longed to go home, but, of course, that was out of the question now. If healthy adults drowned in the river, I could never make the crossing. I kept thinking that I must get over this "upset" some time. I had been ill three weeks now. At last I could hardly stagger to my little *zana* mat bathroom, where I would lie down and retch endlessly. For a week I had retained no food and only rare judicious sips of water.

"It is a bit too late to withdraw my boast that I can take care of myself. This is the time to demonstrate it," I chided myself. I kept thinking that I might be able to retain some toast.

Abubakar and I had worked out a system of baking bread. While my dough was rising, he made a great fire in my "stove," then, when the loaf was ready to bake, we placed it in one of the inverted earthen pots, raked the glowing coals and ashes around it, and let it bake. The bread was burned at the top, but it was baked all the way through. Since he had left, I had had to do all the labor involved, but it had seemed worth the trouble, for toast had been one thing I could eat.

I had not finished the last loaf of bread, since I was eating very little, but bread does not keep under such conditions. So now by pure determination I made myself get up and mix the dough.

Reeling with nausea and weakness, I had to do the kneading in short stages. Several times I had to sit down quickly and hang my head low to keep from fainting. At last it was ready to set aside to raise. Weakness had erased the memory of how I got the fire built. Maybe the children did it for me.

Finally the bread was baked and I cut a small piece of the crust, in lieu of the toast I thought would tide me over until I regained my strength. I nearly wept with frustration and despair when I took that first bite. Because my mind was hazy, or because I had had to interrupt my bread-mixing process several times, I had forgotten the salt! I tried, but I could not force myself to eat even toast made from this unpalatable bread.

I believe it was that evening that Dogo, spokesman for a delegation of scared villagers, came to the door and announced their decision to take me to Maradi. This route was farther than the one I had come, for I would have to ride all the way, but by now the flood had made the former route entirely out of the question. The whole town stood by with sympathy and advice while everything was packed but a few things I had hopefully put aside as food for the journey.

I shall never forget that last evening. The same people who had self-consciously insisted previously that they could only repeat prayers after me now crouched reverently about my door in a spontaneous and earnest prayer meeting. Joy flooded my heart; tears slipped down my cheeks as I heard how intelligently and unfalteringly they were voicing their petitions. These babes in Christ were beginning to stand on their own feet!

"We have arranged with a Buzu for him to come early in the morning and pack all the loads on two of his camels. We will carry you."

Admittedly very weak but still unaware of the seriousness of my condition I said, "Let me start out by horse. I think we had better have carriers, just in case I can't make it all the way. I'll ride as far as I can, though."

Early next morning I got myself ready for my ride.

"The Buzu has not shown up," said Madugu. "We'll have to wait."

Remembering how long my ride had been when I had been feeling fit, I was now impatient to be off. I suggested that I start out with two men who would carry a few things I wanted to keep with me during the ride. Dan Naito said he would help the Buzu with the loads.

Dan Naito had proved himself undependable and not very honest in his dealings with me. At this point, however, I could not afford to remain to watch how he packed the loads, or if some of them were left behind altogether.

"I don't think the Buzu is going to come," said Dogo. "He would have been here by now."

I looked at Madugu. I could see that he agreed.

"We'll have to repack the loads," Dan Naito spoke up again, "and carry them. You had better go on ahead, for it will take time."

"Then make the loads very small and get extra carriers," I reminded him. "So that if I can't ride all the way, they can take over the loads of the four men who will have to carry me."

I was glad when Madugu decided at the last minute to remain behind to see about the loads, and sent Dan Naito and two others ahead with me.

"We'll catch up with you somewhere along the way, or at noon, when you stop to eat and rest," said Madugu.

We were not quite halfway when I tried to dismount for a rest. My knees gave way under my weight and I collapsed in a heap near the trail. I was completely exhausted and glad that I had made arrangements for the men to come prepared to carry me part of the way. The previous night the thought of being carried all that distance, through tall millet and corn fields, had seemed an impossibility. Now, I was convinced, it was the only way I could go on. I was glad that I had ridden at least part of the way.

Kudu, one of my escorts, helped me to the shade of a tree where I lay down, glad that I did not have to make any effort until the carriers caught up with us. After nearly an hour Dan Naito approached me.

"You must try to eat something. We will have to go on." It was about two o'clock.

"I'll try to eat something," I said, making an effort to sit up. "But I am not going on until the carriers come. They will have to carry me from here."

While I tried to eat a few shreds of peaches from the tin that had seemed the most tempting of all my supplies, the men withdrew some distance. They seemed to be arguing about something. They turned away politely when I lay down on my face, retching weakly, unable to eat anything. I stretched out again to wait for the carriers.

Dan Naito and Kudu came back to talk to me, their faces serious.

"We think that the carriers have taken a short cut, and have missed us. They are probably ahead of us now, instead of behind us."

"Can you catch up with them by taking the horse?"

"They might have taken any of a score of paths."

I had rested over an hour, still I felt just as weak as I had when I had reached this place. It was with difficulty that I remounted my horse.

"Hurry!" I urged, estimating the miles we should be covering with the men running at a slow dog trot. "Hurry. I can't ride much longer."

I remember the rest of that nightmare trip only objectively, as though it were someone else. I do not know how many times I blacked out and had to be helped back into the saddle. Once the horse sank knee-deep into the mire, and I had to roll quickly away, out of reach of his thrashing heels. The periods of riding became shorter, the halts more frequent. Finally I could not stay on the horse at all.

"Let me rest a little longer," I panted, lying prostrate on the roughness of a cornfield. "Then I'll hang on your shoulders and walk." Maradi was already in sight. I could not give up now!

I tried several times to walk with the help of two of my escorts, but in vain. I had reached the ultimate of exhaustion. I blacked out as soon as I raised my head. I sank back to the ground, resigned to spending the night in the cornfield where I had collapsed.

I had sent all my things except my small canteen of water ahead by one of the men as soon as the distant town of Maradi had been pointed out to me. I wanted him to swim across the river with a note to Mr. Kapp that I had written the night before. In it I promised to be at the river when he got his note. I wanted him to meet me there with the jeep. It never occurred to me to wait on headquarters for help where I was. In my befogged mind, the river was still an insurmountable barrier.

There I lay in a cornfield near a marsh, in the hot, slanting rays of the afternoon sun. It was time for people to be going home from Maradi market. An old man came by. Another man. There was a consultation. A small crowd was gathering.

"My home is not far," said the old man to me. "You can come to my home."

But how? I could not stay on the horse. I could not walk. Time went by, the crowd increased and stood uneasily at a distance.

A man came by with a chair made out of boxwood. He stopped and offered his chair. I was set on this chair and marched "in state" to the little compound in the middle of fields of tall grain. I had now complicated matters for my friends. Ever since my note arrived, quite some time before, the mission staff had been making every effort to come to my rescue.

In the compound, I was happy just to lie down and rest. It little mattered that by this time even my mosquito net and all my food were probably on the other side of the river. I had only the same small canteen of drinking water, for though I had prepared another container of boiled water, I had seen one of my men contaminate that larger amount of water.

My unhappy hostess was wringing her hands because she did not know how to cook foreign food for a sick white woman. I asked her just to cook me some water. That did not satisfy her. I had to have food.

"But I haven't eaten for about a week," I protested. "It doesn't matter."

She still insisted that she must fix something for me. Knowing the risk of eating anything she might serve, I suggested a boiled egg, for I could keep that clean by eating it right from the shell—if I could eat it at all.

The whole community was drafted into service by the hospitable old man. I heard one man being dispatched to borrow onions (for me, I learned). One woman brought three eggs; a man arrived, out of breath, with eleven eggs that had the suspicious shine of having been snatched from the nest of a disappointed mother hen. Still another, whose quest had taken him farther, was just arriving with more eggs

when Mr. Kapp's messenger came, saying that I would be
carried to the river at once. Swimmers were waiting to take
me across the river where Mr. Kapp waited in the jeep.

I quickly bought the old man's bed, paying him the price
of a new one and hoping he was not including too much "live
stock" with the bargain. I was hoisted up on the heads of
four carriers who pushed through the tall grain over uneven,
slippery paths.

It was dusk when I was deposited in my long, galvanized
tin bathtub which had been tied, on a precarious slant, to
two empty oil drums to make a fairly seaworthy raft. Eight
swimmers shouted encouragement to each other as they towed
me through the swift current to safety on the other side.

After a week of rest and loving care in Maradi, my odyssey
recommenced. A soft bed was wedged, somehow, into a jeep
station wagon—and only a four-wheel drive could have passed
over those *malka* roads to Nigeria. The next day the government doctor at Katsina sent an ambulance to take me to the
airport, where our mission plane came to pick me up and take
me another 500 miles to Bingham Memorial Nursing Home,
in Jos, on September 17.

Some days later, when I was actually convalescing, I raised
my head to welcome Dr. Troup as he entered the room. He
waved me down reproachfully.

"Keep your head down. People with hepatitis must be
absolutely quiet!"

I smiled.

He read my thoughts and answered them. "Your survival
is a miracle," he said.

Perhaps. But I had seen a greater miracle. I had seen a
Mohammedan town that had turned to Christ, delivered from
the tentacles of Islam, because one man had responded to
God's challenge to be a witness.

FIFTEEN

LISTEN—*THE DRUMS!*

And I sought for a man among them, that should
make up the hedge, and stand in the gap before me
for the land . . . but I found none.—Ezekiel 22:30

FAR FROM GIDAN MAGAJI, in an unreached part of the
French Sudan, God had been preparing another miracle
of grace. Long years before, an obscure *malam* had predicted
that some day "believers" would come who follow Jesus only.
Such a declaration, by a leader of Islam, can be explained
only as a miracle.

"Listen to them," he advised his disciples, "for they will
proclaim the truth!"

Among those who heard this advice—almost incredible,
coming from a Moslem teacher—was a man called Galadi.

In the marvelous providence of an omnipotent and omniscient God, Galadi "happened—by chance" to hear the Gospel
when he was traveling in Nigeria. This message of Jesus was
what he had been waiting for. He accepted Christ as Saviour
and received Him also as Lord. The power of the indwelling
Spirit so changed Galadi's life that all in that vicinity were
eager to hear the Gospel that had wrought so genuine a miracle in him.

Galadi set up a boothlike structure in which he held Sunday services. In surrounding villages, he gathered children
and taught them, as *malams* indoctrinate children in most
villages with the tenets of Mohammedanism. He did not

hesitate to let his second wife go when a native evangelist pointed out to him that Christians do not practice bigamy.

Years passed. Galadi was without human guidance and without the Word of God. He was assailed by doubts, and in his anxiety he traveled a long distance to question a noted Moslem.

No missionary knew of Galadi's faith. No missionary knew of his terrible danger. There was no one to intervene, to warn Galadi that Islam's sword is dripping with the blood of Christian martyrs. To seek advice from a Mohammedan *malam* must have but one result!

No man knew—but God did! As He gave tongue to a donkey to warn an erring prophet, as He put blessing into Balaam's mouth instead of cursing, so God caused this priest of Islam to encourage Galadi to continue in the way of Christ! Miracle of miracles!

Galadi lived in a village near Guesheme, and Guesheme was the station to which I had been assigned very shortly after I reached the field, for I had been told that my transfer from Galmi would be to Guesheme. Two rainy seasons had gone by, and still money had not come for the buildings necessary to establish a station. Ray and Doris Pollen, a young couple, had just come into French Niger and were also waiting to go to Guesheme.

When missionaries met for our Niger conference, Ben Van Lierop spoke with urgency of Guesheme's need. With a boys' school on his compound, Ben explained, it was impossible to do much trekking to Guesheme area, for it was 72 miles from his own work at Dogon Doutchi. Ben reminded us that aggressive forces of Islam surround that small pagan area like a besieging army.

"If we do not enter now and take the area for Christ, Islam will enter. Mohammedans are infiltrating right now and," continued Ben sorrowfully, "Galadi, the man who might

oppose them, is dead! It is up to us to keep alive the spark
of faith that Galadi kindled by his glowing testimony."

"How much money is there?"

Strange that the testimony of Christ must be bound by
sums of money. Mother, as usual, had sent in as much as she
could.

"We have enough money to build the boys' quarters," said
Mr. Kapp. "That's all."

"I am willing to live in boys' quarters," I said.

"If there is money for a garage or a chapel," offered Ray
Pollen, "we wouldn't mind living in that while we wait for
money to build a proper house."

"There isn't enough money for even the shell of a building
for you."

The cause was so urgent that all of us were of one mind.
Guesheme must be entered at all costs. We banded together
to pray for funds for a house for the Pollens. The dry season
—the time for building—was slipping by. One month. Two
months. Lack of funds can be as deadly a barrier as was the
vicious torrent of the Jordan River in high flood. But, to the
children of Israel God had given marching orders, "Go!"
They had to walk right into the raging impossibilities.

I offered to go to live in Guesheme alone.

Mr. Kapp, who was district superintendent, faced me re-
gretfully with the grim truth. It was impractical and out
of the question to send Don Darling all the way to Guesheme
with a crew of men to construct the *one* building we had
money for when other stations had funds and were clamoring
for a builder. He would not permit me to go to live in such
an isolated spot alone, anyway.

"You will be 72 miles from your post office and from any
European help," said Mr. Kapp. "Mr. Darling will be here
in three weeks with his builders. We'll have to send them
west—and they will not be able to return until after the next

rainy season. If there is no money, they cannot stop off to build Guesheme station."

Three weeks? If in two years God had not brought in funds would He bring them in now? Time moved on. As one day followed another, our hopes seemed more vain. No one in the homeland seemed concerned. Was God also indifferent?

Then one day while I was helping in the Tsibiri dispensary, someone handed me a note. It was worded like a telegram.

REJOICE. GUESHEME WILL BE OCCUPIED.

Two of our missionary families had sent gifts that would make possible a building of some sort for the Pollens. Don Darling, the builder, had arrived. Because the government had stipulated that Guesheme was to be a medical center, I consulted with Don about using part of the boy's quarters fund for a tiny building just large enough to store my drugs, though the work itself would have to be done out in the open. He suggested I draw a plan.

I had made no plans of any kind until then. All over the field the basic plan for permanent boys' quarters is just a row of rooms, each with a door to the outside, covered with a sloping roof, lean-to style. What is there to plan about that? At best, it would make very hot and very inconvenient living quarters. The tin roof is directly overhead and low.

I started to put my dispensary on paper, though I groaned with the inadequacy of working out of doors in sun or rain. Then I began toying with the idea of shoving those boys' rooms into a square or rectangle of the same floor area that the standard long building would occupy. I enjoy making plans, and soon, with some shoving about of walls, I had a very handy house—though a very tiny one—instead of a row of rooms. I showed my plan to the builder, who said it would cost no more that way.

Don had asked me to draw a plan for a dispensary. Instead, I had transformed the boys' lean-to into the plan for a permanent house with which I was quite content. Now I became enthusiastic. I began to believe that God would also provide a workable dispensary. I believed, now that I had a house, that God would send *something,* but I could not know how much. Time was short. Don was already getting his loads assembled. So, far into the night, I drew plans—four of them —*to fit His provision whatever it would be.*

On the top of my stack of dispensary plans, I placed the one that would be most practical for my work. My extravagant creation included a waiting room that could be used as school and temporary chapel as well. But this plan was larger than my house, though perhaps no more expensive, since it had fewer partitions. This top plan was a dreamer's desire—impossible—but it was the plan I dearly wanted.

God has promised to supply all our needs, but not all our *wants.* This I knew full well, of course, when I took my four plans to Maradi, my knees shaking with my weight of suspense. *Which of the four plans would I have?*

As was always the case, the first thing we did when we got to Maradi was to look for our mail. I had a letter from my Little Sis. I opened the envelope; a crisp slip of paper slid out into my hand. The check I held was so large that when a few minutes later I presented my stack of plans, the builder and Mr. Kapp approved the one on top—the dispensary that I wanted most, and which I really needed for truly effective work. The builder assured us that the chapel, too, would be made quite adequate for the Pollens by using future roofing "pan" to make partitions.

Very soon—by the middle of March, 1953—we were on our way to the station that was rapidly rising. We spent a night at Dogon Doutchi, our nearest neighbor station where lived the Van Lierops, who had been contacting our area occasionally on trek. Seventy-two miles on African bush roads is a very long distance, and it was sundown before we reached our new station. We were almost too tired to enjoy the meal we quickly prepared out of our chop box.

A crowd, buzzing with excitement and comment, gathered around the chapel windows. We ate a bit self-consciously. These wild-looking natives were the people of our parish. Some of them impressed us as looking almost savage, especially the women, who had a very unusual and highly uncivilized taste in cosmetics. A brilliant, brick-colored powder was applied around the blackly accented eyes and was blended into yellow high on the cheek, and then to pale green. Right in front of their almost iridescent faces were thick, black braids that stood out stiffly from their foreheads. But though their styles were a bit grotesque, the expression on the faces was friendly.

The people seemed to take it for granted that, though we had greeted them in their language but in another dialect, we could not understand them. They crowded at the windows and kept up a running commentary on our appearance and actions.

I suppose every missionary dreams of finding the place, suggested in many missionary poems and hymns, where heathen multitudes stand with outstretched hands, crying their desire for the Gospel. I had heard that Guesheme was still mostly pagan, and I had built up fanciful visions of gathering abundant sheaves in a field where I had neither watered nor planted. Guesheme was part Moslem and part pagan, and Galadi, we were to learn, had never actually come as far south as this village. Our people did not even know about him, or about the Christ that he had preached.

Though the entire population did not at once embrace the Gospel we had come to proclaim, even now after contact with the builders, a few people had already declared themselves ready to receive our religion. Light sometimes filters into this intense darkness very slowly, however.

For example, Amali, a petty chief, had repeatedly told Don and others whom he met that he intended to follow Christ. In conversations with me, Amali constantly brought up the question of whether his following Christ would affect his position as chief. One day after I had carefully explained the hope of Heaven and the assurance of our salvation, Amali reverted again to his subject of power as a chieftain. I felt led to ask him how these two things were related.

"If you were given a choice of salvation—which means life eternal in Heaven—and high position here on earth, which would you choose?"

Amali hesitated only a few seconds. "I would choose position."

This poor man was trying to curry our favor, it seemed, with the idea that we had great influence among white people in authority who might be disposed to increase his power or the size of his domain. And yet somehow he was fumbling for what was right too.

Amali came to me one day and asked whether he were doing something counter to the cause of Christ if he helped his friends by giving them advice. By the way he stated his question, I could tell him nothing but that there is no harm whatever in helping our neighbors. Christians should be helpful to others.

Africans are often very indirect, however, and the very fact that he had come to ask about it made me wonder what thought lay behind his query. After he had gone, I asked my boy what Amali really had had in mind.

"He gets his counsels by witchcraft," was Awul's answer.

It seems he wanted my acquiescence to something of which his conscience convicted him as being evil, but for fear that I should advise against his continuance of a profitable project, he veiled his question in such a way that only the native mind could understand his meaning.

Yet the Spirit of God was surely working in him and giving him no peace, for he came back later that day and reopened the subject. He admitted that his power of divination was not of God. I began to understand how dark are the hearts even of those who have not accepted Islam—even hungry hearts.

The wonder of God's patience, grace, and His mercy became plainer to me during those days as I pondered this man's open preference for transient tangibles rather than invisible eternal riches that are realities only to the mind of faith.

Amali's delusion about our own political influence may have been deepened by the fact that our local French administrator from Dogon Doutchi was friendly, and invited us to join his family in a feast of barbecued sheep a few times when they came to the bush on official business with the local chiefs. When we had sliced from the animal the choice cuts nearest the spicy, brown crust, the commandant would wave his arm, and waiting villagers would fall to. The people, including Amali, may have concluded, since they saw us with this official, that we had some connection with government affairs.

The administrator was interested in our affairs, however, though we had no connection with his. One night he inquired about my medical work. I had had trouble starting my dispensary services since I had had to wait almost unbelievably long for a drug order to reach Guesheme. I explained that my work was still very small, since the dispensary had not been operating very long.

"I hope, by the end of the year, to have as many as 100 patients a day," I said.

He looked at me incredulously. "Why, they don't have more than 30 a day in Dogon Doutchi!" he exclaimed. "You are too optimistic. This is bush!"

I did, however, reach my goal, as I had hoped, though that

did not become the daily average of patients.[1] Here, as in Tsibiri, God sent me a few patients who did my advertising for me. The first one was an old man with pneumonia.

"We brought him to you dead," exclaimed a woman of the family, "and now he is well!"

In their eyes, the antibiotic restored him to life as literally as if he had indeed already been wrapped in graveclothes. They had brought him to me with no real hope that the white man's medicine could help.

Marafa, another grateful patient, became my active advertising agent. I found him one day when I opened my kitchen door, lying across my steps. How long he had been there he did not reveal. His face was drawn and ashen gray with pain that, I concluded from his history and symptoms, must be caused by a renal calculus.

I am not sure that my diagnosis was correct. Certainly I did nothing for him except to attempt to relieve his pain temporarily by giving him an injection from my scant and carefully hoarded store of narcotics. If that one injection relaxed him enough for the kidney stone to pass, it can still be put down as a miracle that many doctors would like to see duplicated in their practice. Though he had had repeated attacks before, this was the last one. God intervened when I turned to Him and admitted I did not have the answer.

Though I had not been certain about what ailed Marafa, nor what brought about an alleviation of pain, Marafa was in no wise uncertain about his relief.

"My family had gathered," he told me later, "and waited for me to die, when a paroxysm of this pain struck me. I myself had despaired of seeing another day."

Marafa became my friend and ally. He learned that I was having trouble getting eggs in this new community. From

---

[1] By September, 1957, Joan Jackson, who followed me to Guesheme dispensary, had treated patients from 70 villages, some of them in Nigeria, and had over 200 patients in the outpatient clinic.

that day to the time I left Guesheme, I bought eggs only once. Marafa kept me supplied with eggs—and they were fresh.

Marafa sent me many patients. He came often and there seemed little Marafa would not have done to please me. One thing, however, he would not do, though it would have brought me more joy than all his gifts. He did not accept the Lord of whom I talked to him often until I returned home. He died, soon afterward, victim of a snake bite.

When Na Birni was brought in, I doubted whether I should ever have a chance to tell him about a Saviour who had died for him. Actually I was sorry they had brought him for since he was my second inpatient it would not do my work much good to have him die on the premises.

Ten days before, Na Birni had been bitten on a finger by a *kurege*, a common rodent of the fields similar to a ground squirrel. Now the hand and the leg on that side of his body were paralyzed; he swallowed with difficulty and seemed delirious. His pulse was a mere flutter and it seemed, from general muscular twitchings, that he was on the verge of a convulsion. I checked my books for symptoms of rabies, and for any condition that might have such symptoms. If it was in the books, I failed to find it.

Doris came out to see if she could help.

"I'd let you help me, Doris," I said, "but I don't know anything to do for him—except to pray."

So we prayed together. Then I began the "shot-gun therapy."

I discussed the condition with several of the people who were standing about in hushed groups, hoping to discover whether my patient was suffering from an unusual infection or whether the *kurege* often caused such symptoms. All agreed with our local chief that the *kurege* is as poisonous as a viper or a cobra, and that Na Birni's were the common symptoms.

"Is the paralysis permanent?" I asked.

Two men shrugged, and gave evasive answers. I turned to my own yard boy Naino who was one of the group. He tried to evade my question, too, but I was insistent.

"What about it, Naino?"

"We don't know of anyone who has ever survived a *kurege* bite," Naino finally blurted reluctantly.

Here was a chieftain who was beloved. He had many friends and relatives who remained with him and took care of him devotedly.

"But *you* have to give him his medicine," said his wife. "He's *scared* of you!"

I laughed at the dubious compliment and went with her to cajole or cow him into swallowing the drugs that may or may not have had any effect on his condition. At first he obeyed me meekly; later, when his paralysis lessened, he became unmanageable and seemingly violently insane.

"We'll have to take him home, where there are many men," said his son. I could see his point.

I had seen violent people staked with their knees over a heavy log, both ankles fastened to the log by a sort of metal stock, unable day or night to change position except to lie down, and even that strain made the metal rings cut off the circulation until the feet became edematous and ulcerated. Perhaps my heart stimulants had kept Na Birni alive, but I was not proud of that attainment. Death is preferable to such existence.

Several weeks later, the very sweet woman who was Na Birni's wife brought me a chicken and a guinea fowl. "Na Birni sent the gift," she explained, "for saving his life."

"Was it Na Birni who sent it?" I asked eagerly.

"Yes," she said. "He is much better." Later she brought another guinea fowl, and then another.

"His mind is well now," she said.

Na Birni's village was too far for me to visit him, but one day Ray Pollen had to get another patient from that neighborhood in his car, so I went to see Na Birni. Except for a paralysis of tongue and throat that made it very difficult for him to speak intelligibly, he seemed perfectly well. He kept thanking me for what I had done for him.

I had never had an opportunity—because he had been irrational all the time I had had him on our compound—to tell Na Birni about Christ, so I told him now that I had something more important to tell him than that he was well. But relatives of the patient we had come to see interrupted, asking me to hurry.

"I'll come to see you," said Na Birni.

He came at the time we had appointed, and contrary to native custom he brought his wife. They both listened eagerly, attentively, while I carefully and simply pointed them to the way of *everlasting* life.

Again entirely contrary to native custom, he would turn to his wife. "Do you hear that? Do you understand? This is the truth! This is the Way."

Opportunities in Guesheme were unlimited. Even if I stepped outside my door to set up my deck chair to rest in the shade in the late afternoon, I would barely be seated before I would be surrounded by children who seemed literally to spring from nowhere. They loved to sing and they loved to learn Scripture verses, for they knew that they would get a used greeting card if they repeated them without mistake.

Sometimes they were amazed at how remarkably stupid I was.

Guesheme was a small village with but one unimportant market once a week. It was God's gracious provision that my Little Sis had still consented to give me a kerosene refrigerator, though I had refused to bring one for my second term. Here, as never before, I needed one, for sometimes weeks went by without an opportunity to buy beef. One market day as I was going down to the dispensary for my day's work,

I stopped to ask Naino, my yard boy, to find out if there would be beef in the market that day.

Naino looked at me in amazed incredulity. "But haven't you heard the drums?"

"Of course, I have heard the drums. On market day there are always drums."

Naino's jaw dropped, and he looked at me sharply to see if I were jesting. He glanced helplessly at the inevitable group of youngsters that had collected.

"But the drums are beating *beef!*" shrieked one of the youngsters, less tactful than Naino, who had hesitated to point out that I had been demonstrating frightful ignorance.

Though after all these years, I could not interpret even the headlines—nor the advertising—I had often heard about the efficiency of the tom-tom news service. After the death of King George V, British government officials were duty bound to notify all the late king's subjects of their loss, and used all the tools of civilization at their command to speed the message to government outposts in all Britain's colonies. From bush outposts, Nigerian authorities were commanded to contact all major chiefs to communicate their message. On African trails even the fastest means are rather slow, so it happened that when one district officer arrived to tell a bush chief of the sorrow that had befallen them, the chief answered, "Yes, I know. For two days we have bewailed the passing of our great chief in the land of *Ingila.*"

"Two days!" cried the district officer. "Why, I just got the telegraph message last night!"

"Ah, but the drums! We got our message by the drums."

As quickly as sound could travel, the message had been picked up from one village to be relayed to the next. The tom-toms were quicker than the Nigerian telegraph system handling a message of top priority. How such detailed information is put into rhythm remains a mystery to me, though

I have often listened with wonder at the variety and intricacy of the throbbing tattoo.

I had begun to recognize wedding drums, death drums, and drums for demon worship—*bori*. One day, again in need of beef, I listened to the drums—though with little enlightenment. However, I knew that a cow to be butchered was usually brought into town with a good deal of whoopee, and the wild EEEEEEEEHOOOOOO! that now met my ears was far more suggestive of beef, in my civilized ears, than the sound pattern of the tom-toms.

"It that the butcher now?" I asked, with some diffidence, hoping that my ignorance was not showing too badly. "Will there be beef?"

The boys listened to the *ihu* from the town. At the moment, the drumming had ceased entirely, so one said, "No, but there is some excitement going on." Then, after a few bangs of the drum, Naino said, "You were right. There will be beef."

The tempo of the tom-tom is the heart beat of Africa, and rare was the night that the throbbing drums did not lull me to sleep. One evening, however, not long after sundown, a new and animated rhythm, more intricate and more eager than usual, drew my own pulse beat into its ardent fervor. Its very cadence held a challenge, but there was no hate or blood in the voice of the drums, rather it spoke of reaching out to some mysterious goal with hope and with joyful anticipation. No drummers could long have continued the frenzied beat that filled the very atmosphere with excitement, and all too soon the sound was lulled into a more leisurely rhythm, the vile and sensuous drumming of darkness that is the commonplace of African nights.

Naino had made me more conscious than ever of the meaning of the drums. In the morning I asked him about the drumming of the previous night.

"Those," explained Naino, "were the planting drums.

They were telling the people to get their tools in shape, so that they can plant with the first rains."

Conditioned to the repeated reminders so common to civilized broadcasting, I listened again the next evening. The call to prepare for the planting was not repeated. It was not needed. I would have to wait another year before I should hear the planting drums again.

My house stood on a hill overlooking the village in the valley. The heart of the night was throbbing as a few introductory thumps beat into the stillness of the early darkness. The flickering glow from great open fires cast a ruddy glow on the great trees that grew throughout the town, and reflected even from the smoke that floated languidly about the trees. A radiant web of enchantment cast its spell over a scene picturesque and wildly beautiful.

But my heart ached over the meaning of those campfires, for I knew that about each fire sat young children who were being indoctrinated with the tenets of Islam. I knew that if I walked down the hill and into the town, I should hear the monotonous intonations of Arabic portions of the Koran being chanted in boyish, trustful voices. And I knew that once Islam grips the heart its tentacles cling, and the life may be lost forever to the cause of Christ. I knew. And there was no more beauty in the glow over the trees, for it became the crimson cowl of everlasting death creeping subtly over the land and into the hearts of thousands of undying souls.

Then rose in the darkness a cry and the slow dirge of death as the drums took on the tempo of the moment. My heart froze within me. Had we reached that soul that had slipped away even as I gazed at the smoldering haze?

I thought of the drums that had beaten with such vitality and hope just the night before, calling men to plant, to hope, to live!

Why, I pondered, are there no drums to draw men to the harvest—the harvest that lies spread before me—the unseen harvest of souls? Why should a black man's drum draw all men to make haste for the planting, when the harvest—the eternal harvest—lies all about, unheeded, ungathered?

And then, because my heart listened, I heard a sound— militant, ardent, ecstatic! It was the tread of marching feet, leaping to conquest; it throbbed with a love that passes earthly mediocrity, the cadence of joy over an abundant and everlasting harvest!

Beat—oh, drums!

Beat loudly. Draw into the spell of your call all hearts that have been washed in the blood of the Lamb, all spirits loosed from the shackles of darkness. Beat until love throbs again in souls grown cold and unconcerned for the white harvest that is falling unhindered, ungarnered—unwept. Beat—oh, drums! Beat for God's heartbreak over the unfaithfulness of His sons who grovel for crumbling earth-stores and pass heedlessly by the wealth that endures through eons unending. Beat! Beat for the harvest that now hangs gold to be gathered, for fields ready to cast their yield to the winds!

Beat—oh, drums! But beat not the dirge of a harvest ungathered. Oh, beat not the dirge of the dead!

My heart listened still and above the drums came the sound of a trumpet, and the trumpet heralded the voice of Christ, the Redeemer. Then fell a great hush, and the words came so clearly, so plainly, that only those failed to hear who *would not.*

"Whom shall I send? And who will go for us?"

And in my dream I heard a sound as of a mighty army crying with one voice—a great shout as of volunteers going forth to war. And their words were one.

"Here am I—send me!"

And I stood on the brow of a hill overlooking the village that was like thousands of villages all over Africa. The dream was past; here was reality. Again I heard the wail for the dead and saw the tidal wave of Islam that rushes on because it finds many voices. And where that flood flows, souls will be bound, and darkened, and *damned.*

I listened, and heard but the dirge of the dying—the throb of eternity looming in darkness.

Where are the voices that cry, "Peace—and redemption!"

Listen—the drums!